FREEDOM
FROM
COMPULSION

Carlo
Vigna

How to Liberate Yourself
from the Uptight,
Obsessive Patterns of Living
That Rob You of Peace of Mind

Leonard Cammer, M.D.

SIMON AND SCHUSTER • NEW YORK

MANUFACTURED IN THE UNITED STATES OF AMERICA

1 2 3 4 5 6 7 8 9 10
LIBRARY OF CONGRESS CATALOGING IN PUBLICATION DATA

CAMMER, LEONARD.
FREEDOM FROM COMPULSION

1. OBSESSIVE-COMPULSIVE NEUROSIS.   I. TITLE.
RC533.C35   616.8'522   76–16044
ISBN 0–671–22319–4

ACKNOWLEDGMENTS

During my studies of the obsessive-compulsive person over the past thirty years, I have reviewed, modified and enlarged the concepts of its psychopathology, some of them as signaled by other scholars. To name all the men and women of excellence who have added to this background would entail too lengthy a task. Nevertheless, certain colleagues have contributed so definitively to my formulations of the dynamic process in the obsessive-compulsive person and of the treatment of the obsessional neurotic that I wish to clearly acknowledge my indebtedness to them. I am certain that they will forgive me for not citing or specifying the particular expertise that they offer. Instead, let me quite simply say thank you to:

Paul L. Adams, M.D.; W. Stewart Agras, M.D.; Joseph Barnett, M.D.; John Paul Brady, M.D.; H. J. Eysenck, M.D.; Nancy Friday; W. Horsley Gantt, M.D.; Isaac M. Marks, M.D.; Neal E. Miller, Ph.D.; Leslie Solyom, M.D.; Rose Spiegel, M.D.; and Joseph Wolpe, M.D. My gratitude also goes to the memory and magnificent work of Ivan P. Pavlov, whose genius still lives on today.

Others too have given special help in the preparation of this manuscript. My profound appreciation to Andrew Salter—so perpetually attuned to the subtleties of human behavior—who helped construct the items in the self-rating scales and who read various sections of the manuscript, providing many astute comments which added to its precision and perspective.

Others too have given special help. Alan F. Rappaport, Ph.D., collaborated in writing Chapter 18 and made many suggestions for the development and use of the self-rating scales and treatment logs. Moreover, he reviewed different parts of the manuscript, thus increasing its solidity and value.

Finally, my tributes to Sylvia E. Atkinson, whose moral support and unwavering dedication to this book burned in a bright, encouraging flame throughout its composition; and to Judith A. Kestel, not only for her patience in translating my handwritten first draft into a workable transcript, but for her keen observations of human relationships, many of which have been incorporated into this final text.

Last, and once again, my sincere thanks to Beatrice Cammer, who, as always, gave her unstinting collaborative efforts to the making of this work.

TO
LEON SHIMKIN
FOR HIS WIT, GRACE AND HUMANITY

CONTENTS

ABOUT THIS BOOK 19

PART ONE: RECOGNIZING THE UPTIGHT OBSESSIVE-COMPULSIVE WHO ADAPTS

1. **Are You an Uptight Obsessive-Compulsive (O–C)?**   **23**
   Who Is Not an O-C? 23
   Who Is an O-C? 24
      FOCUS ON THE TRUE O-C 24
      THE BROAD RANGE OF THE O-C PERSONALITY 25
   Are Most O-Cs Uptight? 26
   The Anankast 26
   The Obsessive-Compulsive Personality in Operation 27
      AMBIVALENCE 28
      THE RED ALERT 29
   Measure of Personality Function and the O-C 30
   The P.E.G. Standard 30
      DO YOU FULFILL YOUR POTENTIAL? 31
      ARE YOU EFFECTIVE? 31
      ARE YOU GRATIFIED? 32
   Can the O-C Ever Let Go? 33
   Measuring the Gestalt of the O-C 34

2. **Perfectionism**   **35**
   The Houseproud Woman 35
      PRESERVING THE HOME 36
      Entrapment of the Houseproud, 37   As Your Husband Sees You, 37   Spillover with Your Family, 37
      HOUSEPROUD AWAY FROM HOME 38
      Medal for Merit, 38
   The Houseproud Man 39
   The Completers 39
      THE TOURIST COMPLETER 40
      We're Entitled to It All, 40
      THE FATHER COMPLETER 41

You Can Rarely Be Swayed, 41
THE DO-IT-NOW COMPLETER 41
Tomorrow? Never, 42
Insights to Help the Perfectionist 43
PERFECTIONISM WITH ADAPTIVENESS 43
PITFALLS OF PERFECTIONISM 43
Like O-C Parent, Like O-C Child, 44
EXPECTATIONS AND RATIONALIZATIONS 44
Look for the Midpoint, 44
FRUSTRATION OF THE PERFECTIONIST 45

3. Control   46
The Domineering 46
THE DOMINEERING O-C HUSBAND 47
Domineuvers of the O-C Husband, 47 Sweet
Reasonableness, 47 Domineering with Perfection-
ism, 48
THE DOMINEERING O-C FATHER 48
THE MRS. CRAIG SYNDROME: DOMINEERING O-C WOMEN 49
Domineuvers of the O-C Woman, 50
THE DOMINEERING O-C MOTHER 50
The Subtle Approach, 50 Hitting Out, 51 The
Regimental Approach, 51
DOMINEERING IN THE WORK SETTING 52
Pushing It, 52 Not Letting Go, 52
The Intolerant 53
Intolerance at the Top, 53 Intolerance at the
Lower Level, 54
SOCIAL INTOLERANCE 54
The Classical Prude, 54 Petty Intolerance, 55 The
Intolerant Must Remember, 55
The Stubborn 55
Why Should I Give In? 56 Don't Cross the Boss, 57
Insights to Help the Controlling Person 57
YOU BECAME SCARED . . . 58
. . . AND YOU ARE RUNNING SCARED 58
GETTING UNSTUCK . . . 59
. . . REMAINING UPTIGHT 59

CONTENTS

4. Orderliness 61

The Systems Man or Woman 61
YOU ARE YOUR OWN COMPUTER 61
THE SYSTEMS WOMAN 62
INFATUATION WITH RECORDS 63

The Precise 63
Exact to a Hair, 63　People Arrangers, 64　Precision
as Graciousness, 64　Cash and Carry, 65
I HATE CHANGE 65

The Punctual 66
The Clean and Tidy 66
A PLACE FOR EVERYTHING AND EVERYTHING
IN ITS PLACE 67
Live Tidy, Act Tidy, 67　Your "Inner" Self, 67　No
Fuss, No Muss, 68

The List Makers 68
LIVING BY THE LIST 68
LISTS THAT ENTANGLE THE LIST MAKER 69

The Health Conscious 69
COMPULSION TO BE HEALTHY 69

Insights to Help the Orderly 70
ORDERLINESS ASSURES YOU 70
WHERE ORDERLINESS FAILS 71
TRY A DIFFERENT WAY 72
IF YOU WORRY THE FUTURE 72

5. Hoarding 73

Collectors and Accumulators 73
THE O-C COLLECTOR 73
THE O-C ACCUMULATOR 74
The Clutterers, 75　Muriel's Warehouse, 75　The
Salvagers, 76　"Will I Have Enough?" 76

The Stingy 76
THE MEAN ONES 76
O-Cs Who Beggar Themselves, 77

The Private Ones 78
BEST TO BE TIGHTLIPPED 78
Your O-C Need for Reserve, 79

Insights to Help the Hoarder 79
HOW HOARDING CAN WORK FOR YOU 79
*Miserliness May Be Open-Ended, 80   Safeness in
Privacy, 80*
BUT HOARDING CAN LOCK YOU IN . . . AND OUT 80
The Self-Image of Penury, 80   Dilemmas of Privacy, 80
DEFEATING YOUR HOARDING TRAITS 81
*Substituting for Stinginess, 81   Letting Go of
Privacy, 82*
IF THE HOARDER'S TAIL WAGS THE DOG 82
*Can Stinginess Be Adaptive? 83   Hoarding Your-
self, 83*

6. Compulsion to Work   **84**
The Work Addict 84
*The Project Extenders, 85   The Affluent Too Can
Be Work Addicts, 85*
Vocations That Beckon the Work Addict 86
*Artisans and Technicians, 86   Bookkeepers, 86   Ex-
ecutive Secretaries, 87   Librarians, 87   Middle Man-
agers, 88   Physicians, 88   Theater People, 89*
Insights to Help the Work Addict 89
SOCIETY NEEDS THE WORK ADDICT 90
HOW WORK BECOMES OVERWORK 90
Women Too Are Work Addicted, 91
SUBDUING WORK ADDICTION 91
WHEN WORK REMAINS YOUR OPIATE 92

7. Conscientiousness   **94**
The Conscience-Bound 94
YOUR CULTURAL VALUE SYSTEM AND TRADITION 95
*In Religion, 95   In Marriage, 96   In the Family, 96
On the Job, 97   In the Political Arena, 97*
The Righteous 98
THE WICKED AND THE GOOD 98
THE RIGHTEOUS CAN GO WRONG 99
*The Lecturers, 100   The Censorious, 100   The Con-
demners, 101   The Grudge Bearers, 101   The Vir-
tuous, 102   The Martyrs, 102*

Insights to Help the Conscience-Bound 103
THE VALUE OF CONSCIENCE 103
THE PURITAN ETHOS 104
CONSCIENCE CAN RAPE THE PEACE 105
You Cannot Play Stand-In for God, 105
HOW TO UNDERSTAND COMPROMISE 105
IF CONSCIENCE BEATS YOU DOWN 106
How Good to Be Good? 106

8. **The Single-Minded**   **108**
I Have a Thing About That 108
Compulsive Eaters 109
Compulsive Smokers 110
Compulsive Shoppers 110
Compulsive Gamblers 111
Compulsive Talkers 111
    Compulsive Telephone Talkers, 112
Compulsive Power and Status Seekers 112
    The Mirage of Omnipotence, 113
The Superstitious 113
The "I Must Know" Compulsive 114
Fanatics 115
Manias 115
    Manias as Antisocial Acts, 116
Insights to Help the Single-Minded 117

9. **Measuring the Obsessive-Compulsive's Adaptation**   **119**
An Inventory of the Obsessive-Compulsive
Personality 120
    SELF-RATING OBSESSIVE-COMPULSIVE PERSONALITY
    INVENTORY 121

PART TWO: THE UPTIGHT WHO IS MALADAPTIVE

10. **Maladaptation and the Obsessional Neurotic**   **125**
What Is Neurotic? 125
Understanding the Obsessional Neurosis 126
    DIFFERENTIATING THE ADAPTIVE O-C AND THE
    MALADAPTIVE OBSESSIONAL 126
Becoming an Obsessional 127

11. Thought Disturbances in the Maladaptive   **129**

The Obsessions 129
    HARM TO OTHERS OR YOURSELF 130
    CONTAMINATION 130
    VIOLENCE 131
    SEX 132
    SELF-IMAGE 133
    Complex About Youth, 133
    STATUS, ROLE AND CAREERS 134

Ruminations 134
    RUMINATION LEADS TO IDEAS OF REFERENCE 135

Doubts 136
    INDECISION: ROADBLOCK TO LIVING 136
    DOUBTS AND CONFUSION ABOUT REALITY 137

Insights to Help the Maladaptive with Disturbed Thoughts 137
    OBSESSIONS ABOUT BEING OBSESSIONAL 138
    Obsessions Are Not Delusions, 138

12. Feeling Disturbances in the Maladaptive   **140**

Anxiety 140
    EVER ON THE ALERT 141
    The Anxious Maladaptive Is a Professional Worrier, 141

Phobias 142
    PHOBIAS MEAN LOSS OF CONTROL 143
    Phobias About Illness, 144   *Phobophobias, 144*

Anger 145
    ANGER CAN LEAD TO PARANOIA 145

Depression 146
    EXHAUSTION OF ADAPTIVE RESERVE 146
    SYMPTOMS OF DEPRESSION IN THE MALADAPTIVE 147
    The Retarded Type of Depression, 147   *The Agitated Type of Depression, 148*
    DEPRESSION MAY LEAD TO SUICIDE 148

Insights to Help the Maladaptive with Disturbed Feelings 148
    OBSESSIONALS ARE ANGRY WITH THEMSELVES 149
    SOME OBSESSIONALS LEARN FROM THEIR DEPRESSIONS 149

13. Behavior Disturbances in the Maladaptive   **151**

Rituals 151
WASHING RITUALS 152
BOWEL AND BLADDER RITUALS 153
COUNTING RITUALS 153
BEDTIME RITUALS 155
Checking Behavior 155
RECHECKING 155
Social Checking, 156
Avoidance Behavior 157
AVOIDANCE BEHAVIOR SHUTS YOU IN 158
Repetition Behavior 158
Insights to Help the Maladaptive with Disturbed Behavior 159
OBSESSIONAL BEHAVIOR MAY INTENSIFY 161

14. Psychosomatic Symptoms in the Maladaptive   **163**

Gastrointestinal Complaints 163
My Head and Neck Feel Wrong 164
My Aching Body 165
My Chest Closes In 165
The Telltale Skin 166
Hypertension 166
Insomnia 167
Genital and Urinary Complaints 167
PSYCHOLOGIC COMPLAINTS OF SEXUAL CONFLICT 169
The Hypochondriac 169
THE COMPULSION TO BE ILL 170
The Hypochondriac Is Not Malingering, 170
Insights to Help the Maladaptive's Psychosomatic Symptoms 171

PART THREE: SEXUAL MALADAPTATION

15. Sexual Behavior in the Maladaptive   **175**

Basic Inhibitions 176
THE CONFLICTS OF INHIBITION 177
INTIMACY 178
SHAME 179

SECRECY 180

FANTASY LIFE 181

EMOTIONAL CONFUSION 182

Sociosexual Maneuvers of the Maladaptive 185

SEXUALITY TO BIND THE MARRIAGE 185

Sometimes Is Not Enough, 186

AVOIDANCE OF SEXUAL INTERCOURSE 186

TRYING FOR THE SECOND HONEYMOON 187

LOVERS AT WORK 188

ESCAPE INTO PROMISCUITY 189

FLIRTATION AND TEASING 190

Sociosexual Identity 190

THE SINGLE MAN 191

THE SINGLE WOMAN 192

Limitations on the Single Woman, 193 *When an Active Sex Life Is Cut Off,* 193

ODD COUPLES 193

MARRIED COUPLES WHO LIVE AS SINGLE PERSONS 194

HOMOSEXUALS 195

Sexual Perversions 196

NORMAL VERSUS PERVERSE 196

Insights to Help the Sexual Maladaptive 198

THE CONFUSION OF NEEDS 199

FRIGIDITY AND IMPOTENCE 200

INTIMACY CAN BE YOUR LIFELINE 201

16. Rating Scale for the Obsessional Neurotic   203

SELF-RATING OBSESSIONAL NEUROTIC SCALE 204

PART FOUR: CHANGING YOURSELF

17. How You Can Change   209

Must My Total Personality Be Remade? 209

WORKING TOWARD PRACTICAL CHANGE 210

Motivation for Treatment or Change 210

YOU ARE MOTIVATED WHEN YOU HURT 211

Wouldn't-You-Thinkisms of Motivation, 212

MOTIVATION AND WILLPOWER 213

Your Expectations of Change 214
UNSPOKEN EXPECTATIONS: THE CALL FOR
PROFESSIONAL HELP 215
THE PSYCHIATRIST'S EXPECTATIONS OF TREATMENT 216
Goals in Treatment 216

18. Behavior Therapy   **219**
Modifying Behavior 219
MIND CONTROL 220
Expansion of Treatment, 220
Relaxation Procedures 221
PROGRESSIVE RELAXATION 221
AUTOGENIC TRAINING 223
MEDITATION 223
Transcendental Meditation (TM), 224
BIOFEEDBACK TRAINING 224
Relaxation Techniques with Biofeedback, 226   Re-
laxation and Behavior Therapy, 226
REPORTING TO YOURSELF 226
Learning Procedures 227
OPERANT CONDITIONING: LEARNING THROUGH
REWARDS AND PENALTIES 227
Selective Reinforcement, 228   Aversive Condition-
ing, 229   Negative Reinforcement, 230
DIRECTIVE THERAPY 231
Shaping, 232   Modeling, 233
ASSERTIVE TRAINING 234
Act Out, 235   Feeling Talk, 236
PSYCHODYNAMICS VS. BEHAVIOR THERAPY 236
CONTRACTING 237
Contracting Leads to Empathy, 237   Defusing the
Uptight: A Behavioral Approach, 242   Running In-
terference, 243   Unplanned Contracts: Assurance,
243
THOUGHT STOPPING 244
RITUAL STOPPING 244
Staying Clear of Rituals, 245
REPORTING TO YOURSELF 245

Exposure Procedures 246
SYSTEMATIC DESENSITIZATION 247
Desensitization in Fantasy, 248   Desensitization in Vivo, 249   Desensitization for Other Sexual Dysfunctions, 250
FLOODING 251
Maintaining High Anxiety Levels, 251   Flooding in Avoidance Behavior, 252   Saturation, 252   Flooding in Psychotherapy and Learning, 253   Role Rehearsal, 254   Role Reversal, 255   Flooding Requires Cooperation, 257
REPORTING TO YOURSELF 258
Self-Regulation 258

19. An Overview of Other Treatment Procedures   260
Psychotherapy 260
PSYCHOANALYSIS AND DYNAMIC PSYCHOTHERAPIES 261
ECLECTIC PSYCHOTHERAPIES 261
QUASI-RELIGIOUS THERAPIES 262
SELF-REALIZATION AND CONSCIOUSNESS-RAISING THERAPIES 263
SELF-HELP AND PEER GROUP THERAPIES 263
GROUP THERAPIES 264
Family Therapy 264
MARITAL THERAPY AND MARITAL COUNSELING 265
UNIT FAMILY THERAPY 265
CONJOINT FAMILY THERAPY 265
MARRIAGE ENCOUNTERS 266
Biologic Therapies 266
WHEN PHYSICAL TREATMENTS HELP 267
Treatment for Depression, 268   Treatment for Panic, Anger and Fear, 269   Treatment for Agitation, 269   Treatment for Insomnia, 269
Reaching for Optimal Change 270

ABOUT THIS BOOK

The uptight persons described in these pages may be your spouse, a former President of the United States, a neighbor, coworker—or you. All have one thing in common: obsessive-compulsive (O-C) personality traits.

O-C persons have always existed among us, but their numbers are now on the rise and have become endemic to our era.

Look around you.

Examine our society as it conditions us on a mass scale to the compulsive search for personal, social and national security. See how we are bombarded into uptight living. Health agencies and medical scientists foster our anxiety with alarmist pronouncements. Environmentalists alert us to the dangers of air, water and earth pollution. Accountants dictate the logistics of money and warn us that security lies in keeping flawless records. The police remind us of precautions to take against being mugged, burglarized or murdered. Insurance companies and banks pound us about economic guarantees for living and for death thereafter. Economists reinforce our agitations with woeful recitals of price indices, unemployment rates and similar menaces to our socioeconomic well-being. Social scientists preach of our obligation to remedy matters of racism, education and religion. Always, we are at unease. It would seem to be as Rousseau told us: "Man is born free, and everywhere he is in irons."

The psychosocial foundation is thus well laid for the spread of those who are tense, adrift and congested with anxiety. Assaults to personal integrity, filtering down subtly from corruption in high office, continue without surcease. Gone is bonhomie; we see only hostile encounter. You, the individual, emotionally shaken to start with, find yourself berthed in the culture's mediocrity, which throws more problems at you than solutions. Is it any wonder that you are pursued by a sense of jeopardy, even about trifles? And by threatening omens from every source?

You wish to love, and as the most awesome and unique product of the life force, you should *be* loved. You wish to share, to know the adventures and rhapsody of joined sexual elation. And you wish to be protected from hurts. But ambivalently, you want to somersault at will into being private, perfect and tough. Lacking the equanimity of self-confidence, you decide that the world is out-of-gear and that only you are right, whatever you do, whenever you do it.

So you mime your masters. Because you are righteously determined on control of the self, you program your own robot system of predictable behavior. You become a steel spike, unable to change or to meet the other person halfway; and underneath, your tension mounts, you falter, and your mind quails at your own dilemmas. You are at war with yourself, a love-hate relationship that assures self-destruction.

To spell out the ratios and texture of your uptightness, I have classified the obsessive-compulsive (O-C) as an *adaptive personality* (Part One) and as a *maladaptive obsessional neurotic* (Parts Two and Three). You will inspect such traits as control, perfectionism, conscientiousness, and so on, which are positive when they work for you but, if quantified to that shade or more of excess, can turn into the negative. When the latter occurs, you all too often tear your own life apart and the lives of those you touch on, with maladaptive and devastating effects.

However, throughout this book, especially in Part Four, you will also find the insights that let you read yourself. These insights include the information that will help you to surmount your disabling traits and bring you the freedom you need, for a more passionate and bounteous survival against all odds.

PART ONE

Recognizing the Uptight Obsessive-Compulsive Who Adapts

·1·

Are You an Uptight Obsessive-Compulsive?*

Almost everyone we know is tense and uptight at different times because of one damned thing or another. Life crowds in on us, its problems squeeze and clutch and we all try to cope. Yet, we want to complete ourselves, support our own weight and extract some pleasure out of the bumpy course of living.

However, in fielding the stresses that threaten our security and goals, we often convert into a manufactory of compounded defenses and conflicting maneuvers. Out of this struggle, we may emerge either undamaged, possibly shaken—or so clobbered that we stay perpetually uptight and compulsive. Not a good prospect.

WHO IS NOT AN O-C?

Many people. To be sure, you and some of your friends may own up to a moderate bug, some kind of obsession, a minor compulsion, a few anxieties and fears, and perhaps a peculiar habit or two. For example, you will be uneasy unless you use up the last tiny sliver of soap. Another person is a compulsive latecomer and never dresses for a date before the scheduled time of meeting. I know a colleague who must bandage every rebellious crack or seam in any object of his home and a lawyer friend who swings an imaginary watch on an

---

* *Uptight* is defined: "1. tense, nervous, uneasy; also: angry, indignant. 2. rigidly conventional." (*Merriam-Webster*, 1974 Pocket Books Edition.)

For purposes of space and euphony, *obsessive-compulsive* is abbreviated as O-C in this book wherever feasible. O-C is regarded as interchangeable with "uptight obsessive-compulsive" or, simply, "the compulsive personality."

imaginary chain at a boring lecture. (The speaker would like to strangle him.) And there is the woman who pulls her husband's earlobe fondly whenever he is near. He swears it's getting longer every day.

However, as singles or multiples, such compulsive idiosyncrasies do not mean an O-C personality. They are often laughed off. "That's just my screwball way." Inconsequential in their impact, they merely color the normal tones of a functioning personality. A caveat then—don't judge the whole person by a few harmless quirks that one barely notices.

WHO IS AN O-C?

We can begin by assuming that you are the adaptive O-C, seemingly courteous, even-tempered, often generous. Many admire your efficiency and strong character; you never welsh on an obligation; you are also punctual, orderly and conscientious. How admirable! Moreover, you see yourself as confident and self-sustaining. If this is a fair description of your personality, then you are managing in life and using your O-C traits to advantage, not as liabilities. They do well for you.

What about your punctuality, though? Mostly, it serves you in good stead. But can you allow yourself to be five or ten minutes late when it would really make no difference? Or do you panic at the very thought? And suppose the unexpected jolts you? Can you compromise with a smiling "So what?" and sail through the day with ease? Or does the very word "compromise" stiffen you from head to toe? If so, the chances are that some or many uptight traits pervade your makeup and distort it.

Focus on the True O-C

Such traits would stamp you unmistakably as the obsessive-compulsive whose anxiety plights drive you without letup toward that "radiant shore" of absolute security. No special look distinguishes you because O-Cs are the paradoxes of the familiar. Yet underneath, the quality of the uptight is there. In your own defense, you do what you must do and in your way only.

Does this strike a responsive chord? Ask yourself: How often must others knuckle under to you because you overpower them? In the household? At work? On the social scene? To what extent are they forced to adjust to your priorities? And if they do resist, must they turn and run from the fallout?

Should this be a fairly accurate picture, it is not surprising that you arouse equivocal feelings in them. They may like you, lean on your reliability, envy your self-discipline, pay homage to your organized mode of life. But they must also submit to your dictates and barbs about their "stupidities" and ineptness. "That could be true of me sometimes," may be your reluctant answer, and subliminally, you hear your wife complain: "Why do you hammer at me? And keep so busy being perfect? You're never wrong about anything . . . still . . . well, maybe it is me after all."

At the same time you grapple with specters of doubts as you prowl the catacombs of your insecurity. Only you know that under your competent, authoritarian manner live chronic tension and recurrent misgivings. You may yearn for respite but you cloak all emotion. "I just want to be quiet with my thoughts" (the bell-tone of your anxiety). Your passion to be faultless, and play it sure, keeps you apart. You believe that you are a repository of tender sentiment, that you long to love and be loved, but sadly you lock yourself into your own private hell.

The Broad Range of the O-C Personality

One O-C may be your own office manager whose workers could kill him because he is always right even when he is wrong. Mention an uptight perfectionist and the listener nods. "My mother-in-law. And is she tough to live with." Or it may be the person who sleeps alongside you at night and will never give an inch, even of the bed.

Then, too, there is the painstaking civil servant who checks each detail on your application forever and still pulls at his eyebrows for another five minutes after he has finished your form. It could also be a righteous businessman who sticks to his stale maxim, "It's the principle that counts," even though this stand ultimately shatters the family's firm, his daughter's marriage and many friendships. Most of us have also met the repairman who is uptight about all of life and lets your appliances know it. And do not forget that precise cousin who eats, dresses, works, and makes love according to a fixed orderly schedule. Clocks might be set by his entrances and departures.

ARE MOST O-Cs UPTIGHT?

Yes. While many O-Cs get along in life more or less well, and we call them *adaptive*, you and the myriad others who are the subject of this book remain basically uptight. To what degree? It depends on how you tip the scales of your adaptation to life, that is, how you make your compulsiveness give to you and not take away.

This is where the organism enters.

Like all of us, you are composed of a mind and body strung together with a nervous system. Of this, you are both emperor and subject at once. Only you, the self, can rule this person and, contemporaneously, be ruled. This is the unresolved ambivalence of your O-C uptightness and the heart of your trouble. In your particular theater of life you can show benevolence to the self or act with the despotism of despair. You can compassionate your follies, or tyrannize the individual within you. Your traits may reward you, or freeze you into a funk of insecurity. Along with ostensible success you may pay exorbitant toll to the boss who inhabits you. Thus, you can use your personality for maximum grace or make it into your foulest enemy.

THE ANANKAST

O-Cs are categorized variously as *anankasts* or obsessionals, obsessive-compulsive personalities, compulsives, or, in the full description, obsessive-compulsive-phobic personality types. All of these terms refer to the same O-C uptight, whose character traits are set down in detail later on.

Anankast, as applied to the obsessive-compulsive, derives from the Greek word *ananke*, meaning "fate." Signifying, in its archaic sense, that the obsessive-compulsive was bound to the inevitable decrees of his fate or destiny, presumably tied to the control of a demon of sorts, it thus meant that an obsession was a state induced by an evil spirit. The word "obsession" is derived from the Latin *obsidere*, meaning "to besiege."

Today's O-Cs, in the grip of fixed ideas and compulsive behavior, are besieged and forced to live with a special life-style or suffer terrible panic. Hence, as an uptight person you might be driven to certain actions, not by fate or demons but by ideas and emotions that are unreasonable and unwanted, but which were conditioned into your development.

1. The obsession is the intrusive idea or thought.
2. The compulsion is the act that must be performed.
3. The uptight feeling is the derived emotion.

Understand, however, that simply because you may be an O-C person, you do not exhibit every trait that you will read about as we go along. But you are probably burdened with some portion of obsessive thoughts, compulsive behavior, angers, fears and anxieties.

THE OBSESSIVE-COMPULSIVE PERSONALITY IN OPERATION

The challenge of studying and helping uptight O-Cs who have failed in their adaptations to life or have succumbed to dejection and psychosomatic difficulties has been met partially, and only in recent years, by psychiatrists and psychologists. Uptightness continues to flourish, which is why so many millions live on tranquilizers today.

However, once you understand personality as an integrate of your function, answers other than tranquilizers appear. For instance, have you ever realized how your own personality acts as your basic resource for adaptation and survival? That it both reflects and dictates your moods, decisions, actions and thoughts? Proclaims and at times advertises your successes and failures? Reveals your value judgments and predicts the way you will behave in every situation?

Yet personality is not a standstill phenomenon. It changes, twists and turns in every one of its phases as you progress into a maturity that is uniquely yours. To possess an effective personality one must change, *learn to compromise and to roll with every stress.*

Impossible for you? Yes, as an O-C, flexibility may seem to you preposterous. The fixations (rigidities) that grew out of your anxieties and insecurities, imagined and real, are now riveted into your defensive maneuvers and personality traits, and these create conflicts. Unsettled, they hang on as *ambivalences,* your greatest hazard for adaptation. To resolve them becomes mandatory.

Ambivalence

From the moment you take your first breath society disciplines you. Your individuality will be domesticated even as you resist. From toilet training to job training you learn to temper your impulses and to cooperate with your surroundings. Yet you want "to be me," to feel independent and self-sufficient. Therein lies the ambivalence. You may be fond of your parents, teachers and peers for nurturing and sustaining you, but you resent them for extracting a part of you *at their discretion,* for the common good.

Aware of it or not, as an adult O-C, you are continuing to function in these same contrasts of ambivalent blacks and whites as in your earlier years. It is the rare grays of your mature, benign intervals that confuse others who try to be empathic with your inexplicable moods. At times, exasperated, they would like to take your two heads and bang them together.

Nonetheless, you may be proud of your controlling and perfectionist traits because you see them as strengths. "What's wrong with them?" you ask. "They pump up my self-confidence." Yes, but how constantly must they be exercised, quantitatively and qualitatively? Or are they really jeering at you? Are you as unassailable in your certainties as you think?

Probably not. These "strengths" can act as traps because ambivalence is never absent and whispers fears about the shaky guarantees of your security. In brief, you are on edge because of what you must do but may not want to do. At the same time you heed the voice that tells you not to do what you secretly long to do. As relief for these dilemmas and to use your compulsiveness as an asset, you resort to a swiveling kind of rigidity with perfection as its aim.

The Red Alert

Performing in the above way, whether in work, friendship or sex, means perpetual vigilance. But for this you pay the price of being uptight, using every ounce of energy to keep indefatigably alert to yesterday's currents, to today's perils, and to the shadows cast for tomorrow. You tell yourself, "Never let down for a minute. Watch out for whatever rumbles around you."

In wasting yourself so expensively on vigilance, weariness may set in. Doubts supplant decision, concession is unthinkable, and a lid is placed on talents and goals. True, you may continue to function for a while, or even for years, with this vigilance. At some point, though, you flub your adaptations. No longer can you bull your way past your tensions. You come to a dead end—depression.

Accordingly, how does one judge whether your O-C traits are adaptive or are failing you? At your best, you are effective and productive. But when your worst is in the foreground, you irritate the environment with your hardline rigidities. In the overall do we call this polarized behavior "normal" or is there a middle ground? And if so, how do we assess it? For soundings, let us look into the nature of personality and measure it with that of the O-C by means of a plausible standard.

MEASURE OF PERSONALITY FUNCTION AND THE O-C

A few pages back we spoke of the function of personality (what it does). Here we will talk of its substance.

Simply stated, every personality is a living biologic system, with its inherited (genetic) potentials for responding to ecophysical, cultural and social forces. These forces nurture and condition each expectation and experience. The end result is the personality whose characteristics help you adapt to life's demands and pleasures.

No personality as a whole can stay pliant enough to overcome every stress situation. The bag of mixed traits in any one serves only with qualified usefulness in "getting by." We may manage, more or less well, as normal. But there's the catch. How do we measure that golden balance of "normal"? What constitutes getting by?

The business of estimating the normal has plagued all psychiatrists. Most have concluded that no single statement wraps it up. For my preference, the term *adaptive*, rather than *normal*, pinpoints the problem more accurately. To be adaptive denotes a consummation of your potential and how it is keyed to your effectiveness. Adaptiveness also includes your cup of pleasure and the extent to which your expectations are met. Thus, in order to measure your adaptiveness, and to translate it into terms of mature and successful personality function, I have devised a clinical standard that follows.

THE P.E.G. STANDARD

These parameters, consisting of your Potential, your Effectiveness and your Gratification, are abbreviated as P.E.G. and are explained as follows.

Do You Fulfill Your Potential?

You, like most of us, like to feel full-valued and that you are living up to the best of your capacities.

However, your potential may never totally mature for many reasons, but most often because of psychologic forces from outside and within, which inhibit you. Your inhibited function is apparent as you complain: "The world's going too fast for me. Everything's all too new, too experimental." You sense the reality—that there may be relevance but no real goals, activity but no action, promises but no faithful performance, changes but no improvement, growth but no progress, and corruption, not decency.

You feel expendable and you finally settle for a confined personal security. You decide to play it safe—by ducking out. "I know my own limitations and I make the best of what I am. That's enough for me." But you are not really choosing to circumscribe yourself. What you are after is to reduce your tension by narrowing your sights. If you do not compete, think you, and instead, rely on your compulsive traits, you can bypass the struggle and stay on the comfortable side of your ambivalence. True, this brands you as fixed and static to some and to others aloof and righteous on your elevated shelf. But you have found your niche, which is what counts.

However, with the passing years you scrounge grievously for the self-confidence that you tossed away in suppressing your potential. You now function in the less adaptive column of the P.E.G. standard because the safer but roped-off port held the greater lure.

Are You Effective?

To the extent that you carry your own load within any group you are effective and adapt. No one can survive alone. In one way or another you must cooperate in a family, group, or team of some kind. All adults are expected to contribute, within their abilities, at least an equitable share of what it costs to sustain them. In fact, the

31

state asks: how much and what are you giving to the upkeep of your alliances?*

As an effective O-C you support yourself and participate honorably. "I'd rather die than accept aid or go on welfare. I pay my own freight and keep my self-respect." Thus, you discharge your obligations and consider yourself a responsible citizen. The keystone of your effectiveness is your strict adherence to the status quo as your best bet for survival. But change is always in the wind and you are wary. You therefore count on your compulsive behavior as your bulwark against anything new or novel.

Because you are effective according to the P.E.G. standard, you generally rate high marks here and thereby somewhat compensate for the restrictions in your potential.

Are You Gratified?

It seems to me that all of us are entitled, not only to obtain pleasure, but to lay claim to our full quota of it. Nature herself has given us an inspiring heritage—the capacity to laugh, to rejoice, to know gladness, orgasm, humor, love and other feelings which we call pleasure—in a word, gratification. A fully adaptive person enhances this capacity. The O-C may not.

I know an uptight woman who gives up the pleasure of relaxing to the urgency of her scheduled pressures. "Taking my bath? I'm in and out of the shower in three minutes. Time and duty push on. Once in a while I do treat myself to a long sensuous bubble bath . . . and, oh, what decadence." Numerous O-C women have never experienced orgasm, much less sought it out. "Sex? Who needs it? I'm married eighteen years. We haven't had intercourse in the last six. And that's okay with me. But I do like to be held."

Another O-C calculates the width of a smile he must stretch for each person he meets. Actually he does not enjoy anyone "new."

* Unhappily, the shortcomings of society force many persons into a nonproductive status. Unemployment or disabilities, with the need for some kind of dole over extended periods, exist commonly enough and demoralize the individual.

"Life for me is conventional. Just tepid. I don't cotton up to people. My wife tells me I should practice making up chit-chat. Well, maybe I am dull, but who says I have to work at being a bore?"

How not to feel dismay for a person with so meager an affinity for his fellows! But he is telling us that he is an O-C and does not care.

Many O-C persons suppress any talent for simple conversation or whatever else there is to be enjoyed. One sees them shut off, not to dream, not to imagine, not to search out, not to innovate, not to feel more than their concept of the social mores dictate.

CAN THE O-C EVER LET GO?

Yes. Under selected conditions you may be the kind who is ebullient, merry and genial. One O-C bachelor composes witty palindromes and limericks to entertain his friends. A beguiling O-C widow who is an accomplished raconteuse can rescue a sagging party with her gems of narrative and timing. She is much sought after. So is an O-C steelworker who loves to sing folk songs to his own guitar accompaniment. And an O-C laundress I know takes her fun in roller-skating derbies and rock concerts. You may find your pleasure in cards, folk-dancing and the like.

Still, pause a moment. Isn't it characteristic that, above everything, your real gratifications come from the conscientious discharge of duty well done and from conduct so orderly and perfectly disciplined that you continually congratulate yourself on it? If this is true, you are closing off all entry into the humanness of emotional exchange, and derivatively your score on the P.E.G. standard will register low for Gratification.

One can hardly say, then, that an uptight O-C personality makes for a lusty individual. You miss out on too much of life's rapture. The elixir of joy is not your drink.

MEASURING THE GESTALT OF THE O-C

The P.E.G. standard proves out when we bring Potential, Effectiveness and Gratification into a biosocial context for living. We audit the degree to which each one of the triad has been programmed into your O-C personality, gauged with and against each other, thereby disclosing the level of adaptiveness. For practical purposes, the evaluation places you in one of two categories: adaptive (Part One) or maladaptive (Parts Two and Three).

However, such assessments variate. The repertoire of O-C traits is, after all, limited. Their significance lies in the network that binds them to your general compulsiveness. The ensuing equilibrium, after each stress that you experience, either raises or lowers the weight and predictability of your uptightness.

That some O-Cs adapt well for long periods of life testifies to the human's tolerance for punishment. But if, like many, you are prone in your uptightness to living on the edge of maladaptive troughs, then you will fall into dysfunction repeatedly, i.e., decompensate.

You may want to ask: How long can I ride my own uptightness? What is driving me? And what is it doing? To myself? To my family? My friends? To others? Can my O-C traits be changed? How? Succeeding portions of this book will attempt to answer these questions for you.

· 2 ·
Perfectionism

Within the basic rigidity of the uptight obsessive-compulsive, the drive to be *perfect* stands out as the imperative activating trait.

Most people, at one time or another, carry a perfectionist on their back whom they fend off with anger or humor, rarely with insight. The perfectionist can, as one husband put it, "be a pain in the behind because that's where you get it when every chair in the house is for show and not a comfortable one to sit on."

The compulsion to be perfect combines with other related O-C traits, but we start with the houseproud woman.* It is she who most clearly exemplifies the more obvious facets of perfectionism.

THE HOUSEPROUD WOMAN

We will assume that you are giving a dinner party. From past experience your friends know that your home will be a masterpiece of cool elegance. It is, because you have spent the past week having the silver polished, the napery freshly done, and fretting about the centerpiece and each place setting. "Maybe the Lalique birds would be better at each end of the table. But they might overshadow the floating flowers in the jade bowls, so no one will notice them."

---

* It will be noted later that many refer to the houseproud as "a Mrs. Craig." They do this without recalling the origin of the catch phrase or its more essential import of control as seen in Chapter 3.

You try seven different ways. Agonized by indecision, you throw yourself into the final details with tension straining at your neck and back. Then comes the moment of dolor. Will your guests comment on (meaning, rave over) your home? Anything lacking? Is it gracious? "How can I be sure . . . it's such a headache . . ."

As you welcome Margaret, your first guest, you absently adjust her sleeves and pat her hair in place, the way she doesn't like it. During the evening your darting glances everywhere bring a protest from someone. "Why can't you sit down for a few minutes, dear? Relax and enjoy it with us." But like most houseprouds you seem to have peripheral vision; you know that all the ashtrays have been used and only four smokers present. Tight-lipped, you keep emptying them after one cigarette is stubbed out in each.

When someone drops a bit of hors d'oeuvre or spills a drink, you hold your breath. Then, to the rescue you go with a cloth and little cheeps of dismay. The crisis over, embarrassment lingers on but you pull yourself together with a wan smile, only your damp eyes showing portents of further calamity. After dinner you whisper to Margaret, "Please, darling, don't sit so far forward on that chair. It spoils the mat of the velvet and it's just been recovered. You don't mind, do you?" Margaret agrees but with reservations. She is fond of you in spite of . . . oh well . . .

Preserving the Home

The moment everyone is out you dash ahead to clear up. Happy again, you wash and store each pot, pan and piece of silver and place every dish in its own cellophane envelope. You vacuum the rugs and put back the clear plastic covers on the upholstered furniture. (Your father has been heard to murmur, "The hell of it is, they crackle.") Your husband wonders, why, in God's name, must the place always be restored before sunrise? You would retort blithely: "No one can imagine the comfort of waking up next morning with everything exactly as it was before. We wouldn't even know anyone had been here."

Entrapment of the Houseproud. Your energy as you tackle your household each day is a marvel. You miss nothing and make it all look so easy. The cleaning woman never does the kitchen "right" so you take it on yourself. If asked, "What about the plumber? Are you right behind him making sure that he picks up every scrap of refuse that he drops?" you answer simply, "I don't like the plumber there at all."

One sighs for you, locked into your pathetic world of choredom, no songs of delight, words and music only of your things and their museum status. You are the vintage O-C perfectionist whose career is your home with its voice directing: "Keep me always in perfect alphabetical order."

As Your Husband Sees You. An electrical contractor who does well, your husband likes his well-kept house, your thrift, your decorum and, above all, your reliability.

For himself, he thinks of how great it would be if you could let him bring home a few of the boys for beer and pizza to watch the ballgame on TV. He cannot imagine just tearing a bag open and eating right out of it. He saw cold cuts devoured this way at a friend's poker party and was shocked. "My wife would never allow that," he blurted out. Instead he gets your constant message: the takeover of your beautifully conserved rooms would be tantamount to inflicting wanton abuse upon them.

On the whole you get along together except for his occasional good-humored gibes about your fussiness. At times he objects to the way you pick on the kids and harness them to your house routine. But he will add: "I've got to hand it to her. She's right in there with both feet to protect them when they're bawled out by some dumb teacher or a storekeeper who accuses them of making a disturbance. Right or wrong, nobody better say anything against her children. She's a real tiger mother, she is."

Spillover with Your Family. Your mother, herself an O-C, may be pleased with your traits; your father, taciturn and a bit sour about you. Your sister waves you off: "I guess you mean well, but you're just a nut about your house," while brother regards you with mellow indifference, as does his wife. When your back is not turned, the twins pretend to be "good, quiet, and orderly"; the youngest child abides by your every rule in order to curry favor and win approval, possibly another O-C in the making. But your teen-age daughter rebels or just drifts away when you rant about "that pot party you went to, and I know you're taking the Pill, and why can't you wear a bra, especially with those breasts sticking out to there and the nipples showing?" Still, you never overlook having a snack ready when they arrive after school.

Houseproud Away from Home

Another houseproud, you are off to stay at a resort hotel for a week or so with your husband. It is your custom to refuse your rooms until they meet your perfectionist standards. They cannot be home unless: the lamps all match; the upholstery, drapes and bed-spreads harmonize to your taste; the pictures and mirrors integrate with the period of the room. Including a miscellany of ashtrays, bibelots and other objects, the changeovers you insist on add up to twenty-six items.

Up and down with the assistant manager you trudge to the storage basement and spend the entire day in refurbishing. You are on an expensive vacation but you feel good, knowing that you have satisfied your claims even though you are ready to drop with fatigue. When your husband returns from the beach and sees the finished place he beams. "That's my sweetheart. Everything perfect." You smile back tiredly and order dinner in bed. Your husband leaves to meet his "pickup" at the gambling casino.

Medal for Merit. "First prize of show" for houseproud goes to you for your valiant efforts in protecting your Oriental rug to the death. Grimly, you have trained your dog to wipe its four feet on a special mat at the door, and to patter on hind legs near the walls on the bare floor, then down, rest, patter—down, rest, patter—until it reaches its own turf in the house. Poor dog. Poor you. The only winner here is the rug.

THE HOUSEPROUD MAN

Although a male O-C, you can be just as houseproud as a woman. Your uptightness centers on what you consider your departments. Perfectionist about your car, you find the tiniest scratch on it excruciating. You work endlessly to clean and oil your golf clubs, keep your barbecue and fireplace implements "ready for inspection," and become obsessed about one speck of sediment or a floating bug in the swimming pool. Your yard is always immaculate and only you can paint the deck of the veranda or the garage floor without a blemish.

But what if your wife is a more casual sort? Her "sloppiness" torments you. You nag her about leaving bras and hose on the chairs, the toothpaste tube unrolled, or misplacing your pliers. You can drive her up the wall as she tries to follow your rules for a perfect household. She says, "I don't understand him. He can be so darling when he wants to, but he's been chipping away at me for years. Sometimes I think he'll break me in two." She would like to dispute your accusations about her carelessness, "but he'll never listen and I would have to screech and go into hysterics. That would turn me into a shrew." What is her alternative? None that will work, and this is your secret weapon in remaining the perfectionist overlord of your home.

THE COMPLETERS

Perfectionism is expressed when O-C men and women must complete every task to its ultimate and faithful end, receive their due to the last jot, refuse to defer what "will have to be taken care of anyway."

Have you ever watched an O-C carpenter at work? He matches

every molding with infinite pains, finishes the corners with loving care and sands the edges to a velvet mat finish.

In the same way an O-C housepainter leaves no islands or streaks, however small, and cleans all the hardware exhaustively until his work glories in the perfection he demands.

A dressmaker of O-C bent will make certain that every stitch in the garment is locked so that it will never never pull out or ravel, no matter whether the owner wears it to the grave.

Such completers are of the genus Mr. Fixit, whatever their major vocations, and one explained: "You don't need to have a halo to know that a job worth doing—as somebody said, I think—is worth doing well all the way to the end." Most perfectionists are completers, but the models that follow reveal their need to complete as their overriding signature.

The Tourist Completer

You are the O-C lawyer who remonstrates with your wife while on a guided tour of France. "But, Gladys, there are two places in the tour book that the guide missed. Can't we go back and at least get a few camera shots of them?" It is 4:30 P.M. and everyone on the bus is saturated with the statistics of an all-day trek through historic sites. Gladys had been enthralled but now she gives you a glazed look. "I guess if the tour book mentioned the spot where Napoleon's horse peed we'd have to snap that too."

We're Entitled to It All. You argue that every promised item on your tour schedule should be covered. Only then will you be getting full measure. That's what makes the trip a success. "After all, I paid for it, didn't I?" And now you feel defrauded.

So does your wife, for her reasons. In order to attend every tour that you wanted for full value, she has missed the joy of dawdling in outdoor cafés, roaming the bookstalls, dancing in Montmartre or just sitting in the Tuileries, chatting with a bench neighbor and using her halting French. Secretly, she never forgives you for depriving her of this chance at a fling of pure hedonism.

40

Thus, for both of you the memory of the trip rankles. You refuse to compensate your feelings of incompletion by drawing on your recollections of the vivid and extraordinary sights and sounds that you *had* experienced. The latter fade. Only your resentment at being balked by not accomplishing every detail of the tour remains. "It was coming to us."

The Father Completer

When you, as an O-C father, lay down the law at mealtimes that no one gets dessert or is allowed out to play unless they "clean the plate," do not think that you are using logic in the name of completion. No, you are simply playing this role as a substitute for common sense, blind to any allowance for variations in tastes, appetite, metabolism or social needs. Your wife, more adroit, learns to anticipate the discord that will poison the evening and starts to feed the children before you arrive home. At this point, imperceptibly, familial unity begins to falter. You feel it and say, "I don't understand my family. Why do they act as if I'm some kind of a dictator? . . ."

You Can Rarely Be Swayed. Everyone in the house knows that whatever task you have started must be completed. If you are repairing a faucet, watering the lawn, sorting your coins, or listening to the weather reports, all must hang in midair. Your train runs on the track—no stops, no flagging down for the unscheduled. Granted, you are not totally unreachable. Occasionally, you can be wheedled into delaying your account books for an early start on a family picnic; you make this exception only because it is Frankie's birthday and the weather is good. The children expel their breath at your leniency. It is so rare.

The Do-It-Now Completer

The finish-the-job compulsion finds its corollary in now-is-the-time. This trait is a first cousin to that of the houseproud, who must

41

fly around putting her place in complete order before she can go out. What must be done must be done *then and there*.

Some persons function on the do-it-now compulsion with different rationales. A small tear in the seam or a loose button must be fixed instantly, no matter what. "Suppose I lose the button. Then I'll have to replace the other five. It's the 'stitch in time' idea. Anyway, if it's repaired I don't have to worry. Put it off and the worrying gets worse."

Are you the boat owner who feels compelled to wipe down the hardware with fresh water the moment you dock? And if you delay a minute, become irascible with yourself and your guests?

Or maybe you are the do-it-now wife who must make the bed as soon as you and your husband are up, to "get it out of the way." When he is finished shaving he wants to sit down to put on his socks but you shriek: "Don't! You're mussing the bed after I just made it," and he slinks off to the kids' room to finish dressing. At the table, you are a plate snatcher, clearing off feverishly while your husband's fork is still in his mouth with the last bite of food on it.

I also recall a telephone installer, the most unruffled of men. When asked to verify his work, he assured me that for over twenty years he had had his exact routine for completing every job "on the spot," and never left without triple-checking the bell, wiring, dial tone and all other details. "I do it now. Otherwise I couldn't eat supper tonight."

Tomorrow? Never. The do-it-nower may be further extended in your father completer role previously mentioned. When your son tries to build a box kite you take over.

"But, Dad, I want to do it. That's the fun."

"You'd never finish it."

"I would, next weekend."

"Too late. You'll have the weeding. When you work on something, get it out pronto because . . ." Your lecture drones on.

You worship your motto: "Never leave for another minute what you can do this minute." Tomorrow is a filthy word. You nail it down. "There's no time like the present. Tomorrow I might drop dead and it would never be finished. See what I mean?"

INSIGHTS TO HELP THE PERFECTIONIST

Sticking with the principle of perfectionism as a life guide gives uptight O-Cs a stimulus-response of consequence and probity. Such agreeable images are the psychologic support of their adaptive strengths. Thus, perfectionism need not always be a one-way street to trouble.

Perfectionism with Adaptiveness

Houseproud is not an accident of language. It means what it says: pride and security in the perfection of housekeeping. This trait can often serve you profitably. When you maintain your possessions with diligence, they become heritage items. You avoid replacements, live within your budget and, in this area, without anxiety and with some euphoria—like "polishing my brass candlesticks until they glow like golden tapers . . . what a thrill . . ." Or a houseproud man will say, "My place is my castle. If it's flawless I feel anchored and safe."

As a completer, running your life to the requirements of your tasks gives you the comfort of honest toil. It accelerates you to waste no time and leave no loose ends. You can then wipe your mental slate clean for the next item, avoid muddle and exult in your top-to-bottom performance. At home, should your evening meal be delayed, you stay placid and cool. Your perfectionism is working for you because you keep it where it belongs.

Pitfalls of Perfectionism

However, this trait contains its own perils. Built into it skulks the need to overdo. Look into your own perfectionist self as parent, spouse, worker or social being. In your houseproud fervor you deny your husband the use of his home for his social wants. With your children you substitute sham virtue and cookies for empathy and fondness. Friends and intimates? Some may admire your housework perfection but others write you off. "She must be a horse."

As a male perfectionist your security symbols of "things" may be a ball and chain, your "castle" a jail, so chilled that you must stay wrapped in your uptight garments against anxiety. You tend to be stony with your mate, and you walk a tightrope between half-buried guilt and the need for absolution. Thus you save secretly for some jewelry as a surprise, but you are really hell-bent on having your way, and think, "Maybe this will get her to live up to my standards."

Like O-C Parent, Like O-C Child. In your parental role your perfectionism demands that your child be predictable and conform to impossible disciplines. You want a quiet good child because you believe this means good mental hygiene. For whom? To eliminate your headaches, back pains, or whatever else? Are you satisfied only when the child is reflexive and compulsive in obeying your edicts? This very forcefulness may rob the youngster of authority, creativeness and innovation. It is a putdown of a dreadful kind, because when children ingest the diet of uncertain, insecure and anxiety-ridden nutriment fed by adults, they convert their emotions into O-C mechanisms. These may be lifelong.

Expectations and Rationalizations

Try reorienting your expectations to a better compromise in preserving your possessions. Can you rationalize that, after all, your things are inanimate—for use, not to adore? Can you transfer that sensuous delight in your dishes and crystal, or car and swimming pool, to the taste and smell and feel of people, and not reserve it just for objects?

Look for the Midpoint. Call upon your resource of flexibility to alter a position, mechanically at first. Later, it "comes natural." Does it really matter if your husband's friends mar the table? Have it redone. And do you know that he has steeled himself to approve of you because "after all I have to live with her." Does he indeed? Have you ever suspected that he resents your orders? That he feels belittled? As things are, he may leave one day. Perhaps he is only waiting for the children to be grown.

Men too have their sensibilities and could cry when hurt. Since you would be the first to run to his defense, protect him from the hurts that you impose. Do not believe that it is chic to kick your husband in the teeth. Old-fashioned caring is still the best tranquilizer for marital tension with only affectional side effects.

Frustration of the Perfectionist

If you find that you must struggle to camouflage your perfectionism, it is no longer working for you. At the very least you are embarrassed by your personality and the floating indifference you sense in family and friends. They fancy that you are an uptight perfectionist, yes. But that you are basically an obsessive-compulsive eludes them. They do wish that you would ease up on your tiresome amalgam of worries and fears, whether about yourself, your house, or your fanatic completer drive.

So do your children wish it. Conditioned by unwholesome pressures, one or some may grow up as links in the chain of existing O-Cs. Their smoldering angers may then descend on you. Older now and less resilient, you will be unable to withstand your progeny's staggering toughness in hammering you with contempt and dissociating from you as well.

These facets of perfectionism constantly threaten to choke off your adaptive comfort and make life a dance over hot coals between trepidation and panic. As the P.E.G. standard would measure your performance, maladaptation and perhaps depression await you just around the corner.

> Anxiety, your sting smarts in perfection
> and makes a nonsense
> of finding sleep or peace.

· 3 ·
Control

To remain as adaptive as possible, in your O-C uptight function, you define your identity and status with exactitude, budget all your resources, including physical energies, save regularly, and place fixed limits on purchases, goals and, too frequently, pleasures. This is the self-discipline of your control which, more than any other trait, signals your obsessive-compulsive personality in action. Yet, while self-control is preeminent, *control of the other person and the environment* runs a close second. This means that only by gaining jurisdictional command, that is, overbearing power, can you relax your uptightness. Control of the self and others, rather than *living with*, becomes your essential style of life.

THE DOMINEERING

Ordinarily, when we specify a *dominant* person, we are designating an individual who is master of a situation because of superior competence, intrinsic merit or the *authoritativeness* granted by expertise.

In contrast, as a *domineering* person you hold sway by your own mandate of *authoritarianism*. For example, you may be an adaptive O-C, but if a secret lack of confidence eats into you, then you must lean on your dogmatic leverage, rather than on your abilities and skills. This is called *reaction formation* and compensates for your self-doubts. Jockeying for control of your fellows, you exercise overbearance, disrespect, acerbity and the like . . . all unaware.

The Domineering O-C Husband

You may work long hard hours for your wife and children, fixed on giving them every possible advantage. But as an O-C controller, you expect total compliance with your judgments and directives since, "I know best for all of us."

You can sour your wife's joys and freedoms. You saddle her with excessive duties, from assisting you with your paper work to servicing your elderly parents. You also suspend her interest in returning to college. "Ridiculous. Why do you want a degree at your age? Where will it get us?" In sorrow, you imply that she is deserting your needs. "Be a help to me and understand that things must be done my way."

She caves in and asks, "Am I forgiven?"

You pat her. "Sure, after all, you're a darned good girl."

Is she humiliated by her apologies? "No, they're just words—to make him feel magnanimous and relaxed. I do love him, I suppose."

Domineuvers of the O-C Husband. Domineering maneuvers need not be enforced with a club. Small putdowns can also maintain your sovereignty. For example, you are the husband who tunes out your wife's chatting by flipping on the radio, going to the kitchen for some fruit or diving into the sports page. She trails off, hurt. Or when you are leaving for a party, she may stop to kiss you and ask impulsively if you like her dress. It all seems a nuisance, uptight as you are about prompt arrivals. You brush off the kiss and mutter, "I guess so. Let's get going." Quite effectively, you have dimmed her light.

Sweet Reasonableness. Another man domineers his wife, the proud owner of a boutique, by showing her "on paper" the insignificance of her profits. "Besides," he points out whimsically, "in my bracket I can't afford the taxes on them. Give the place up. You're such a great wife. Isn't that enough for you? It is for me, pet."

47

Domineering with Perfectionism. One woman explains gravely, "Believe me, I'm married to a kook who wants to come home to a superclean house. Not one cozy little germ flying around. He thinks he's the perfect father, too. Nothing out of a jar for his baby. Everything daily fresh. And when he arrives, he wants his dinner on the dot. Why can't he take a little time off for me? . . . just to feel each other up and down for a minute? He's forgotten how we made that baby."

Or maybe you are the O-C who constantly badgers your wife about her week's menus, which of your sisters to telephone or what kind of dress to wear next day. You may also go over the refrigerator every night. "Look at those leftovers. Money doesn't grow on trees. The least you can do is make sure no food goes to waste."

Your wife says wearily, "They'll be tomorrow's lunch."

You grunt and dismiss her, but you never connect your harassment with her chronic fatigue and "nerves."

The Domineering O-C Father

Perhaps it is your daughter, now a thinking young woman, who is bucking your control. You rarely praise, much less encourage her talents. She writes poetry and plays the guitar, but you charge that she is frivolous and maybe "messing around too." If she would take on a greater share of the household work it would make more sense. You do not bite, you gnaw, gradually eroding her into your ideal of good behavior because you cannot divest yourself of role fixation as Big Chief of Family. When your daughter finally leaves home, you are baffled, angry and frightened.

You might also take a look at one of your neighbors who is a controlling O-C. Remember when this man's teen-age son broke his wrist while wrestling at school? And his father refused to buy him a sling? "Use an old scarf. You shouldn't have been horsing around like that anyhow. Why weren't you fixing the glass in the basement window instead?" He might have been saying, "Do as I tell you and don't get into trouble because my stomach can't take

CONTROL

it." Did his harshness repel you or did you secretly empathize with him? An honest answer might clue you in to yourself.

The Mrs. Craig Syndrome: Domineering O-C Women

Among our great classics in the American theater is George Kelly's play, *Craig's Wife*, which appeared originally on Broadway in 1925. Fifty years later the theme is just as fresh, and Harriet Craig remains the paradigm of the uptight obsessive-compulsive woman.

The very term, "a Mrs. Craig," which you yourself may have used, has crept into our lexicon to symbolize the houseproud woman (see Chapter 2). Mrs. Craig lives in her self-imposed milieu of inhibition. She is righteous, perfectionist, insecure, and devoid of any warmth. What is less understood is Kelly's portrayal of Mrs. Craig as the epitome of the controlling woman.

The play highlights her strategies for ensuring security. She dominates all who cross her threshold, keeps surveillance on them, including her husband's movements and telephone calls. She chokes off his friendships and exploits his healthy tolerance to keep him from penetrating her crafty aims. She grasps into her own hands "the control of the man upon which the guarantees of my security are found" and emasculates him. While she may hunger at times for affection, her anxieties dictate that only her possessions and the enslavement of those around her offer safe destiny.

She does not want the man. She despises him. Equally, she scorns the subjective reality of her marriage. Solely, it is the façade that counts. In her words, "I'm interested only in the impression on the popular mind and the respect of the community we have to live in."

In suppressing her husband, she reinforces her dominance and presents him instead with a beautiful and orderly home as cold and sterile as herself. But the cat's-paw does not remain forever quiescent. Mr. Craig, disillusioned by the vital deficiencies of his marriage and unable to accept them, at last leaves his controlling wife and her "home."

49

Domineuvers of the O-C Woman. Today, we see the same intra-marital callousness by domineering mates who fail to counterbalance with honey and spice in enough segments of the marriage.

You may personify the blatantly controlling O-C wife who keeps your husband reeling on the ropes. His grievance? "She makes me feel like a worm and it gets me mad. I say, 'Laugh, listen to a funny story,' and she says, 'Shush, you'll wake the baby.' I say, 'Let's have a drink,' and she says, 'You're a wino like your brother.' I ask her, why, when I come home and kiss her, she don't kiss back? She says, 'Maybe because I'm a receiver, not a giver.' I say, 'Let's make love,' she says, 'You're sex crazy.' "

You do not see that inwardly he is suffering. In living by your standards only, you are assaulting his entire person. Such onslaughts account, in part, for the high divorce rate today of those married ten years or more.

The Domineering O-C Mother

In the broad spectrum of middle-class families, you may be the controlling mother who will raise an O-C child.

The Subtle Approach. Although verbally warm and affectionate, you are, like Mrs. Craig, fundamentally inhibited. You evade sexuality and tend to diminish men, especially your child's father. In striving for control, you teach your daughter to be polite, morally proper and ultracautious in her trust.

But not for you the direct approach. "That way you lose them." Your authoritarianism takes over after some minor infraction; for openers you make a simple appeal. "Susie, I know you love me and want to be thoughtful of me." Susie is bewildered. "Sure I do, Mom." You then lecture her solemnly on the importance of your welfare as her main concern. "It is only mother who will truly love and stick by you." To accede to your needs her behavior must constitute total devotion. Susie is hooked. Should she ever fail to be "thoughtful" of you, i.e., the model child you demand, she will be violating her love and allegiance and, even as an adult, develop guilt. The earlier this conditioning begins, the more certain that both mother and child will feed each other's uptightness and O-C patterns.

Hitting Out. Perhaps you are the O-C mother who, in your desire to control, throttles your son's exuberance and makes him toe the line. For instance: with threats of sickness ("You will suffer because you are bad"); of separation ("I'll leave you—or give you away"); of isolation ("I'll lock you up in your room"); of death ("You'll die like your friend Sandy"); and of similar calamities that will subdue him and lay the groundwork for future anxieties or phobias.

Possibly you use other expedients for control when he erupts into mischief and frustrates your demands. You may reject him overtly ("You are nasty and don't deserve my attention"); you withhold love or gifts ("I won't kiss you goodnight," or "Don't expect a birthday present"); you threaten indifference ("You'll have to ride home on your bicycle. I won't pick you up").

Conversely, you dole out affection and approval only as the child bows to your will. Thus, conformity is fixated and development stifled when generous love is not given. This "happy, good" child learns to toady to you for applause and rewards. Later, he will do the same with relatives, teachers and other superiors. He never becomes self-confident or plans independent goals and interests appropriate to his potentials. He lives in the mold set by you. (See Operant Conditioning in Chapter 18.)

The Regimental Approach. You may be a third type of O-C woman who declared right after marriage that you were the boss. And you are. Typically, you raise your children in the style of a Marine drill sergeant. You order them to bed—a pointing finger at the clock and a stern, "Okay, kids, BEDTIME!" You expect them to obey to the split second. No storytelling, no tucking in. The trumpet blows. The toy soldiers must disappear.

51

Domineering in the Work Setting

Uptight O-Cs, from the corporation president down to the mail-room clerk, occupy space in every office. If you are a middle manager you embody the controlling superior, who demands total allegiance as a protection against your dormant insecurity. You set the ambiance, the schedules and the pace of the work.

You may consider it your duty to poke your nose into all established routine. Mail must go out at the time you designate (it always has); the files are to be cross-referenced your way (even if it makes no sense); you continually modify the form of letters (and when a ballup ensues, blame the stenographers); you create office schisms and power struggles (oblivious to them). One worker muttered: "When he walks in, the whole place gets crudded up."

Pushing It. If you are the supervisor of a fleet of delivery trucks, you hustle your drivers into fast and reckless performance. Time, time! They end up with ulcers. Holding the power to fire or make a damaging report, you also harry them with implied blackmail—intimations of their personal affairs, of gambling, indebtedness or violations of minor rules.

Your ploys are familiar to all except the top executives, who are busy putting pressure on you. This augments your uptightness and defensive tactics. One sees this dehumanizing process in many corporate setups where tight control signifies production, profits and power but, equally, frayed nerves and torment for many.

Not Letting Go. You were the O-C director of photography who fenced in your total enclave. Eminent and meticulous, you wanted memos in detail of whatever took place. You could not resist supervising all moves of your associates, explaining gently, "Just trying to help." Each man was expert, some near-geniuses. Yet you took pains to study, okay and initial each step of their work. Did you fear their competition? Not a bit. But to relinquish any part of

52

your authority would have been to wrench off a limb. Control, ipso facto, was the watchword.

In an academic setting you may be the sedate college professor who speaks in uppercase. "Sometimes people Resent me as being Arrogant and Domineering. They say I'm Bound to the Regular Order of Things. It's Axiomatic, though, that this is the Firm Ground on which we Exist. I am the Department Head and it must run My Way. Very well, the others Dislike me. That is Unsettling. Who wants to be Disliked? Sometimes I could Cry. But I know I would look Grotesque, so I Blank it out. I think Mine is the only Right Way."

Stopped by caution, fighting alterants, you implode with gall and heartache. You do not see that our current civilization, clamoring for great change, is yet trying ferociously to preserve conservatism's strengths. In your uptightness, you hang on to its sores and its desperation.

THE INTOLERANT

Since you cannot control the behavior of your friends and strangers, numerous situations may turn you gradually into a restive, carping person. Whether at the apogee of power or in the lower echelons, you emerge with the canker of intolerance, an O-C spin-off of control. As such, you become obsessed with "law and order" and absolute governance in all affairs. You want dissent obliterated at any cost.

Intolerance at the Top. A supreme example of intolerance warring on criticism is recorded in a macabre episode of Queen Elizabeth I's reign. One of her loyal Puritan subjects, John Stubbs, printed his disapproval of her prospective marriage to a Catholic French duke; her reprisal was swift. She ordered that his hand be chopped off. Immediately after the amputation, he raised his hat in his other hand, swore fealty to the Queen and England, and fainted away.

Elizabeth, as most rulers, felt threatened throughout her life. Her intolerance shielded her anxieties and protected her enormous might, a trait evident in some of our current leaders. Believing only in their own virtues and lofty motives (translated "control") they have suppressed all other judgments, thereby vindicating their own.

Intolerance at the Lower Level. "No, sir," said one small business-man to a poll-taker, "I'm not changing my mind on anything. We need real laws and a lid on people's thoughts. Being too open-minded only lets in rotten ideas and the political rabble."

His teen-age son was leaving. "Pop," he yelled back, "you need a lubricant. I can hear your ideas creak."

His father's face fell. "See? No respect today. That's what I mean."

Social Intolerance

Much of the day-to-day transactions of social intercourse can arouse intolerance and impel you and other O-C uptights to anger, fear, or similar emotional distress.

The Classical Prude. You may find yourself struggling against stimulation for pleasure, even the mildest of erotica, which you apprehend could arouse your prurience and sexual fantasy and, in turn, escape your control. Your strengths might thereby be sapped by an undertow of desire—and you would feel undone! Powerless to endure those who carry off such prerogatives of freedom with sunlit joy, you are repelled by the overt sensuality of a coworker and her gay references to affectional exchanges, sexual romps and party play.

Or you may be the staid headmaster of a prep school, bound in grimly devoted wedlock, who condemns a younger colleague for sporadic infidelity to his marriage. The younger man tells you, "It's none of your fuckin' business, sir."

Still, you are not pleased with your inhibitions. But frustrated as you are by an inability to cater to the senses, to achieve social ease, or to be electrified in sexual outlets, you would stifle anyone who adapts to a more piquant and informal way of life.

Petty Intolerance.   In minor situations, your intolerance is often expressed with scolding, murky snubs or peevishness. Somehow, you always manage to disrupt the peace. You may center on dinner guests who spill soup on the tablecloth, or you condemn dogs and dog owners. Maybe your special irritants are frowsy nephews who are coarse and impolite. If you are an ethnic or social snob, you disdain minority groups who "should know their place," also majority groups who "are too permissive with minorities"; and you maintain a running bias against all salesgirls, merchants, cab drivers and service people who "answer back" or who are "out to cheat" you.

The devil of it is that some of this may be so. But the excess emphasis, the sole preoccupation with the negative and the petty, betray you as an intolerant O-C. You live in an indigence of cheer, dulled to the echoes of your intolerance; you lose the tender charity of those who want to like you but cannot.

The Intolerant Must Remember.   Although aware that no one can alter the past, you may still cherish it jealously as your bedrock of experience. You dredge your memory, savoring old wounds of insult and rejection. But these recollections may not be accurate. The good things are inked out as you select your painful *reactions* to the events, rather than the events themselves. Moreover, you preserve letters and mementos to "prove" what happened in the past exactly as you must recall it. Such specificity of recall, reinforced by your accumulated evidence, bolsters your intolerance and the craving to control "those responsible" for past suffering.

THE STUBBORN

Most of us have encountered obstinate O-Cs who will hold out forever to get their own way. A pretty nurse said: "When I'm fixed in a mind-set, I can't be moved. That's how I am and nothing will change me."

There are no two sides of a problem to muddle you when you are a stubborn O-C, only one—yours.

Why Should I Give In? "I'm head of the house. This is my job," is your dictum when you insist on carving the turkey your way, and as always, it ends with a chopped-up mess of meat and bones. But you have proved that you are top guy in this house and no one had better say you nay.

As a controlling O-C your obduracy can appear in many other ways. You may be the young man who will not call your auto club for a tow because you must get your car out of the ditch by your own devices, even though it is in danger of turning over.

There is also your headstrong daughter, a true O-C, who decides to repaper the bathrooms with her boyfriend's help on the Sunday that you expect your families to dinner.

It could be your housepainter, ordinarily the sweetest of men, who rejects all of his wife's appeals for red doors on their home. "No way. They'll fade to pink after a few years and that means redoing them."

Perhaps you are the dogged O-C who won't wear your dinner suit for a "black tie" affair, then blames your wife for not insisting, when you arrive and feel foolish because all the others are in black tie.

Would you be the O-C woman who stubbornly refuses to cut short your long-distance calls "just because my husband wants to keep the bills down"? You say, "After all, it's my mother I'm talking to."

If you are the spouse whose wife suggests that the screw holding a loose bracket is now firm and in just right, do you rebut: "No, it needs that one extra turn to make it real tight"—and shear off the head of the screw? Your wife could either laugh or slug you, but she is too busy offering comfort and excuses of "bad luck" that you need for your mulish judgment.

Finally, perhaps you are the man I once noticed who went into a fury and demanded that his fiancée return and enter the building through the door that *he* was holding open for her. No matter that she was already halfway through an adjacent door being held open by the other couple.

Don't Cross the Boss. Those who must contend with pigheadedness try to circumvent it. One wife simply lays out her husband's dinner suit and states categorically that everyone will be in black tie. Another woman threatens to throw out the dinner if her husband does not come up from his workshop in ten minutes. She did this once and it helped. He remembered it for the future.

However, a gentle and tolerant husband is stymied. "What is it that makes me afraid of that little woman when she's being so stiff-necked and I want to disagree? It might be as small a thing as how to open a letter. I know she loves me but it's just that shuttered look of temper and disapproval . . . it's easier to say, 'All right, you do it.' "

Stubbornness is not an endearing trait. When an individual retains a fixed judgment on any matter, it serves mainly to reinforce control over a situation or another person. But it also betrays the fragility and sometimes an early breakdown of the O-C's self-confidence.

INSIGHTS TO HELP THE CONTROLLING PERSON

As a controlling O-C, your resourcefulness gets things done. Compulsively, you organize and expedite your projects, often with great ingenuity. This is your adaptive strength. It appears to give you proof positive that you are anxiety-free and, in short, a doer.

Still, we have the other side. When you practice your control, you are shooting straight for controllership. It is a disconsolate truth that the O-C is a failed person in finding the love and sureness that create a high confidence level. Here is where you sense your lack; all the more you must fight for a tight grip on any and everything.

You Became Scared . . .

. . . and this is why you are racing in a contest with yourself. Possibly this trait was provoked by early imprinting of rejection by one or the other unloving parent, or by the tyranny of a sibling or class bully, or by emotional deprivation and loss (broken family, death, school changes with excessive mobility), or perhaps by helplessness in facing the demands of capricious adults. Any or all of these could have sensitized you to uncertainties in every human relationship. You shrank in value.

Hence, brain circuits carrying reinforced messages of frustration were always on the ready to be triggered into explosive outbursts. But you were forced to control them by reaction formation. Ambivalence, as a push and pull, came on stage.

. . . And You Are Running Scared

You are, in fact, trapped. To be psychically at ease and to compensate for the vacuum left by doubts, you now sacrifice the dividends of partnered and egalitarian living. One O-C reflected, "I suppose I like feeling angry and frustrated. It fits me like an old shoe." While you need love and joined hands, you subordinate affectional emotions as the least important to your vitality. You rationalize that control and hubris offer more.

For example, let us say that your worthier self would like to support your wife's ego needs. Yet you are afraid that she will usurp your authority or that others will think you a sad sack or a uxorious jerk. If single, you long for intimacies that will banish aloneness. But you also want to be free of commitments because, like most O-Cs, you are "a private person." Actually, you are trying to finesse your ambivalence with the notion that control means being "true to yourself." Therefore, whether domineering, intolerant or stubborn, you intimidate others. You accuse them of contentiousness, distortion of issues or competitiveness. Ironic. You are more nearly describing the projections of your own autocratic say-so. You want the last word.

Getting Unstuck . . .

You can gain freedom from your demon of uptight control. An adaptive, happy life requires giving. A first step is to learn how to make deliberate overtures. Most recipients find this irresistible when it is real. In giving what the other person wants and taking what that person offers, a harvest of benefits results. Constraints are broken in geometric progression: contact of mind takes place, and without further signals, affability and respect envelop the relationship. (See Contracting, in Chapter 18.) Such sharing permits those who love you to bring support when you need it most. Alienation is obviated. You pool resources, and the weight of "going it alone" is lifted. You are eased.

Consider a simple way of testing your need to control. The next time you find yourself in an ugly conflict and your quarry says, "Oh, what the hell. All of this isn't worth the argument. Let's forget it." Must you then fire off more shots about previous resistance and refuse the accommodation? Or can you take a deep breath, let it out slowly, nod, smile and abandon the fracas? It might surprise you to feel a surge of genuine confidence because now you have gained true control of self in its profoundest form—generosity distilled from adapting to the other person.

. . . Remaining Uptight

What if you cannot compromise, yet life's events and pressures make you forfeit control? One sad man summed it up: "When I brood about the possibility of losing the helm, I squirrel around in

59

my mind about how to whip my attitudes into shape again so I can't be faulted. Finally I get tired of being on guard, then tired of being tired. Feels as if I've lost my cushion."

The cost of maintaining such rigorous control and vigilance may be functional hypertension, other psychosomatic ailments or severe desolation (see Part Two).

While adaptively effective and often close to the high of your potentials, as a controlling O-C you cannot entwine yourself in the gossamer filaments of joy or fun. This inhibition wrecks your pleasures. Thus, you lower your gratification score in the P.E.G. standard. You are unpopular because others sense that you do not savor the ordinary delights of belonging to the human race.

> Where go you sorry creature . . .
> Gripped and compelled, tension held
> unbend or break.

· 4 ·
Orderliness

To be systematic and regular, to follow a prescribed course and to plan ahead produce the low hum of euphoria and honor for orderly obsessive-compulsives. They marshal and pace their tasks briskly, with no shortcuts, as if some arcane force had wound them into motion; their orderliness becomes another deputy of control.

A number of overlapping subtraits within orderliness will be described in this chapter. As seen in life, no sharp line distinguishes them, but in order to strike their special tone, we discuss each as a constant under separate headings.

THE SYSTEMS MAN OR WOMAN

In today's mechanized culture, you, the orderly O-C, are a prize catch for any employer. You define and program all operating procedures for large and small companies. From your job specifications, the cogs are developed that make the corporate wheel. Its hub of nerve centers is then activated and the ponderous system rolls.

You Are Your Own Computer

Long before IBM gave birth to computer technology, you were the efficiency expert. Your routined traits flourished and also drove you to schematize your own life.

For example, a consultant engineer whom I recall spent hours at home cataloguing references, worksheets and memoranda. His papers, books and technical bulletins were bound and shelved perfectly. "Look at this. Isn't it beautiful? Everything in its nook, nothing ever misplaced."

Your system may cover different ground. You inventory your personal possessions, from furniture to cuff links, and label your pipes with origin, age and date of last use. You keep accurate ledgers, too, on income and expenditures by the day, week and month. Your enthusiasm for data input includes purchases of groceries, shoelaces and whatnot, as well as the big-ticket items. At a moment's notice you can compare a week's cost of living with the same week one to ten years ago.

"I am a creature of method and routine," you say, as you practice your far-flung efficiency. Living becomes a game of order for you. At meals, you divide your meat, vegetables and starches to "come out even." When smoking, the last match must ignite the last cigarette in the pack.

True, with these rigidities, you may show up at home as a despot, but in your estimation you are a paragon of solidity. You are uniform! No matter that your wife may sometimes blanch with apprehension. "Now, what did I do out of turn? Will 'he' find out?" The household must run on schedule, all accountable to you. She fumes: "And you try living with that."

The Systems Woman

You may be among the many women who thoroughly enjoy a computerized psyche. "I love working in the accounts office. We have computers and everything always comes out to the penny. It's so satisfying."

If a homemaker, you explain, "I do everything with a plan in advance—sewing, laundry or shopping at the supermarket in the order of the aisles." (See List Makers later in this chapter.) Your system for folding linens? "The bathroom towels must be done in thirds, the kitchen ones in fourths. The sheets and pillowcases are squared, table napkins are triangled, and my husband's shirts stacked in alternate directions for solids and patterns." You may also divide every week's cash allowance into separate envelopes. Each, with a record on its face, is inviolate and self-supporting. No borrowing from Peter to pay Paul or the Avon lady.

Infatuation with Records

As a doting lover of orderly living you glory in your matchless records. They pin you down to hard-headed realities and stiffen your *amour-propre*. At times, you may get charged up with a mystique of their value to posterity, identifying them with the clay tablets excavated from ancient Babylonia and Egypt which recorded domestic life in those periods. You muse wistfully on Samuel Pepys' ten-year diary or the Duc de Saint-Simon's twenty-volume history of the court of Louis XIV, and you dream, "What a book my records would make."

One O-C man confessed that at times he had a sense of being transmogrified. He saw himself as a huge metal receptacle of files, but in which he, plain Joe Smith, could not be found. Pride inflated him. *He* was the system. Then he would shake himself, deflated and fearful. He must not get lost, he must dig out of his records and find himself.

THE PRECISE

Within orderliness, precision may be your absolute in every way. You clean and wax your car each Sunday morning at nine A.M., fetch the newspapers, trim your hedge to perfection and mow the lawn. Your bedroom lights go off at a fixed time; the hour you and your wife return from any party is just as precise. You are so regularized that you take your two-week annual vacation on the same date at the same place, every year without fail.

Exact to a Hair. I once watched an O-C woman avidly rule off the double doors of a custom-made cabinet to see if the width of the wood grains matched to the millimeter. She also measured the *design* of the piping on all the cushions of her sofa. When a fractional difference appeared, indiscernible to the eye, back the cabinet or sofa went. This continued for a year, when the seller disinvited her patronage.

You may find your own preciseness offended by a picture that is out of line on the wall. You must level it, even when visiting or waiting in your doctor's office. Or if your wife relates an incident to friends, you are impelled to cut her off in order to rearrange the sequence and give your more literal version of it.

Perhaps you are a middle manager whose passion is the precise care of all office equipment. For months you may have been pondering over your files. Finally, you call a meeting of your subordinates and fix them with a basilisk stare. Your hands grip the desk nervously. "Let me remind all of you that we are not living in the Stone Age. We operate at the highest peak of civilization. From now on, no papers are to be filed with edges sticking out of the folders unevenly. Brooks, rivers and cowpaths meander. Files must be straight and go by the ruler." Nodding of heads and then escape. You feel a surge of triumph at having spoken up. Then the anxiety. "What about the next time a sheet pokes over the edge?"

People Arrangers.   Let us suppose that you are the uptight precise hostess whose itch to arrange your guests comes to the fore. Nothing must go unorganized. *The crime is helter-skelter.* You shepherd one couple. "Do sit there, won't you?" To someone else, "Oh yes, the sofa will take three easily," or "I wish you'd join Mildred and Jack. You have so much in common." (They don't.) "No, I'd rather you didn't stand here at the bar. Sort of crowds the room, don't you think?" You leave nothing to chance, and while you gamely strive for a cordial climate, the ear detects vibrations of strain.

Precision as Graciousness.   As a precise O-C, you are at your best when you send a gift. Like most compulsives, you tend toward money and things as symbols of security. Since it is not easy to give

64

of yourself, you proffer a gift. It is perfect for the occasion and the best in quality. Your personalized wrappings and a note written in your own courtly fashion reveal the effort at affection behind it.

You also entertain exquisitely, making certain that all introductions convey full information about each guest's accomplishments, interests, status, and so on. You seem to wrap everyone in warmth and to want to serve as the conduit for your friends' pleasure. But such O-Cs as yourself are the exceptions. You are extraordinarily adaptive; and entertaining, with precise attention to food, wine and decor, is your compulsion. It may spring from a sublimative fondness which you can rarely display in a more intimate setting because your fastidious habits preclude the responsibility for another. Those like yourself seldom marry and generally are nonorgasmic persons. Yet you are mature, especially in social effectiveness.

Cash and Carry. You adhere closely to a cash basis and pay bills promptly, a trait welcome to creditors. One O-C pays his rent a week before the first of the month. "Why wait for the bill? I know it's coming." In a restaurant you leave a fifteen percent tip, to the penny; and when with friends, you pay only your exact share of the check. Although you cannot bear to be cheated, whether in time, money or services, you are equally pained if you defraud, and you spend every thought and effort to correct the most minute error.

I Hate Change

Do you choose your next day's clothes the evening before? And if the weather changes overnight, do you then castigate the forecaster with bitter telephone calls of reproof? Probably yes. It is also fairly certain that if you are ever dislocated from your accustomed habitats, you feel caught in quicksand. Only your "regular" waiter, hairdresser or salesperson will do. You may even grow as livid as the woman who cried wildly after coming from her dress shop, "So they had to remodel it. The sofa was so comfortable . . . and why did they repanel the place? That pretty wallpaper, with the mirrors just perfect for privacy . . . it was the same for fourteen years but now it looks new and peculiar. It will never be right to me again. I HATE CHANGE!"

THE PUNCTUAL

To be inordinately punctual is to revere orderliness in terms of time. Like money and other material things, time plays a substantial role in the psychologic anatomy of orderly persons. Simply that it can be measured as a verity tells the punctual O-C that it should be respected. You may assert, "I must always be assured in making any appointment that I won't have to wait. I'll admit that I demand immediate attention and service. I get to the airport way in advance so that I won't have to stand in line for checking in. If my luggage isn't down at once after landing, I threaten to see the baggage-master." And you fidget, stalk about and glare at your watch while matters are being rectified.

However, punctuality for O-Cs also includes deference to others' time. If you are a nine-to-five employee, you assume that you are to work those eight hours because they belong to the boss. You arrive a few minutes before nine and never dream of leaving until a bit after five. Somehow you are not the favorite of the office.

Should you, perchance, be a few minutes late, you are distraught and launch into a jumble of explanations. You may not recover your poise for the entire day.

THE CLEAN AND TIDY

As a conditioned attribute of merit for your O-C traits, knowing that your body, clothes and surroundings are scrubbed clean can banish your uptight anxieties. You say, "I can't tolerate one hair in my wash basin or a smudge on the mirror. My stomach doubles up until I've tidied them. Then I'm fine."

You spray your bathroom and kitchen with the newest antiseptics. However, your clean and tidy neighbor begs to differ. "I prefer old-fashioned ammonia. Even the strong smell tells me it's better. And don't forget, my floors are so clean you could eat off them, anytime." She also hangs each day's wearing apparel in the open, overnight, "to let them breathe the germs away." Not to be outdone, you wash the undersides of all closet shelves and zero in on every kitchen cabinet screw with metal polish. If an onlooker exclaims, "The things you get to," you reply, "Doesn't everybody?"

A Place for Everything and Everything in Its Place

Unlike the houseproud you do not dote on display, beauty or good taste. Your place can look as ugly as an old toad. But neat, trim and sanitary it must be.

We can envy your complete absence of mess as you work. The floor is swept between chores. Magazines are neatly stacked according to date. You place the telephone in a cabinet out of sight. The world globe must be spun to its original position; footstools, toaster, teakettle, soap dish, and books are returned to their proper spots. Sofa pillows are lined up like soldiers on parade. Where the houseproud will artfully arrange her pillows as if they had toppled a bit by chance, because she nurses the illusion that her home looks "warm and lived-in," you would rather your place looked as if humans never inhabited it—or had to.

Live Tidy, Act Tidy. You enjoy being ultrafastidious about yourself and justify it. "Suppose I were in an accident. I wouldn't be found dead with underclothes not freshly laundered."

One O-C tidy-clean woman wasn't nearly so outraged about her jewelry being burglarized as she was because the robbers had eaten sandwiches and coffee in her kitchen without washing the dishes and leaving the sink clean. "Slobs."

Your "Inner" Self. "Don't clutter me up with the facts. I like having a tidy mind. Take this nonsense about protected species and world food shortages and poverty levels—conversation pieces. I keep my ideas plain and simple. Living is smoother and neater that way."

No Fuss, No Muss. An excessively tidy-clean man whom I met avoids sitting down at a party because he refuses to crease his trousers or jacket. He perches on the edge of a chair with his legs partially extended; to sip cocktails he raises his arm from the shoulder rather than bend his elbow fully to avert wrinkling the sleeve. When he leaves he removes his jacket and tenderly hangs it on the hook in his car. One might think this performance droll—but not if it were realized how helpless he is in the clutch of his compulsions and that once at home he sags from muscle tension due to the strain of his sartorial postures and his friends' raillery. "Goofed again" is his last glum thought before sleeping.

THE LIST MAKERS

"I've got a little list . . . they'd none of 'em be missed," as Gilbert and Sullivan's Mikado had it, could serve as the contrapuntal theme song of O-Cs who are compulsive about their list making.

Living by the List

We all use memorandum pads or appointment books, and many of us could not get along without them. However, as an uptight orderly O-C, you may compile daily lists for every minuscule task ahead—to mend or purchase clothes, to "do" the closets, the drapes, the second set of dishes, buy bus tokens tomorrow, put out garbage, and replace the plastic liner. You also prepare guest lists for parties, date and gift lists for birthdays, anniversaries and holidays, plus lists for children's entertainment, lessons, car-pooling, whose turn for bridge nights—and last on the list at nine that evening, "Do next day's list."

Lists That Entangle the List Maker

The deep-rooted insecurity of O-C list makers intimidates them with being short-changed if they fail to obey every listed commitment. For example, one housewife had second thoughts about an item she had listed. "Like someone told me about hiphuggers. Frankly, I don't have the shape for them, but after I put them on the list they would holler at me until I got them. So I had to buy a pair to cross them off the list—and off my mind."

You may be a list maker so befogged in trivia that if asked to take off for a movie or to greet an unexpected caller you answer with a vacant gaze. This was not on the list. How do you now account for it as an entry to be scratched off? In effect, the list is dictating what not to do. It robs you of unconstrained, even impulsive choice.

If you should complete all the assignments listed and have a brief moment of relief, do you next feel dejected realizing that they are finished? But then, with sudden joy, know that now you must start a new list?

THE HEALTH CONSCIOUS

For you, orderliness in health means never being sick, and prima facie, you do appear to be either a very healthy individual or at least a noncomplainer, pushing to adapt. At the other extreme, we find O-C complainers (see Chapter 14), who suffer many psychosomatic ailments that relate, in some way, to their fears, anxieties and tensions. There too is the hypochondriac, whose compulsion is to be ill and who cannot tolerate being well.

Compulsion to Be Healthy

Predominantly, you are a self-controller. No one can tell your body how to behave. Verbally well, you must never allow disorder to foul your life. But illness strikes (if only a miserable head cold), as it does at all mortals. Stoically, you refuse to accept it and will not pamper yourself. Your denial of illness is noted when you rarely, if ever, accept medication. Given a prescription you do not fill it. And that is final.

The intense emotion with which you minimize your distress suggests that to sacrifice orderly control is a greater agony than the illness. Seen by you as weak or careless behavior, you do not intend to reward the illness by surrendering to it. A radio dispatcher told me, "You could never believe how that pain zig-zagged up and down my leg, doctor. But nobody would ever have guessed." Put your way, either you do it with willpower and wait for nature to heal, or you ache in silence.

INSIGHTS TO HELP THE ORDERLY

From the foregoing we can acknowledge that orderliness may well coordinate many disparate forces, remove guesswork and help achieve goals. You might say, "To do a job haphazardly is costly in time and money."

Orderliness Assures You

Systematization, documents, memoranda and precision can be indispensable for adaptive living. They are also needed for information retrieval in any scientific research, in merchandising and in educational fields requiring infallible record systems; for medical reasons, especially where children are concerned; and for tax purposes (a must should a return be challenged).

If you are a stickler for punctuality, that too buttresses your orderly existence, while it is evident that to be clean and tidy saves hours and aborts mounting tension when you must search for that misplaced item. And, as you may point out, "People never walk in and say, 'Oh, what a clean house you have.' But how they would talk if it ever looked dirty." Nor can shopping and travel lists be ruled out as aids to living.

Finally, your health consciousness may induce you at times to give comfort and sympathy to another's illness, thus lowering your defenses a bit in that person's service. Temporarily, you are permitting your uptight self a respite.

Where Orderliness Fails

Keeping systems and records that contain no intrinsic worth for your survival may defeat you. Each bit of O-C devotion to a precise life-style both reinforces and lulls you into a false sense of security, leaving you unable to deal with stress. You become entombed in your orderliness.

Doesn't punctual mean dependable? Not always. You rationalize that it soothes your time-conscious family and friends. But does it in the long run? To the contrary. You create a conditioned expectation that you cannot always fulfill. What if your plane is stacked up, your car caught in traffic, your train stalled in a tunnel? The household falls apart. "John must have been mugged, run over, had a heart attack. He would never be late without calling. He'd find some way."

Clean and tidy involves the same implacable dynamic as precision and punctuality. It can be just as deleterious and constrictive as all other varieties of orderliness.

List making is addictive. One woman says: "The trouble with my lists is that without them I'd never get anything done. But then the lists take up all the time I'd have for doing my work anyway." You have canceled out. One can test for addictive list making. If you ruminate about the list and always study it in full before tackling the next task, you can be sure that it is compulsive and taking charge of your life. As a double check: Do you constantly revise it? Are you driven to keep it complete? Is it your security symbol?

Flight into health antagonizes those around you by deprecating their frailty and contrasting it with your own high threshold for discomfort. You may also be playing an unaware game of trouble when you dismiss as "nothing" an infection or an injury that later may impair your well-being.

Try a Different Way

What would you say to a resolute turnaround? Too drastic? Nonsense. Not with your self-discipline. You can enter the battle to reshape your behavior for a fresh start. Break loose from your systems and precision traps. Convert from an unyielding machine to the humanness of error. Establish your self-trust by reexamining your unaided strengths and lean on the pluses that you uncover. You may be astonished at their quantity and quality. I will discuss operant conditioning in Chapter 18, as a method of behavior modification; but until you study it, challenge yourself to give up those habits and traits of orderliness that now dominate your life and, incidentally, pull your face into wrinkles and lines.

If You Worry the Future

When you assign priorities to the major needs in your life, this is adaptive. But like most O-Cs, you probably tie in "coming events" with the present through *anticipatory anxieties.* Your judgments may then be compulsive and not that astute. In the process you generate a demand for absolute order in life to counteract your anxiety. This in turn drives you to want constant control of what is ahead—which is impossible.

To the extent that orderliness becomes the pith and marrow of your personality function, it also becomes the index of your uptight way of adapting to life's stresses.

> *To relax?—why yes*
> *But let us govern it and be easy*
> *only at the intervals so designated*

· 5 ·

Hoarding

Forged into your O-C value system is the psychologic need for money and possessions. This material stuff represents immutable security to you. It also takes precedence over all that is voluptuous. In hoarding your possessions, you attach profound emotions of self-importance to their real and symbolic worth.

COLLECTORS AND ACCUMULATORS

Art dealers have capitalized heavily on this need to hoard. You may recall Lord Duveen, a master salesman who motivated such wealthy men as Andrew Mellon, Henry Clay Frick, Andrew Carnegie and scores of others to gather collections worth staggering sums. These assemblages of art are now contained in museums and libraries, bearing the owners' names and giving them the deathlessness they sought.

Millions of persons, in a large or small way, have been stimulated to support a collecting industry. The Franklin Mint, porcelain factories and the Post Office are among those who spur on O-C collectors with first and special issues of their products as the lure.

The O-C Collector

Perhaps you are the O-C who hotly pursues stamps, coins and medallions, china, paintings, sculpture, old bottles, lacquered boxes,

73

or any other body of rarities. Your hoard exhilarates you and offers the cachet of Collector.

You may be found within any social, economic or cultural stratum of society. Exceptionally, and only as Collector, do you abandon your customary aloofness in order to display your treasures, to buzz to everyone about the chase for them, to imply their cost and, possibly, to hint at your smuggler role in getting away with a foreign antiquity. Your audience duly panegyrizes, although an expert among them may spot a manufactured dud but let you rest in blissful ignorance.

By contrast, you are the old O-C friend of mine who guards your hoard against intrusion. "Top secret" is your rubric. One day, in a weak moment, you allowed me to view your spectacular collection of airplane models. You opened the glass case and I handled one of the miniatures. I saw you grow ashen and break into a cold sweat. This was real terror. Your hoard was in deadly peril. Quickly, I returned the model. "Come on now, let's get your adrenaline down —try to stop shaking. I promise never to touch it again." You locked it away and ushered me out. I had blown it. Never again would I get into that room. Otherwise, you are still the most amiable of uptights and my valued friend to this day.

The O-C Accumulator

No central artistic or cultural theme need be the criterion of accumulations, which may consist of exotica or attic junk. The compulsive principle remains the same—acquisition of booty for the sake of acquisition. The most catholic accumulator of all time, the former publisher William Randolph Hearst, remains legend. Owner of an enormous tract of California land, he purchased a conglomeration of things—from disassembled castles and small boxes, to the complete collections of others (contents unseen)—and erected a wedding-cake palace to house this heterogeneous mass.

The Collier brothers also set a collecting fashion of sorts. A recent news item, recalling their compulsion, reported that a malignant stench had alerted neighbors to a wealthy suburbanite; she had been accumulating all her rubbish and garbage in her house over several years.

The Clutterers.   If you are an O-C woman who attends do-it-yourself classes, you accumulate all the yarns, tools, cookbooks, pots and pans, fabrics and other paraphernalia required. The rage for the craft passes. So does yours, but the materials stay forever. "Suppose they came in handy sometime?"

You may be an artist clutterer. You acquire brushes, paints, supports, sprays, palettes, and other equipment in quantity which you will never discard. Or, as a camera bug, you buy every new model, adding it to your old ones. If a homecrafter, you purchase each tool manufactured. Used or not, you hang on to it all.

You may also accumulate objects invested with fuzzy import. An O-C World War II veteran, you haunted Army and Navy stores for sales. You bought 104 T-shirts, 12 cents each; 5 Japanese swords, $1.85 each ("It's a nice item to have"); 90 khaki undershirts, 8 cents each; 90 overseas caps, 40 cents each (to cache your hundreds of pocket combs); and a dozen hunting knives, 39 cents each (you do not hunt). Still, the total costs of your binges were minor and as a salesman you adapt effectively. Lots of clutter but no harm done.

Or if you are the counterpart of an O-C doctor I know, you hoard every scientific journal, reprint, medical magazine and drug brochure you ever received. Your apartment, country house and office overflow. These issues are piled on tables, shelves, behind drapes and under furniture. You never refer to them, mostly because you cannot find the one you want.

Muriel's Warehouse.   You have been hoarding for years and do not know it. So far you have assigned three rooms, closets, basement, attic and other areas for your "temporary" discards. Temporary? Twenty-five years? You keep your children's baby clothes, cribs, carriages and whatnots. After all, they are in mint condition and your unmarried daughter may yet have a baby. She is forty. You also cling to your haute couture clothes. "The styles might come back at any time."

You also save your husband's original golf clubs and sports coats, broken-set dishes (for ashtrays and pin holders), lamps, desk accessories, frames, pots and pans, curtains and drapes, all packed into old luggage, mother's steamer trunk and the children's camp lockers.

The Salvagers. As an O-C fix-it-upper, hoarding draws you to leftovers like a magnet, certain that you will find useful scraps. And you do. A miscellaneous screw or nail is retrieved from a broken box. Odd electric parts or wires come in handy. Obsolete furniture with its seasoned wood will make *something*. At times you scavenge happily in your neighbors' junk piles for choice tidbits.

"Will I Have Enough?" Here you demonstrate your anxiety through excess: You may be the O-C bachelor who purchases six tubes of toothpaste when only one is needed, a dozen cans of soup, tuna fish or other staples; the single girl who hoards fifty pairs of pantyhose; the housewife with 140 boxes of detergents; or the married man with almost 100 shirts, some in their original cellophane wrappers. "Thirty-five of them I've never had on my back. But this way I know I won't ever run out."

THE STINGY

You cannot forgo the delights of saving and owning, any more than you can slough off your other O-C traits which synthesize with the control gauge of your personality.

The Mean Ones

Hoarding can act as the *primum mobile* of stinginess. Dickens' Scrooge pattern of the O-C who gives little of the self still stands.

For example, your wife inadvertently depicts you as a churlish pinchfisted O-C. "He says that I'm immature and a spendthrift, that I don't understand that money is lifeblood. Every night he follows me from room to room ranting about the cost of things and where to buy for less. I told him to stop being so busy being rich and talking poor." Later, I learned that she had understated you. You say that no one is worth more than a two-dollar gift and spending money on beauty, sentiment or romance should be outlawed. And if someone asks you for a favor? The usual reply would probably be, "Sure." Not you. This could be a trap. "We-ell, what is it, first?" You deflect the answer and make yourself scarce. You cannot give even a token willingness to help.

Or perhaps you are another kind of person, petty and cheap, but for yourself only. "I never buy newspapers. I pick up a discarded copy of *The New York Times* and *Wall Street Journal* on the commuter train and read them coming home. Saves maybe $100 a year. Makes sense to me."

You may be the Detroit housewife I met who flings wide your closets, fat with silver, china and linens. You also hoard stacks of records and tapes which you never play, barroom stools, lamps and bric-a-brac. Devouring them with shining eyes you chant: "All wholesale, wholesale. And the floor samples, *less* than wholesale." You drape your meanness in the vestments of hoarding. Seldom do you bring your things out for use. But you are using them every day as security emblems, exulting in your shrewd bargains that make every penny scream. It is horrid and "wondrous strange," yet somehow poignant, that you can find no other certainties or pleasures.

O-Cs Who Beggar Themselves.   Some miserly persons never let go of their money for a minute. We hear of those who died of malnutrition in penury yet with $20,000 sewn in their skirts or hidden in the mattress, or possessing bank books revealing tidy sums. Such rich paupers need the assurance of money in the hand more than food in the stomach.

THE PRIVATE ONES

Privacy is here linked with hoarding because it is a trait of retention found in most O-Cs. You who keep apart, do not join groups, withdraw to be unobserved, are hoarding yourself. You remain as secretive as possible without offending others.

One O-C woman laid down her dogma. "I rely on myself. I do not impose and I don't want to be imposed on. I'll share in the community where proper, but I don't want the community to share in me. My privacy is my genteel right to do as I please. And I please to be secluded." Her husband told me: "One night I heard an intruder. I let out a bellow to frighten him off. My wife woke, scandalized. 'Fred, please . . . Shhh. The neighbors will hear you.'"

Privacy is your cult to ward off unfavorable comment. Ostentation, which could invite criticism, is not for you. Indifferent to the fizz of life, your paramount concern lies in a finical and conservative anonymity.

Best to Be Tightlipped

You shut people out so that no one ever knows your weaknesses, affections, sensitivities, or even the ordinary facts about you. You are the soul of civility but you evade all that touches on the personal.

In relating an anecdote you are "objective," quote others and admit to no opinions of your own. Having seen a play you refer to the critics for judgment. You fear that praise might invite contradiction. This would intrude. You keep voice and face deadpan. Others can draw their own inferences. In an entire evening, your new companion knows as little about you at midnight as at dinnertime. (If you are an O-C woman of this ilk, further dates may not ensue. But this may be what you too want.)

In clamming up because you are unable to give, you discourage

78

those who cannot guess where they stand with you. They then become defensive, sensing that they are also being forbidden to give.

Your O-C Need for Reserve. On immediate impression, not every O-C appears reserved. At first acquaintance during a five-day conference, you seemed an outgoing man of grace and presence and of sparkling wit. Then came the subtle change as you noticed, over the days, that your colleagues were bringing you too close to comradeship. You rang down the curtain, the air grew chill. You had retreated to your real abode of privacy in far-off country.

INSIGHTS TO HELP THE HOARDER

Hoarding, collecting, miserliness and stringent privacy have a place in your uptight way of life. These behavioral devices may ease your psychic apparatus but, unless tempered, go on to extremes. At modest levels, however, they can be adaptive and you can use them as such.

How Hoarding Can Work for You

If you love rummaging in junk shops to salvage something good from something marred, this penchant might bring you a new vocation—the restoring of antiques, for example. You earn a living this way and satisfy your creative spirit at the same time.

Suppose you were born to wealth. Your exhibited art collections offer enchantment to multitudes, and you are gratified. But another individual, whose very riches may have deprived him of developing his own identity, requires, not plaudits, but self-respect and accomplishment. One member of a renowned family collects and studies butterflies. His data on their habits, breeding and survival resources contribute to the knowledge of entomology. *His* collecting earns him scientific recognition and authority, thereby reinforcing his sense of personal worth.

79

Miserliness May Be Open-Ended. Your philosophy of "living close" can also determine that nothing anywhere should be wasted. You perceive that when man finds a balance with nature, man survives. If you topple this balance, nature dies and so does man. This awareness, keyed to your hoarding trend, may specify you as the ideal activist in a program of environmental protection.

Safeness in Privacy. As an O-C you need privacy as you need food. You may harbor deeply concealed secrets, mostly hurts of your youth—the scorching rebukes, the acid tirades which resulted in fears and ambivalences that dominated the spiral of your growth. You guard these emotions against sordid discussion. It is safer to be private. But how do you tolerate your tight seclusiveness? "We can't all be the same. You have your wife. I have some acquaintances and my sister and brother. We're mostly apart but we get along; we never pry into each other. And we're content."

But Hoarding Can Lock You In . . . and Out

You were the uptight O-C woman on a cruise when news of a storm at home was broadcast. Seized by hysteria for the safety of your house and art collection, you took a plane at the next port to return home and inspect for yourself. Your two children never entered your thoughts.

The Self-Image of Penury. Within hoarding, the subtrait of parsimony drives you; rich or poor, you may be discontented with yourself. However, your real poverty lies in the distorted mirror of a lowered self-esteem. You hope that your hoarded possessions or your penny-pinching will miraculously oblige you with inner security. It is dismal to note the small hooks that you must bait in order to fish for the general encomiums you crave so dearly.

Dilemmas of Privacy. You are torn between the fine balance of your sensitive need to reach out and commingle and your compulsion to stand aside. You cannot afford to let your potential for a panic response or disinhibited emotion be tested. Should you see an erotic movie which is later discussed you may react with a tingling in your loins, but you fight to remain impassive. "Yes," you concede, "sex is part of life. But need it be talked about?" You fear that such stimuli could rock your self-control. Your wife says of you, "Anytime he gets shaken up—that's when he digs himself in and goes it as a loner for a while. Fine company he keeps."

Defeating Your Hoarding Traits

First step: Overcome your paralysis at the mere mention of reducing your accumulations. Second step: Note how they cripple your mobility. Then start to unclutter. This is best accomplished with help. Mark off the superfluities and leave the house. Let spouse or friend unload them on a charity or a thrift shop. (And do not buy back. You just rekindle the hoarding habit. See Role Reversal in Chapter 18.) When you return you may feel shocked, as if in a reactive depression of loss. Your footings are gone. But relief will follow and later you will barely miss your hoarded security symbols.

Your finest pieces remain, and when not elbowed by the lesser rubbish, they show up as gems. This will mark you as the true connoisseur. Build your Collector reputation on that.

Substituting for Stinginess. To give up close-fisted living requires a personality upheaval through the mental mechanism of substitution. You shift your value system from a money orientation to a human one.

You were the most miserly O-C I had ever met, satisfied that your marriage was childless because "raising kids is too expensive." Caught off-guard one day you let your wife persuade you to act as foster parents to a boy of nine for a three-week vacation in your home. The social organization hoped for adoption but most people wanted a baby. Young Eric brought an aura of cheer into your household. It grew lively and you became fond of him. One day leavetaking came, but at the door Eric hesitated. "I couldn't help but wish I might have stayed for good. Only, I guess I'm just too old."

Later I heard the outcome of the tale. When the child spoke you were transfixed. Too old? A boy of nine? In that instant, the discriminative centers of your brain must have mobilized to perceive this inhuman paradox. The deadlock of your meanness broke, not in maudlin sentimentality but in outrage. What was wrong with a world that could throw a boy of nine on the scrapheap as "too old"? You brought him back, made room for him in your heart and pocket, later adopted him. The changeover was not easy. Only as the magic of getting pleasure from giving pleasure suffused you did the happiness of an open hand take over.

Letting Go of Privacy.   When a distrust of people sours the flavor of living it is time to remodel. (See Shaping in Chapter 18.) Have you ever tried to share some intimate facts, let the other know that you too can feel rotten about life's stresses? Maybe you don't measure up as great as others? Perhaps you never achieved your chosen career. But why must the pangs dog you forever, keep you from sizzling with laughter and fun? Why not let yesterday decay and your inhibitions of privacy with it? You have nothing to lose but your uptight tensions.

Ask yourself: How well do you know your mate? What stratosphere do you drift off to in your heavy silences? Try talking and listening instead. Hear your voices speak. Bring alive the small drama of letting your hearts touch. Open your arms and learn to become a spendthrift in giving of yourself. Banish privacy. Go public. (See Chapter 18.)

If the Hoarder's Tail Wags the Dog

You could be the O-C widow who waited for your mother to die so that you would inherit all her things—piles of them, on top of your own things, further to crowd your home. To reach the sofa one trips and climbs over stools, tables, chairs, cabinets. Visitors

82

are now few. Your place gives them claustrophobia. While your things seem to offer you love, they are really leering at you in mockery, because you belong to them.

Can Stinginess Be Adaptive? Yes. If you are indigent you are forced into economic prudence. Or if you are someone of sufficient means but niggardly, you prefer buying day-old bread because it is cheaper and just as filling. Biting on the saved pennies rewards your miserliness more than the taste of fresh bread. That is your O-C adaptation.

Hoarding Yourself. You cannot accept communal fellowship, whether in sharing a joke, a beautiful scene or even a moment of sadness. You live only for your possessions and your reclusiveness. Aloneness comes upon you and you are now an atrophic social being. Of all deficits, loneliness is the most devastating and the most vulnerable to maladaptation.

> *Lock the gates*
> *disturb not my things which are but me*
> *Ask me for nothing*
> *or I shall give you only emptiness*
> *and with myself, of you, be free . . .*

· 6 ·

Compulsion to Work

Many O-Cs have learned that to help them relax, work surpasses tranquilizers. Not only does it drain off uptightness but it brings monetary gains, purpose and stature as well. "Also," an O-C adds solemnly, "it keeps you out of trouble. Remember? 'Satan finds some mischief still for idle hands to do.'" Yet the O-C may become as addicted to work for relieving tension as others do to alcohol, drugs or nicotine.

THE WORK ADDICT

You may be an O-C of middle economic level who is committed to the doctrine of unremitting toil. Whether shopkeeper, white-collar employee, or a professional, you deplore anything less than a sixty-hour workweek as plain sloth.

What if you are the one-third partner in a liquor store, whose wife says: "Norman is a slave to that place. He's supposed to take the one-to-nine shift, but when new merchandise comes in he's right there at ten A.M. to check the deliveries and rush them to the shelf. Naturally, his brother Fred leaves for the day, and my nephew Buddy is also no slouch at buck-passing. Either his kids must be taxied to the doctor, and if not that, he waltzes off to the ball game. Norman gets the full load and I think he's off his rocker to take it."

Your reply? "What can I do? Buddy's family has a lot of sickness. We're fortunate, all healthy. Okay, so maybe Buddy should get a man to cover for him. But how do you find a stranger

you can take your eyes off of?" Your wife puts in, "I don't buy
that. Look at us. Married almost twenty years and never a vacation. It's a big deal when they close over Labor Day. He's up and
down like crazy for two days because he can't go in to the store.
It's a sickness with him, only he doesn't know it. He's a workaholic."

The Project Extenders.   The need to "be at it" constantly may
consume you. A divorcée and legal secretary, you take on leadership
of a girl scout troop, enroll in evening graduate courses and do part-
time interior decorating. Your father despairs. "There's no joy in
her. This frenzied go-around she's on . . . I see her burning herself out." You reply with the fierce rhetoric of the uptight O-C.
"The ant hill must be piled high, the beaver must build its dams,
the moles dig their runs. I despise aimless living. Keeping busy, doing, making, that's the only thing that counts for me and makes
me feel good." But your tight mouth, strained and unhappy, belies
you.

The Affluent Too Can Be Work Addicts.   You are a corporate
chief in your middle sixties who pushes desperately to stay at the
peak. You contend: "Joe Kennedy made the point. If you're not in
first place, second place means you're a loser." A palatial home
awaits you in Acapulco but you never holiday there. You are a two-
thirds theatergoer because you must leave early for bedtime to make
an early office arrival. "Best time for getting the work going." While
you grab an occasional vacation, your average day, with five projects
to juggle, conferences, and three-way telephone parleys, may add up
to at least twelve hours. "It keeps me young," you say, "and stops
the juniors from crowding me out." But overwork? Wearing out
the battery of your nervous system? "What about your wife and
children?" You slump. "I try not to think of that."

85

VOCATIONS THAT BECKON
THE WORK ADDICT

An urgent problem confronting most of the young is future work. What to go after? For many, especially those cheated out of education, the choice is limited. Obviously you take what you can get. "Moonlighting" and overtime must compensate for the economic squeeze. For others, even during unemployment stress, the options are wider. The O-C, to control his own destiny, makes an early choice.

A sampling of typical vocations that call for your O-C traits in more or less degree follows. Almost invariably, your choice will identify you as an O-C because it requires just your kind of diligence and work addiction.

Artisans and Technicians. I cannot conceive of a tool and die maker, battling possible errors with calipers or electronic devices of tolerances within millionths of an inch, showing up as anything but a work-addicted perfectionist. You nod, clearly in this category. "Of course. Good Lord, one tiny blooper could mean enormous losses in dollars and maybe lives too."

Whether you are a diamond cutter whose one slip on the facet of a rare gem might be fatal to its value, or the final inspector of instruments that ensure the safety in air travel, your precision must be razor sharp, thorough, rigid (and stubborn). Exactitude is the watchword.

At the same time these exquisitely developed skills carry a drawback. As the severity of your training continues, it proliferates the circuits of previously conditioned O-C traits that brought you to such jobs. Work addiction and the compulsiveness that rivets it into your personality can hold you in captivity forever.

Bookkeepers. For the most part, it is the O-C single woman who adopts this career. With your affinity for it, you are now a full-charge bookkeeper in total command of your department, always constant and infallible as, for example, with your payroll. Even if it keeps you to midnight, it will be ready for the morning. That you are blessed by those whose spending always outruns their wages gives you a sense of benevolent omnipotence.

Your love for the work lies in its certitudes. The debits, credits and complex accounts that you record in weighty ledgers all strengthen your O-C compatibility with your material interests in life. Hunting down errors fascinates you: "And when I find one, do I pounce. I feel like a heroine." This mundane world of arithmetic boundaries helps suppress your sexuality and evanescent worries. Its snug familiar schedules gentle your uptight nervous system and keep your spirits settled.

Executive Secretaries. Whether male or female, as secretary to a prestigious figure you are probably considered a gift from heaven. Of sterling loyalty, you anticipate your employer's needs before he does, and you are a scrupulously mute confidant. Ever available, your time, your thoughts, are owned by your boss, whether it means coming in an hour earlier or taking his call from a bar at three in the morning to send an urgent cablegram about a scintillating idea that has struck him, to "beef up" next week's conference. Should illness ever send you home to bed, you cry. Suppose Margy, that nitwit from the steno pool, messes up your files. And forgets his coffee, and his wife's anniversary flowers and his girl friend's jeweled pin. "My God, she might even get them mixed up."

Librarians. If you are in a career of library science, you generally call to mind the somewhat unfair image of the drab spinster or the shy retiring bachelor. But such labels would hardly convey your true essence as an expert librarian. It is your O-C personality, narrowed by the rigid devotion to your work, that creates this impression. Happy only in lavishing your scrupulous care, patience and affection on your catalogued books, any longings for human intimacies are waived. More frequently than not, marriage is a poor rival. Who would want an intruder in such a paradise of non-

87

threatening volumes on their miles of shelves? Only a non-O-C perhaps.

Middle Managers. I include you here if you are an O-C office manager, minor executive, or some other coequal. You may be frustrated at the squeeze of your middle management and its frail tenure. You are aware that you shoulder the responsibility without the authority to enforce it, especially where nepotism grins. You often tighten with rage. "How do I get some competence out of that Perkins idiot if he knows that I can't back up my directives?" But you dare not raise the issue. "Too slippery. They'd have my head on a platter." So you throw your allegiance and O-C discipline into the breach. You take on the work.

Your immediate superior also assesses you correctly as the compulsive subordinate on whom to dump the whole load. Knowing his own inability to handle it but with no intention of being chewed to bits in the organization's teeth, he banters you into accepting the burdens. And you do. As an uptight worrier you even feel relieved that you can dispose of them efficiently. Although you have been exploited because your reliability is a byword, somehow your work-addiction trait is gratified.

Physicians. Most physicians in every specialty of medicine are O-C personalities. Medical exigencies attract, mandate and *condition* their compulsive drive to be thorough and dependable.

As a practitioner yourself you know what nonsense the words "office hours" are. Behind the scenes you go on ad infinitum as you consult with referring doctors and relatives; you give persistent attention to the merest thread of a hint in the patient's history which could change the diagnosis and make correct treatment a greater certainty; you teach, you reply to lengthy professional correspondence, and you study the social factors of your patients' environments. Numerous medical journals must be read to keep abreast of new learning. Great chunks of time are thus consumed and—you are work-addicted.

As one of my colleagues put it, "In one day, no matter what the specialty, a doctor makes more crucial decisions for a patient and the family than do most people in other fields over a year." Your O-C traits are reinforced by this absorption.

Theater People. The universal concept of those in the theater as mercurial creatures of temperament stems largely from publicized and often fictitious gossip. The other side of the picture is rarely glimpsed, that of the grimly dedicated work addict whose obsession with excellence may know no limits. Even if you are not a pronounced O-C when you enter the acting profession, you soon acquire its fears, superstitions and compulsive maneuvering in order to deal with the apprehensions that characterize it. In fact, your uptightness mounts in almost direct ratio to the uncertainties of your work. Inwardly you are wrenched by a lack of confidence, even disbelief, in your ability or looks, and by a morbid disquiet about the future.

Nevertheless, despite your tautness and the seeming hysteria that swarms backstage, control prevails. As professionalism governs you, your inner weaknesses are conquered. Reprimands about a false step or a wrong timing may be thick as flies, but they enrich and pervade you. Compulsiveness heightens when the theater becomes your world. Your work addiction grows. Little else matters.

INSIGHTS TO HELP THE WORK ADDICT

Productive work is the most natural energy outlet for anyone. All biologic, social, economic and psychologic forces combine to motivate work, which is an action. To make a decision and take action counters threats to survival. It may even thaw out the individual who is frozen into a panic state. It discharges worry, frustrations or similar stress. "Full steam ahead" mobilizes the potential excitement of aliveness which all beings need to go forward and provides an excellent antidote to a suspenseful state of mind.

Society Needs the Work Addict

As we have just seen, nearly every occupation contains its own intrinsic demands for certain characteristics in its workers. If you are the extroverted person who can verbalize nonstop with conviction, you do well as a salesman but not as a research librarian. Or as one with mechanical leanings, you feel better as a lathe operator, not as an account executive in advertising.

Many personnel managers know that particular jobs can be handled only by an O-C work addict, although you would never see this requirement on an application form. If you fit this compulsive work pattern, you are in distinguished company. Some heads of state, senators, bank presidents and their like could never keep afloat emotionally without work addiction to buoy them up.

In literature you may recall Thomas Wolfe and Eugene O'Neill who gave their blood and health to their compulsive work addiction. In the arts we can observe some of Seurat's paintings in pointillism whose textures of confettilike dots were compulsively disposed over the canvas and architectonically developed into meticulous color fusions; or Dali's perfectionist techniques embracing precision of shade and line in his surrealism and ultrarealism; and farther back, the medieval band of mosaicists whose deliberation in matching small bits of stone or glass into an extraordinary art form seems perhaps to coincide with the theological rigidity and terror of the period that put every life in personal jeopardy.

How Work Becomes Overwork

It sneaks up. You may be a young and vigorous O-C man, habituated to working hard "for my future." You start off enjoying it but your motives change. Also, your logic puts in an oar: Only if you stay until eight or nine P.M. at the office can you keep tasks from spilling over into the next morning. But does it occur to you that more reasonable hours would generate higher efficiency through the following day and make Jack a less waspish person at home?

Such compromise with psychobiologic urges for diversion go ignored, now that you see the chance to climb fast and close to the top. The frenetic notion of being the "youngest" in the upper reaches of your field displaces a gracious view of life and the simple delight of a warm loving body beside you. Other qualitative changes take place. Your wife is frustrated and disillusioned. "There's no fun in him anymore. Sex? Either he's too tired or he can't make it. Sometimes I think he'd like to move his bed into that office. No more companionship. No friends. It's all fallen apart and he doesn't even know it."

The final pitfall. You begin to see your work as escape from a querulous woman who throws you into confusion and dull despair. Only when back at your desk do you find your psychologic and physiologic tensions relieved. From then on you swill your work the way an alcoholic drains the bottle. You are fully addicted.

Women Too Are Work Addicted. The son of an O-C career woman astutely defines her work addiction. "My mother sees even an hour's idleness as unproductive and sinful. Her problem is an overactive sense of duty. She's so busy proving that she's worthwhile, she doesn't know how to waste time constructively. I guess her early disenchantments won't let her relax. To be perfect she must be 'getting things done.' Me, I shoved off from there."

Like many other work addicts this woman cannot indulge in humor or the small leisure of gazing and marveling at a redwing in flight. This is "doing nothing" and would menace her intactness.

Subduing Work Addiction

Work addiction is one of the least malign of O-C traits and the easiest to give up. Your difficulties arose when you deprived a mate, parents, children or others of a balance in relationships. Your overwork habits flawed them. To slacken off, then, becomes an obligation.

True, work addiction claimed you first. Now your talents for recreation and enjoyment must be practiced daily. If vacationing "without purpose" is too drastic to begin with, go where you will find something moderately productive to do—gardening, helping a friend add a wing to his house or fixing a boat dock. At the same time work at being a bit lazy. If your body and mind have forgotten how to enjoy the rewards of relaxing, then rewarded behavior will be aversive to you at the start. But man is a sensitive instrument and you can relearn.

Start with noticing everyone. Distribute generosities, don't pocket them. Applaud others' successes—out loud. Deflect malice wherever you see it. Delight in the wit of your mate. Evolve a counteraction to a friend's disappointments. Pause to watch a child's experiences drift, fumble and fructify. These are the melodies and arpeggios of life, and their interplay the orchestration. Sprinkling this new selflessness through your days will ultimately detoxify you from your uptight compulsive work addiction. (See Relaxation and Learning Procedures in Chapter 18.)

When Work Remains Your Opiate

You recognize your ambivalences and know that overwork is a mixed blessing. You enjoy the compulsion yet resent its bondage. By default you give up family and ordinary pleasures, social and sexual. An embrace becomes perfunctory. A kiss is pursed and closed. Even divorce may be accepted with guilt ("I'll take the full blame"), rather than accommodate to a new life pattern.

When you need your work addiction it means that you are afraid of "the outside" and the unforeseeable. But emotional health demands the use of experience, expectation and inspired uncertainty. Call it hope, or call it the adventure of the future. We must learn to live with it.

As an O-C, however, you believe that only the armature of. structured solutions in the present and for the future will do. Thus, living solely in your work, fixed into the static certainties of the now, you stunt yourself. You do not accept the challenge of curiosity and mature anticipation of what might come. When you stop dialing maturity you stop growing.

> Work the day through to blood and bone
> except
> . . . maybe off for two minutes
> for a fastmeltingicecreamcone.

· 7 ·

Conscientiousness

In the turmoil of rapid change today it is more usual than not to meet indifference on all sides. The needs and sentiments of others are trifling to the self-centered. It seems fine, indeed, to come across the "good" person who abides by the rule "always follow the voice of conscience." But it is also dismally true that many such individuals are obsessive-compulsives.

What is conscience? Genuine conscience is your feeling tone about your system of beliefs. The more you are indoctrinated to obey the laws, moralities and other cultural values of your society, in short, its traditions, the more you will regard the imperatives of your community as your pillar of strength. These imperatives are your conscience; it impels you to contribute to society in the knowledge that society is then obligated to contribute back and to protect you.

THE CONSCIENCE-BOUND

Reliance on conscience values is commendable—but there is the "overdo" to consider. A total reliance on the conscience, while providing a sense of benediction, will personify you as the O-C person who must never overlook a duty. Indeed, it must be so. Were you to lower the bars, your ambivalence would sweep you into doubts and guilt. You adapt well, then, so long as you leave no room for compromise or in the least way offend your conscience. But you

94

may also become the indurated O-C (perhaps the intolerant man or controlling woman) whom we have already met.

Your Cultural Value System and Tradition

In psychologic terms, conscience represents the full sum of ingrained societal values and traditions. These act as your guide. Your roots suck nourishment from them. Montaigne said it simply: "The laws of conscience, which we pretend to be derived from nature, proceed from custom." Freudianism would put it that you invite the "superego" to dominate your personal identity. Thus, you are conservative to the hilt and you will act predictably in order to freeze the social process into stand-pattism. This is your base line. Automatically, you oppose change (to you, turmoil), even when your orthodoxy may produce foolishness, unworthy decisions, abnegation, or major upheavals in your life.

In Religion. Adherence to conscientiousness is bred into every religious practice. O-C sticklers who follow all major and minor dicta range from bishops and sextons to you, the uptight parishioner. Some may dub you a fanatic. Still, you may well find the solace in your devotions and church attendance that nothing else gives you. But what is the extreme?

For example, there you are, an outwardly demure and sensible young matron, inwardly confused about hell and mortal sin. After seeing you on several occasions I conversed with the young priest at your church. He was plaintive: "She comes to every novena; her church attendance is so repetitive that one thinks one is seeing double. She was *just here.* Doesn't the Lord say she has a home to take care of and other family duties? What ails her, constantly dwelling on her sins? To be pious, yes, but does God insist that the conscience torment his children?"

Which is what is happening to you, young lady. You had told me how you had shoplifted the lipstick. But you returned it. You played bridge on Sunday, and you flew high with your husband one afternoon on the living room sofa. Not only that, you dropped the steak on the floor and never washed it off.

Distressed little person—sincere and devout but also compulsive and uptight. Because you are bound to a howling conscience, you never have a moment's peace, and will not, until you learn to drag it off your back and put it firmly in its place.

In Marriage. As a conscientious O-C husband, you regard sex, child care, attention to parents, and so on, as disciplined behaviors. The socioeconomic and emotional sobriety of family living motivates you to this; affection and romance are incidentals, to be almost ignored. You consider your sexual life a marital assignment, to be regulated and routined at specified intervals, thus avoiding the fault of "gluttonous lust."

As an O-C wife you, too, may perform sexually, according to your conscience calendar. But this is not truly conscience. It is your O-C inhibitions showing, disguised as self-control and restraint. Both you and your mate are the victims.

In a different context, I think of the conscience dilemma that descended on an O-C school principal. "Ten years of marriage, then my wife finds a casual bedmate. In the divorce, I gave her custody of the kid. How could I handle it as a single man? But she made a marriage sacrament and should have stuck to it. Now I've got no home or family. So who's the father? Me or that man she lives with? They've taken away my parenthood. . . . What? Yeah, she begged me to forgive but do you think I could ever go inside of her again? She's a slut and my conscience wouldn't let me. I'd be violating everything I was ever brought up with."

In the Family. You are the sister of a browbeating O-C who keeps everyone, including collateral relatives, off balance. When he brings his children back from camp, family ties say that you, also an O-C, should visit them and you telephone. "No, we have to unpack and there's too much to do." Later, he calls you. "Okay, you can come over." But now you are going to the theater. He is outraged. "What? And you won't even see them after they've been away all summer?" You wilt and agree. Regardless of angers or impositions, as two uptight O-Cs, your actions are always geared to appease your duty-laden lives. Early conditioning has chained you to each other and conscience shrills that after all, this is flesh and blood and it must come first.

On the Job. As a conscientious worker you base your integrity on the code of the old crafts and guilds. "An honest day's work for an honest day's pay." Or, as an office employee you explain, "I hand in my bimonthly report one day early or my conscience would murder me. That's in case I should get sick or have to go to a funeral. At least it will be in on time."

Another instance: you are the compulsive civil servant who is always on guard never to blot your copybook. Fearful of initiative or your own judgment you must check every detail with your superiors. This is why you function best in a tightly stipulated bureaucracy. One observer noted: "Most people in government get paid for a full week of work which they could do easily in a day and a half. Their 'conscientiousness' uses up the other three and a half days."

In the Political Arena. You may be an O-C congressman, senator, or grand panjandrum of any political group who jealously secures the stanchness of your adherents "for the good of the Party," your main concern. Laws become obsolete but you arbitrarily fight their reform. Were you to check your voting records you would discover that you are playing both sides of the ambivalence equation; you think yourself faithful to your constituents in the name of political conscience, but when organizational loyalty conflicts with the desires of those who voted you in, you choose the former.

Moreover, you learn to swallow your own platitudes as High Truths. You feel upright and honest, a myopia that can be sadly comic at times. A Minnesota newspaper reported on a congressman who visited some 500 Indians at their reservation where they lived in bleak poverty. "My good friends, I'll work to get you better housing," he thundered in glorious demagogy. "I'll see that you receive

97

relief and federal grants." On went the speech. After each burst of promises, the Indians shouted, "Oom galla galla."

With the ceremonies over, the congressman noticed some bulls nearby. "Magnificent. May I get a closer look?"

"Okay," said the Chief, "but be careful you don't step in their oom galla galla."

THE RIGHTEOUS

Conscientiousness is rigidly supported by its affiliate—righteousness. Detached from its origins in sometimes moral and laudable convictions, righteousness then becomes an aim in itself.

We have occasionally heard stories of highly principled men and women who go to great lengths to gain their point. A recent news item told of a man who is spending thousands of dollars to defend his stand in not paying an unjust tax that amounts to less than $17.00. "It's because I'm right," he proudly informs the press.

To be unerring and good all of the time borders on the superhuman. "God laughs in heaven when any man says . . . 'I am never caught at fault or doubt.' " None of us, including the O-C, attain saintliness. As a righteous person, you are vaguely aware of this. At the same time, you feel propelled by God-given directives. But when you take that extra step "beyond," and believe that you are ordained to obliterate all the Bad and to command only the Good, righteousness can savage you to evil. (In recent history, this track led to the ovens and gas chambers of Buchenwald and other concentration camps.)

The Wicked and the Good

Righteous evil is the theme of Victor Hugo's *Les Misérables* in the person of the compulsive police inspector Javert, who spends five years pursuing Jean Valjean. Ultimately he catches his prey, and Hugo describes all the emotion of his righteousness and inner joy. The excitement of his moral success transcends him. The following is an extract from the book.*

Javert at this moment was in Heaven; without distinctly comprehending the fact, but still with a confused intuition of his necessity and his success, he, Javert, personified Justice, light, and truth in their celestial function of crushing evil . . . he protected order, he drew the lightning from the law, he avenged society, he rendered assistance to the absolute. There was in his victory a remnant of defiance and contest; upright, haughty, and dazzling, he displayed the superhuman bestiality of a ferocious archangel in the bright azure of Heaven. The formidable shadow of the deed he was doing rendered visible to his clutching fist the flashing social sword. Happy and indignant, he held beneath his heel crime, vice, perdition, rebellion, and hell; he was radiant, he exterminated, he smiled, and there was an incontestable grandeur in his monstrous St. Michael. . . . Probity, sincerity, candor, conviction, and the idea of duty are things which, by deceiving themselves, may become hideous . . . they are virtues which have but one vice, error. The pitiless joy of a fanatic, in the midst of his atrocity, retains a mournfully venerable radiance. Without suspecting it, Javert, *in his formidable happiness, was worthy of pity, like every ignorant man who triumphs; nothing could be so poignant and terrible as this face, in which was displayed all that may be called the wickedness of good.* [Italics mine.]

The Righteous Can Go Wrong

We have the righteous and good here today in many uptight O-Cs. Often called sanctimonious hypocrites, they are the determined moralists, the power-hungry, and the Archie Bunkers.

* The Heritage Press, New York, 1938, p. 282.

The Lecturers. Such O-Cs are the angry persons who reinforce their righteousness by lecturing others. You were the young girl whose outburst about your mother, an attorney, sent you into a storm of tears. "She always ranted to us on the virtues of good manners, of the importance of proper greetings and of a well-tempered voice and a clear conscience. Yet *she* was forward and brazen at parties. She scorched my friends with criticism. She hated every driver on the road and swore at their wrong turns or weaving. She said they had no conscience. Her! who bragged about her own driving and lightning reflexes, doing exactly what she condemned them for. She lectured against everything—doctors, books, makeup, music, whatever hit her mind."

Today this same girl flares up with righteous fury at people in subways or buses or on the street if she does not get immediate right of way. No, she is not mimicking her parent. Rather, she is reflecting the belittlements and contradictions she suffered, with no consoling indulgence to counterbalance them.

The Censorious. Omnipotence and grandiosity may also be implicit in the righteous, as in Dionysius the Elder, Tyrant of Syracuse some 2500 years ago, who castigated his son for his debauched conduct but was himself a notoriously licentious and profane man. This righteous father, in turn, influenced his son, who became the second O-C Tyrant of Syracuse.

It is of more than casual interest to note Richard Nixon's stern statement at a press conference in January, 1973. "Those who served paid their price. Those who deserted must pay their price and the price is not a junket in the Peace Corps or something like that. . . . The price is a criminal penalty for disobeying the laws of the United States." Yet this righteous man erased the palimpsest that stated his oath of fidelity to his country and rewrote it with his wrongdoing in office and obstruction of justice. He saw no discrepancy between his own ruinous activities and his censure of the draftees who were dedicated to the principle of noninterference in Vietnam. (There are some who view Nixon's downfall as an epic drama of fate. But it is hardly that when one realizes that the essential quality of the Aristotelian concept in Greek tragedy was lacking in this poor creature: nobility.)

The Condemners. Within your righteousness, along with other O-Cs, you must condemn even when events summon you to ready compromise or open-ended decisions. Whether it concerns your daughter who lives with her boyfriend, or Personnel who override your racist decisions about employees, you remain hard and impenetrable as flint. To you, your righteousness is indisputable and will allow you no concessions.

In your community, you may be the self-appointed crusader. You drive not only to scour your own impure thoughts and fantasies but to suppress those of your peers, family and everyone else within your orbit. You must "clean up" and condemn movies, TV, magazines, the library's books and sex waywardness. You fight the acceptance of homosexuals and equal privilege for women. You would love to shape your fellowmen's behavior into pliant designs, more pleasing to you. The means you take for this may be warped, but fidelity to your convictions justifies them. You are the benevolent protector merely exercising your goodness. Like Savonarola? Torquemada?

Then again, in a social setting, if you are a more subtle condemner you make no overt comment on a social guest who strikes you unfavorably, but your Laodicean gaze travels beyond her (and she feels like a cipher). You are fond of saying, "I never have an unkind word for anyone. I just keep quiet." Yet an irksome twinge of guilt may, out of the blue, prompt you to send her flowers.

The Grudge Bearers. Possibly you may be one of the righteous who keep a special memory-bank to store the accumulated resentments of a lifetime. They may be directed at a person, a situation or generalized. "So I'll remember not to get hurt again." You also have your antennae out for slights. The barest touch is a brutal elbowing, the faintest dissent an arrant insult. (In recent history the most notorious incident of grudge-bearing was revealed in the White House "Enemies List"—another kind of hoarding which may verge on paranoia.)

Old grudges can pop up blindly in a current situation. At the supermarket you were the middle-aged shopper, about to check out two overflowing carts. Another housewife with only one item timidly asked permission to pass through. Plumped with indignation you refused. "No, *this* is how it's always done. You wait your turn. Anyhow, no one ever gives me a break." Then and there you expended quantities of emotional energy on muttered justifications, reinforcing all your past grudges in life. When reaching home you perceived no link with the antacid you needed.

The Virtuous. The constrictions of your uptight O-C virtue may also convert into the bullies of righteousness.

You strike the authoritarian note, starting with your child. "All children must be well behaved and agree with every word the parents say. After one warning they should be punished for disobedience. I know how frantically I obeyed my parents. And now I'm grateful for what it taught me, and I pass it on to my children even if I have to beat it into them."

In another setting, you are the widowed mother who shows disgust for your married daughter's discreet love affair. You know the girl is locked into a ghastly marriage, that your son-in-law is unfaithful and lost to all decency, "a bum," and that your daughter needs some tenderness and dignity. Yet you brand her a whore, unworthy of her little son's love. In your righteousness lurks anger because you never acquired the fortitude to disavow your chastity and dispense with your miserable marriage. Hoping to give you some insights, your daughter writes a short piece of fiction, germane to her own problem, for the magazine to which she contributes. Your sour comment: "I didn't know you wrote that kind of smutty stuff."

The Martyrs. You are the O-C woman who said recently on the telephone: "I'm going to let it all hang out. You wouldn't believe it, but here I am with a breaking back, waiting on my husband hand and foot, who's in bed with the flu, and running between him and my son in the other room, who also has a fever. And the maid away. My mother came to help but I sent her home because I had the trays and medicines all organized. It was my job to get my family well. All I could do was suffer through it, even with my back killing me. We're not exactly poor and it's ridiculous for a woman in my position to be drudging like this . . . no one would ever do it for me. But I have to think of my conscience. When it's all over, everyone will be fine except me. Will anyone ever appreciate it? Never." Your O-C martyrdom swells.

INSIGHTS TO HELP THE CONSCIENCE-BOUND

As an O-C bound to your conscience, you are certain that doing everything "right" guarantees that you will never do anything "wrong." You dare not live in the dirty gray area of "giving in"; to compromise with what is right would signify a loss of moral strength and the threat of guilt and shame.

Yet, how to reconcile this belief with the reality, since all through life everyone, if not a total recluse, must somehow learn to accommodate to others' (and their own) flaws.

The Value of Conscience

At the start of this chapter, I noted that conscience may be defined in terms of your feeling tones and your system of beliefs, and how you were indoctrinated into, and conditioned by, the values of your society.

With further reinforcement of this conditioning, the spread of value judgments that you had imbibed zeroed in to the specific. You converted "Society wants me to do this" into "I should do this." You were thereby enabled to develop empathy and secure your survival through the group by contributing of yourself. This view of conscience (the indoctrination of the child by society and its growing need to cooperate) is often neglected by psychologists and social scientists who are preoccupied with the individual's needs, to the exclusion of society's needs as a whole. Theologians, however, have long accredited conscience with the quality of co-operativeness and have used it for stabilizing and matching both individual and social needs.

As an O-C, then, when you are adhering to the conscience dynamic of the societal value system, you are adapting effectively despite your uptightness. For example, you would never enter into criminality; you believe in justice and a working social order; you deplore those who do not observe moral codes, who are underhanded, or who shirk their duty—all praiseworthy attributes and rising to a good level on the P.E.G. standard.

The Puritan Ethos

Nevertheless you are a product of the American cultural tradition, which developed under the Puritan ethos and still remains within its grasp. The very words and thoughts—such as *control, discipline, inhibition of pleasure, perfection, casting off evil*—spell out some of today's compulsiveness as it stems from the traditions of Puritanism. From this conflict between yesteryear and now, many uptight O-C personalities have been spawned.

You personally may often be kind, even an endearing person in many ways and "someone to like." But with one foot on Puritan ground and the other in today's revolutionary social values and stressful technologic change, you are understandably confused and ambivalent. I think of the uptight insurance agent who lamented: "A friend the other day said I worked my conscience overtime as if I were grabbing for an Emmy award. Why? What's wrong with observing the right codes? Like never covering up a fraud or watching for moral laxness in your children? That's our tradition, trying for perfection. What's conscience for if not that?"

Conscience Can Rape the Peace

When your righteousness breaks out excessively, it fires antagonism. You jolt others into pugnacity, you sound holier-than-thou and, what is worse, so final.

To exemplify: You may not have noticed that, within your household, angers and pent-up bitterness have gradually been seeping in; family ties have started to shrink and gaps in communication widen. If your daughter chooses a man of another religion, you ordain, "Nobody in our family ever married an outsider, and no child of mine is going to break that record." But she does and you vow never to see her. Ultimately, in despair, you realize that your other children too doubt the veracity of your love, that they are searching for a way out of your righteous grasp.

You Cannot Play Stand-In for God.   The matter is, you have lost your ability to discriminate between what is right and what is wrong in a given situation. You are equating only what is good or bad for your way. Righteousness has destroyed your objectivity.

You cannot play God, disregard others' sensitivities and believe that righteousness entitles you to club others into submission. This leads you far aground. Comes a time when you almost have the urge to destroy people in your fever to make them understand "the right things for their own good." Yet when you catch a fugitive glimpse into this brutalization of your spirit, you loathe yourself and cannot understand how you could reach such abominable depths.

To live with nature as nature intended, you must learn how to compromise and how to make compromise your perennial companion.

How to Understand Compromise

Change is a law of nature to which we must adjust. Tradition itself is an ongoing phenomenon that constantly tests the new. Rules and regulations are modified in the very process of being. Some may appear in shadows and stray breezes. But we stay alert to them.

Start with the assumption that no absolutes exist for right or wrong. At best you consider what is good for you and others as a *totality* under given conditions, and then compromise.

To remain pinned to your judgments alone means that you are in Looking Glass Land. The more you push to live with traditional righteousness, the more you stay in one place—but you are really going backwards because the changes in life are passing you by.

Try to phase out your conscience to humanitarian levels by updating your value judgments. To be silk is better than to be sandpaper. Ask: "How much 'give' was in me today?" Pick up your rewards in the richness of compromising with people who were taught to comply with rules different from yours—an exciting prospect because your panoramas broaden. (See Chapter 18.)

There is no magic to finding compromise. It simply means learning to adapt, that is, to accept the other person's failings and, yes, even to poultice them if need be. This is conscience working at its highest level.

If Conscience Beats You Down

In such case, your conscience is acting as the emotional lash that conditions your judgments. It will never let up. You do not see this, however, because of the small unseen wings that beat about your head—the angels who accompany your righteousness at all times.

How Good to Be Good? It has been noted by psychiatrists that people who inhibit or suppress particular behaviors (sports, sexual intercourse, dancing, marriage) which they desired at one time but rejected develop into hidebound and castigating persons about these activities in others.

You reveal some of this in your role of young matron with two children. Working at home designing fashion jewelry, you like your creativeness but chafe because it is almost your only outlet. Discontented, you describe your friends at parties, "smoking pot and laughing when there's nothing to laugh at . . . personally I think they're all miserable. They think they're escaping. They don't realize how embarrassing it is to someone like me when they start feeling each other up while they dance. It's indecent." You cry. "But me, I don't do anything wrong. I'd worry that the goblins would get me. I'm good and respectable. I can't even let go that way with my own husband. Sometimes I wish I could and get my juices going."

But you're afraid? Because your inability to "let go" justifies your righteous stance? You yourself summarize the ambivalence. "My husband says I'm too prim and proper and I suppose he's right. I guess I'll lose him someday. It's stupid to be like me. Maybe that's why I like to think all the others are so terrible. But pot *is* a copout and drinking or taking Valium is just sick. Though maybe I am too. The trouble is I don't have any fun out of being sick and they do. How the hell can I learn to just ginger up and do what everybody else does without seeming like some freak. And I keep wondering what Mom would think. I wish I'd stop feeling in my conscience that I'm the one who is right . . . and yet I do . . . and yet I don't . . ."

> Love me for my goodness
> Say that I am prime or I'll despair
> and slide into that wanton joyous sin
> that others find so good and yummy-ish . . .
> To be in.

· 8 ·

The Single-Minded

In the preceding chapter we discussed O-C traits as they can serve your adjustments and, conversely, as they cramp your progress toward mature adaptation. In another perspective of your personality, however, you may be characterized by only *one* compulsive trait, incontestably urgent to you. Call it *the single compulsion*.

I HAVE A THING ABOUT THAT

The particular obsession or peculiarity, superstition or discreet habit, minor as it may seem, is a genuinely compulsive trait, not merely an eccentricity like those described in Chapter 1.

What if you are a fervid vegetarian? Your dietary strictures may just skirt the obsessional (or possibly fanatic) even though no O-C traits stand out elsewhere. Or perhaps your thing is avid card-playing or a daily gym workout, rigorous, demanding and undeviating. Or maybe you are a car buff who rehabilitates old automobiles with compulsive attention to the last detail of the original model; your mind is in a ferment until you have traveled hundreds of miles to the place recommended by the G.O.B. (Good Old Brotherhood) where that final piece of authentic decorative chrome awaits you. It may cost enormous energy output, but this is your compulsion.

While you may indulge your single pursuit with untold passion (or greed), mostly it is shrugged off by others as "your thing." It seems to declare your freedom to fly your own flag. Only infrequently does it hinder your adaptations.

COMPULSIVE EATERS

"When I get nervous or upset I eat comfort foods like candy, ice cream, cake, nuts—anything delicious that I can cram into my mouth." This is how you explain your overweight.

You may also be among the O-Cs who eat addictively, adding pound on pound. You sneak "nosherai" between meals, go on day and night binges, take soft drinks and coffee for the stimulant (caffeine) which provides a mild lift from your depression or fatigue. (This needed stimulation also attaches to alcoholism and drug abuse, subjects too complex and extraneous to discuss within this book, except to note that one of their components is the trait of compulsiveness.) With no control, and self-deprecatory, because in your eyes you are repulsive anyway, you say, "Why fight it? It won't help." Your psychosocial problems, as unresolved as the alcoholic's, generally relate to the void of love or whatever else is lacking in your emotional diet. Food is your substitute.

Or you may be the compulsive dupe of bad habit who must cater to your appetites for sensuous dishes and drink. Along with many gourmets and non-uptight persons, you eat for sheer pleasure. It is your thing, but you stuff yourself and get dangerously fat. You are one among a plenitude of Falstaffs and Nero Wolfes. Look around in any restaurant.

Another category of overeaters encompasses a large group with hormonal, metabolic, neurochemical, and other physical imbalances which disturb digestive and absorption activity. Be sure that your problem is not a medical one before calling yourself a "foodaholic."

COMPULSIVE SMOKERS

If you are typical, your smoking began in adolescence or a bit later, possibly as a declaration of adulthood. Encouraged by manufacturers who want you to infer that smoking means sex and virility for the male, romance and sophistication for the female, smoking is now your compulsive addiction. Reinforced by its tension-reducing effects, it seems to satisfy a number of psychologic and social needs. But what of its maladaptive consequences in the toxic damage of emphysema, circulatory disorders and heart ailments? And today, you have a new stress to contend with: More and more, smoking is frowned on and forbidden in public, so that you feel irritable and guilty each time you light up.

To quit smoking requires the positive in motivation plus willpower (much easier with your O-C discipline than you think) *once you have made up your mind to extinguish this noxious habit.*

COMPULSIVE SHOPPERS

Man or woman, your thing may be shopping, which in many ways can be an impediment in your life. "But that's my fun," you say. If you think so and can afford it, yes. You zoom in feverishly on such items as the latest cooking gadgets or stereo sound equipment, and if it is clothes—shoes and sweaters one season, blouses, slacks, shirts, ties, the next. You look and buy without letup, often to maintain your reputation as an authority on all merchandise produced. But your shopping is really addictive and may border on the obsessional.

How often have you dragged your husband through stores, flea markets and bazaars in your travels looking for special "buys" or antiques? Or your O-C husband had you wait in a quiet fury while he probed for every tool, clamp and drill in a hardware store or pored over endless shelves of secondhand books?

Carried too far, compulsive shopping encroaches on the leisure of vacations, causes neglect of family, and may even throw the compulsive spender into a nightmare of unpaid household bills.

COMPULSIVE GAMBLERS

Bank clerk, manicurist, salesman, ranch hand, baby nurse or taxi driver, when your thing is compulsive gambling, you are teetering on the crest of maladaptation. Considerate and gentle otherwise perhaps, in this respect you are comparable with the compulsive eater or alcoholic. You blow all the savings on horses, cards, numbers or the stock market. Violent arguments, unkept promises and ultimate penury often smash up marriages or other alliances, due to your thing. You cannot hold on to winnings, ever, and this reaffirms your drive to gamble further in order to recoup your losses. Your most frightening thought when you wake up in the morning, uptight, palpitating, is: "My God, where do I get my betting money today?" Embezzle? Steal? Maybe even from the kid's piggy bank?

No clearcut psychologic formulation explains this gambling compulsion. Some believe that its risks represent a revivification of the child showing off to take a dare or the adolescent yearning to do something "world-shaking" in a sensational sweep of luck. The obligatory response to lose may also express self-flagellation for not achieving the maturity to stop gambling.

COMPULSIVE TALKERS

Are you one of the army of talkers who wear down anyone within earshot? As you gabble without punctuation? Possibly you are the mother described by an elder daughter: "She talks without pause, especially in the morning, when she asks a thousand questions. Never waits for answers. She inquires about anything just to get her voice going."

Your daughter likens you to Amanda in Tennessee Williams' *The Glass Menagerie*. The utterances go this way: "I wonder why Emma Lou slunk down the back street and didn't walk past us, right out in the open?" You overflow with instructions; you also slip in vague slander and gossip spiked with namedropping, flights of imagined expertise on any subject, or random sparks of non sequiturs. You ask that a new dress, hair style or recent weight loss be noticed, but never stop for approval. "You do really love it, though, don't you?" Over and over again.

Sometimes you try to face yourself "honestly," and end by wondering whether you are just liked for your conversational gifts. Foolish inverted woman, hoaxed by your dim field of visibility.

Compulsive Telephone Talkers. At a friend's home one evening I saw that the telephone was off the hook. The hostess said, "My sister-in-law's on the phone. Don't worry, I have my eye on the clock. She'll be winded in ten more minutes. Then I'll pick up the receiver and make listening noises."

"How long will she go on after that?"

"About another twenty minutes."

"And altogether?"

"One hour. That's how she visits."

COMPULSIVE POWER AND STATUS SEEKERS

We know that heads of state vie with one another in hot and cold wars to dominate spheres of influence. Hard-nosed leaders and politicians at every level in government, industry and labor compulsively seek to expand their power. The Watergate revelations and the mini-Watergates of innumerable politicians, many of whom ended in jail, testify to this.

As an O-C private citizen you may operate within corporate

mergers for competitive squeeze plays, to be top man in the executive pyramid, or to amass an astronomical fortune. Though lower in the scale, the adolescent gang leader fighting to reign over his "turf" is little different. All bear witness to the compulsion for seizure of control and absolute power at any level.

The Mirage of Omnipotence. Some people have been so bruised by disparagement that now they spoil for power over others for power's sake.

You may be the O-C who combines self-image and complexes into the role of "First Man There." Riding in your taxicab one day I became aware of your race to get in Post One every time the light stopped you. It turned green and off you took wildly, though it meant throwing a nursemaid and child into paralyzed terror. Whenever you were stuck in second place you brayed your horn without pause because the car in front refused to sprout wings.

In a different situation, you are the steaming uptight status seeker who must beat everyone out in snagging the VIP who recently moved into an estate nearby. You spend hours of time on elaborate plans to get the jump and snare the newcomer as your social discovery.

Obviously such small plays will not ripple the earth much. For you, however, who must satisfy your status "thing," social competitiveness seems to ease your tensions. At bottom, however, these maneuvers, requiring all your vigilance, feed your uptight adaptations the more.

THE SUPERSTITIOUS

A marked emphasis on superstition may be your single compulsion. While it is difficult for any of us to live with doubts and torments of the unknown, many persons, confronted with happenings of Good and Bad, invent and believe in vibratory guardians who will range the Good Forces on their side and ward off the Bad. Our primitive ancestors did much the same.

Today, as an uptight O-C you too may bog down in the Bad portents and compulsively try to preserve yourself against them. Such common harbingers of bad luck include broken mirrors, whistling in theater dressing rooms, black cats and certain numbers (13 is universal). The Good Force magic protectors comprise "knocking on wood," tossing spilled salt over the left shoulder and, if a garment is donned wrong side out, spitting before changing it. Those who fear travel may carry a St. Christopher medal, Greek holy flowers, mezuzahs, amulets, or a painted glass eye (the better to outglare the one worn by Fate).

You could have been the twenty-year-old college student, always beleaguered by a low-grade anxiety and nebulous omens of disaster, who had been adopting many of the Good Force superstitions and trying to circumvent the Bad. One day, you grimly chose a term paper subject, "The Evil Eye." On completing your research you felt almost euphoric. "I've discovered that practically everybody's afraid of an Evil Eye or something like it. That means I'm not such a nut after all." An uneasy solution but the sophistry worked for the time being.

Nonetheless, superstitions, though generally innocuous, can lead to avoidance behavior (afraid to do this, afraid to go there) which we will discuss in Part Two.

THE "I MUST KNOW" COMPULSIVE

The archetype of the inquisitive, you are the woman with an "I must know" complex. You pry into everyone's affairs. When told simple facts, you demand sources. You relish gathering unlisted telephone numbers and must always know what is going on; you hug yourself because the others do not know and you can tell them. Mention a first-rate author and you say wisely, "But, oh, what a lush." You take your small place next to Big Brother in the computers of government, industry, banking and credit, who can tear our social fabric apart. Like theirs, your troublemaking potentials rank high. And yet, a kindly soul at heart, you would be horrified were you to realize the havoc you wreak through what you consider your harmless little bent of curiosity.

FANATICS

Fanaticism of any kind is an obsessional state which probably originated in you by way of a childhood or adolescent *ism*: idealism, faddism, sophomorism, antiestablishmentarianism, or whichever. Hampered by a lack of experiential learning, you compulsively structured a tight thinking perspective to form your conduct. For example, warmongers who settle issues only by violence, terrorists and militants who must reform others in their image, and joiners of vigilante groups have never outgrown the essentiality of gang survival. If you have remained at some early level of maturation, you too may be prone to a brand of fanaticism.

Like most O-C traits, fanaticism intensifies with a chancy existence, especially when the environment shifts to rectify its social homeostasis.

MANIAS

Should your personality oscillate between the adaptive and maladaptive (Part Two) categories, you are the borderline person who seems "so normal" that no one would ever suspect the single flaw in your makeup which, in fact, may barely incapacitate you. This compulsion is called a mania.

Single manias (*monomanias*) are specific, odd behavioral acts which conform to all the conditions of a compulsion. The behavior is irresistible; the uptight person feels a release of tension after the act; the act was not premeditated, yet the person knows that at some future time he or she will repeat it.

Kleptomania (the compulsion to steal) usually appears as shoplifting,* but such acts also include stealing from an individual (often at school). When undiscovered, the person continues on his untroubled way. You were the stewardess who stole cuff links from a man you dated casually, only to give them to another just as casual date. One model walked out of a showroom with a fur piece that she never wore. A wealthy man shoplifted useless items and sent the merchandise back with anonymous apologies. But he had no regrets or remorse. He had done his thing.

In another kind of compulsion your single thing may be sexual conquests (nymphomania in women, satyriasis in men). These episodes "prove" your desirability. Bibliomania (immersion in books) may evince your urgent need for universal knowledge or to kindle a self-image of erudition. Apparently, such single compulsions satisfy you emotionally. If your curiosity and exuberance in childhood were met with ambiguities in behavioral rules, these manias often supply the buoyance and excitement that were drilled out of you at that time.

However, at some point, compulsions and manias bring you to a fork in the road. You may resent being shackled to your thing even when it does you no harm; yet secretly you enjoy your trait and delight in its execution. Which road to take, then?

Manias as Antisocial Acts. Some manias are believed to be silly and childish forms of criminal impulses; witness the compulsive practical joker. Many others, born of hatred, jealousy, fear or frustration, can result in the compulsive act of real crime, unless reason comes to the rescue and deflects the uptightness that is actuating it. (See Aversive Conditioning in Chapter 18.)

The true criminal is secretive and wants to pursue his course, whereas you, the maladaptive O-C, fear that you might replicate a real criminal act and hurt someone against your better judgment. Such thoughts torture you, and you may report them in order to be stopped. The roster of compulsive single acts or preoccupations

* Shoplifting is not always motivated by kleptomania. People steal from stores and other persons for a variety of reasons, including economic need, antisocial angers, boredom, and so on.

with the single subject contains both ordinary and exotic manias. Most are benign; others can send the O-C into maladaptation when exercised beyond sober reappraisal. A partial list follows:

Books: bibliomania	Numbering: arithmomania
Bullets: ballistomania	People: anthropomania
Cats: ailuromania	Pleasure giving: hedonomania
Children: pedomania	Sexual pursuit in men: satyriasis
Counting: arithmomania	Sexual pursuit in women:
Crowds: ochlomania	nymphomania
Darkness: scotomania	Sexual stimuli: erotomania
Dirt: rhypomania	Sleep: hypnomania
Dogs: cynomania	Small objects: micromania
Drinking (alcohol): dypsomania	Stealing: kleptomania
Fire: pyromania	Sunbathing: heliomania
Food: sitomania	Talking: lalomania
Heights: acromania	Touching: haptomania
Horses: hippomania	Touching fur: doramania
Names: onomatomania	Travel: hodomania
Newness: neomania	Wandering: dromomania
Night: noctimania	Words: onomatomania
Noise: phonomania	Work: ergomania
Nudity: gymnomania	Writing: graphomania

INSIGHTS TO HELP THE SINGLE-MINDED

Your single dominant O-C traits rarely exclude other personality features. As a compulsive gambler you may also be patterned with a sotto voce motif of perfectionism, drowned out by the more raucous pitch of your gambling.

The psychodynamics behind this single-minded behavior may occasionally point to a specific rewarding experience. "Sunbathing cured my acne," says a young man. "Now I love to lie in the sun all day. You can't get me out of it." He could also be signifying a substitution for a bitter trauma or a galling rejection that he experienced which he attributed to his blemished appearance.

Or maybe you are the O-C daughter of a beautiful mother with whom you competed obsessively. Then you went on a dietary regimen to acquire an extreme slimness like your mother's. Presto! You won a coveted part in a high school play because of your lissom figure. Your triumph was reinforced by a herd of males in hot pursuit for dating. Now you see yourself as the personification of female sexuality. Your diet, not jealousy of your mother, has become your thing.

The same obsession developed in a woman who could not forget her youthful years when she had been teased mercilessly about being fat. Now she counterreacts to the point of dangerous emaciation. Similarly, superstitions, fanaticisms or manias may range from bizarreries to destructive behavioral handicaps.

When single-minded traits remain nonthreatening they can screen you from anxiety and even give you a glow of pleasure. Thus, like many O-C persons, you cannot tolerate the thought of abandoning your single compulsion. You are afraid to let it lapse. *It must be done.* This is why even the *single* trait may sometimes become the nexus between an adaptive pattern of living and one of maladaptation.

> *The idée-fixe*
> *pursued with guile or bile*
> *or even Heil*
> *May use such means*
> *as make the end, the end.*

· 9 ·

Measuring the Obsessive-
Compulsive's Adaptation

The normally adaptive person exists only as a theoretical ideal. No one is so perfect that he or she can adapt successfully at all times and under every circumstance. Some do well, with a high confidence level most of the time, and appear reasonably content. Many can adjust only to a portion of their lives. Different demands or a new setting may cause a previously stable person to decline and become maladaptive. This is why adaptation should always be measured within a specific context of living.

Most of those with obsessive-compulsive traits described throughout Part One function satisfactorily as energetic and competent although uptight persons. You yourself may live productively and not beholden to anyone. This influences your O-C traits benignly and helps to soothe you into a feeling of safe good humor. Your polite self-esteem is also an aid in ignoring any imputation against you as unworthy criticism. While one young woman called herself a "normal neurotic," most O-Cs do not think of themselves as out of gear. Perhaps you would not readily acknowledge that you are an O-C, although you might agree that others think so and maybe with some reason.

For example, when we evaluate your traits we find spotty distortions in your interpersonal relationships. Lurking within you are all the ambivalences of envy and fear of your superiors, cool respect for your peers, loftiness and indifference toward your inferiors. In your need to affirm your security symbols, your expectations and standards, and to maintain your perfectionism, orderliness and conscientious identification, you emit a complacency that maddens those who must deal with you. As you are also a controlling compulsive, you try to function on a purely cerebral level, burying your emotions deep. You say, "I keep myself bottled up and make sure that I'm on top of every situation." This invites suspicion and distrust, voiced by coworkers who are aware of being cut down and realize that you hold them cheap. They eye you askance. "That type is a killer. No feelings."

You are faintly attuned to their alienation but cannot grasp its core—that you short-change the art of civilized fraternity. While you may be effective and often close to the high of self-support, your interpersonal associations lack kindness and good cheer. This inhibition suffocates your pleasures and potentials. Yet you silently beg the refinements of enlightened humanity for yourself.

AN INVENTORY OF THE
OBSESSIVE-COMPULSIVE PERSONALITY

Taking the foregoing as a whole, then, how does it integrate and add up?

Following is a self-rating scale that I have devised for you to inventory your O-C traits and score the intensity of your compulsive drive.

The questions used in this scale are distilled from well over a thousand case histories out of my practice and from many willing subjects outside it. They represent a statistically correct balance between the frequency and the vigor of various traits that relate to the obsessive-compulsive personality. The scoring has been validated by computer analysis, and the margin of error is well within acceptable scientific confidence levels. Answer the questions honestly, do not try to cheat, and rate yourself as of the day you take the test. Then ask your mate, friends or coworkers to rate you in turn. You may be surprised at the diversity in scoring and perhaps see yourself for the first time through the eyes of others.

Self-Rating
Obsessive-Compulsive Personality Inventory

Circle appropriate number for each of the following statements. Total your score.	None or a little of the time	Some of the time	Good part of the time	Most or all of the time
1. I prefer things to be done my way.	1	2	3	4
2. I am critical of people who don't live up to my standards or expectations.	1	2	3	4
3. I stick to my principles, no matter what.	1	2	3	4
4. I am upset by changes in the environment or the behavior of people.	1	2	3	4
5. I am meticulous and fussy about my possessions.	1	2	3	4
6. I get upset if I don't finish a task.	1	2	3	4
7. I insist on full value for everything I purchase.	1	2	3	4
8. I like everything I do to be perfect.	1	2	3	4
9. I follow an exact routine for everyday tasks.	1	2	3	4
10. I do things precisely to the last detail.	1	2	3	4
11. I get tense when my day's schedule is upset.	1	2	3	4
12. I plan my time so that I won't be late.	1	2	3	4
13. It bothers me when my surroundings are not clean and tidy.	1	2	3	4
14. I make lists for my activities.	1	2	3	4
15. I think that I worry about minor aches and pains.	1	2	3	4
16. I like to be prepared for any emergency.	1	2	3	4
17. I am strict about fulfilling every one of my obligations.	1	2	3	4
18. I think that I expect worthy moral standards in others.	1	2	3	4
19. I am badly shaken when someone takes advantage of me.	1	2	3	4
20. I get upset when people do not replace things exactly as I left them.	1	2	3	4
21. I keep used or old things because they might still be useful.	1	2	3	4
22. I think that I am sexually inhibited.	1	2	3	4
23. I find myself working rather than relaxing.	1	2	3	4
24. I prefer being a private person.	1	2	3	4
25. I like to budget myself carefully and live on a cash and carry basis.	1	2	3	4

COLUMN TOTALS _____

TOTAL SCORE _____

Scoring

25–45. Not compulsive or uptight.

46–55. Mildly O-C. Your compulsiveness is working for you, and you are successfully adaptive.

56–70. Moderately O-C. You are adaptive but uptightness has crept into your personality function, and you experience uncomfortable days of high tension.

71–100. Severely O-C. You are adaptive but quite uptight, insecure and driving hard. You have many days of nervous tension that should be eased off. The closer you are to the rating of 100, the nearer you come to playing brinkmanship at the ragged edge that borders on exhaustion of your adaptive reserve and a slump into depression.

PART TWO

The Uptight Who
Is Maladaptive

· 10 ·

Maladaptation and the Obsessional Neurotic

All workers in psychiatry, psychology and sociology have found it a major problem to spot the turn at which a condition glides from normal to abnormal. In maladaptation of personality function, just how, for example, do we assess and quantify the amount of precision or cleanliness that is adaptive (normal) or maladaptive (obsessional, i.e., an impediment to living—or being "sick")?

WHAT IS NEUROTIC?

Ask yourself: When do you think your list making goes too far? At what stage does checking, twice, thrice or more—of water taps, the stove, window and door locks before leaving home—seem obsessive? Do tension and frustrations sweep over you and phobias close you in? Are you embittered and disaffected? In sum, do you become so uptight in dealing with most life situations that you decompensate below a "normally neurotic" level? In such case, you are poorly immunized to fresh stresses as they arise, and one might say, psychologically, that you are incapacitated. You may dispute: "Yet I produce on my job and I manage somehow."

Agreed. Your life may be seasoned with some pleasure, and objectively the median social standards of adaptation in most societies would not fault you, high-strung as you may seem. But subjectively? Only you know how much your obsessional fears dilute your self-confidence, how abrasively your anxieties grapple with you and make you feel as if you are "going crazy." But no such thing. You are an obsessional neurotic who is treatable. It is your full contact with reality that ratifies your "saneness." Let us see what is really happening to you.

UNDERSTANDING THE OBSESSIONAL NEUROSIS

The latest edition (1968) of the *Diagnostic and Statistical Manual of Mental Disorders* used by the American Psychiatric Association defines the *obsessive-compulsive neurosis* (obsessional neurosis) as a disorder "characterized by the persistent intrusion of unwanted *thoughts, urges,* or *actions* that the patient is unable to stop."

Symptoms of an obsessional neurosis may fall within three categories: *insistent thoughts, uncomfortable feelings, anomalous behavior.*

1. You may perceive your insistent thoughts as ridiculous. They are called obsessions, ruminations or doubts.
2. Your uncomfortable feelings include phobias (fears) and worry; anger and frustration; the tension of uptight alertness to safety in your surroundings; and, in the outermost phase, a state of depression.
3. Your anomalous behavior encompasses drives to perform certain rituals, to check and to recheck, to avoid, or to become entangled in repetitive speech or movement. It also means living with a variety of psychosomatic symptoms.

Differentiating the Adaptive O-C and the Maladaptive Obsessional

Before we discuss obsessional symptoms in their separate categories, we will review the O-C person of Part One who appears to adapt satisfactorily and will note the distinctions between this individual and the obsessional neurotic who is maladaptive.

THE ADAPTIVE O-C

You know that you are precise, orderly, conscientious and perfectionist. You approve of your traits.

You are proud of your rigid, disciplined and controlling behavior.

You enjoy your attention to detail and order, constantly examining and reinforcing it.

You rarely doubt reality and are righteously sure of your rational approach to life and people.

You are productive, take pleasure in your work and feel no need to apologize for your unbending ways.

You feel in command of your life and retain a fair measure of adaptive reserve.

THE OBSESSIONAL NEUROTIC

You know that you are suffering from and trying to resist your intrusive thoughts, ritual acts, phobias, self-doubts and vacillations.

You find your obsessions and rituals depressing, unpleasant, burdensome and time-wasting.

You try to camouflage your need to check and recheck, and dislike your repetitive and avoidance behavior.

You are uncertain of your sanity and painfully troubled by your recurrent doubts of reality.

You have insight into your compulsions as silly, unproductive and handicaps, but they must be discharged.

You loathe your obsessions and consider yourself to be enmeshed in a maladaptive jumble with no reserve energy.

BECOMING AN OBSESSIONAL

The obsessional neurosis can break out at any time during a life-span. The greatest probability lies between the ages of fifteen and thirty-five, with the peak of onset at fifteen to twenty years of age. This is true of both males and females.

In about 60 percent of obsessional states, the roots of the disorder lay in the O-C personality traits to start with (Part One). Malignant psychologic extensions in O-C personality function were and are then seen as decompensations; we term all symptoms that follow as maladaptive or anankastic O-C traits.

The remaining 40 percent of obsessionalism seems to emerge as noncoping patterns in persons who are traumatized by overpowering stresses. These may be a result of an acute heart attack, surgery, social and economic upheaval, or loss of a dear person. However, any event, even occurring only once and seemingly incidental, that threatens security, welfare, survival or previous adaptation to a way of life may precipitate the obsessional mentality.

In short, we take special note that the obsessional neurotic *includes the maladaptive O-C who has slid involuntarily from his adaptiveness* (Part One) *into the state of maladaptation* as it will be described in the following chapters.

> *Don't drift to such climes for the ride*
> *It's windy and hurty and bleak*
> *and you find you're into high tide*
> *When . . .*
> *Oh Lordy! the boat has a leak.*

· 11 ·
Thought Disturbances in the Maladaptive

Obsessional thoughts that push into your consciousness against your will are usually distasteful, absurd and "rubbishy." At times, they are idle curiosities or metaphysical ponderings. Often, they appear as blasphemous or bursts of obscene ideation, alien to your personal beliefs. You complain, "I don't know where such horrid thoughts come from or why they keep spooking me." They arise out of nowhere and you are scared that you have lost control of your mind. This trend in itself spreads your anxiety and intensifies your obsessions.

These ogres in your skull are better understood when we divide them into three main facets of your mental function.

The obsessional state
—dominated by the *obsessions* themselves
—dominated by *ruminations*
—dominated by *doubts*

THE OBSESSIONS

Recurring obsessions are persistent and unreasonable thoughts. They cannot be dismissed and rarely give pleasure. The aggregate of obsessions seems to be endless. Many such thoughts are bizarre, but they fall into determinable configurations.

Harm to Others or Yourself

Are you the young mother who thinks obsessively that you might injure your child? That if a knife lies exposed you will suddenly stab the baby? Or if the window is open you might throw it out? You love your child and would certainly protect it, but your obsession with infanticide undermines trust in yourself. You hide the knife or close the window. Soon you cannot prepare meals or air your house. You have become maladaptive.

Other obsessionals say: "Sometimes I have this strange thought that if I touch a person he'll die." Or you are beset by the conviction that your thoughts "affect" the timing of events with far-reaching destructive consequences. You feel responsible for accidents, deaths and crimes totally removed from you.

Or perhaps your obsession focuses on a pair of sneakers that you own. "I get the thought that my hand will come off if I wear them and I know that's stupid." These and a host of similar obsessions about harmfulness are common symptoms of the despairing O-C and frequently result in *avoidance behavior* (Chapter 13).

Contamination

Fearful thoughts of being contaminated, developing a hideous illness or carrying germs to another showed up in you (now a twenty-eight-year-old married woman) in your early years. Your thoughts about contamination have surfaced in a new way; you are certain that you smell peculiar odors from the electrical outlets, and you spray perfume into them to cover the "odor."

By chance, you hear that perfume is flammable and you become obsessed with the possibility of fire throughout the house. Lacerated with suffering and guilt, no explanation on the improbability of this hazard can assure you. You forbid anyone to use the outlets (even after they are replaced) for fear of a spark. When your warnings are ignored you fly into hysteria.

You were the obsessive young man who constantly feared being "dirtied" just by looking at garbage pails, ash cans and other waste receptacles. Even remote thoughts of such containers sent you into panic. You finally began to follow a staggered, alternate route on city streets to avoid your "obstacles" and reach your destination.

I also recall the middle-aged construction worker who told me: "I've got this nutty idea. If I ever look at the doorknob at home I think that my hands are smudged. Then I can't touch my coat because I'll get germs on my neck and face. It makes me shaky. I suddenly feel that my lips are infected, and if I kiss my wife she'll be diseased."

Or maybe you've noticed your likable young nephew with his germ phobia who cannot ride in subways. "The seat might be contaminated. I don't know why buses are okay."

You are the young matron obsessed with contamination from your husband's laundry. You use double plastic bags in the hamper and surgical gloves while handling his underwear and shirts. You spray the washing machine after each use and scrub your hands at least twice when finished. These procedures have lengthened—first to two hours, then longer and longer. If anything touched by your husband goes down the incinerator, you pour disinfectant into the chute opening.

Violence

Thoughts about violence can be dreadfully distressing when they force themselves into the mind of a normally gentle person. You are just such a fifty-year-old housewife, part-time librarian and prize-winning gardener. Your obsessions, which you call your "punishing thoughts," involve dead children, horror accidents, beheadings and decay. Violent images of death followed by rot all around you keep recurring. You do not know why you should be scourged with such gruesome suffering. For years you stoically endured your mental torment, afraid that revealing your thoughts meant divulging yourself as insane. You finally summoned the courage to do so.

A young man, indifferent to religion generally, you find your thoughts revolving about sadomasochistic religious practices such as presiding over a Black Mass in which a nude woman is tortured. Obsessions of violence may also be self-directed, as in the case of another person who says, "I can't go near a railroad track because I might jump in front of the train or someone else might compel me to do it." (Fear of losing control.)

Closely allied to these areas are the obsessional's apprehension of some act that, while not a physical atrocity, might yet violate social sensitivities. One woman becomes obsessed with the idea that she will undress in church; a man is terrified that he will hoot and yell at a symphony concert; another woman is sickened by a mental image of herself laughing or clowning at a funeral cortege.

Sex

Many obsessions focus on sex. Unlike stimulating sensual fantasies, these obsessions are usually repugnant. A prudish girl pictures vivid scenes of "kinky" sexual behavior in revolting postures; a decorous businessman cannot rid himself of desires to take part in "perverted" sexual acts involving several partners, some animals; or an adolescent must fight off the urge to masturbate in public.

You were the formal, elderly woman who complained that "dirty" words and phrases kept invading your mind. To boot, all the words seemed to go with rape: undrape, dilate, ejaculate, masturbate, violate. In a similar predicament a professor of history is plagued by "sexual limericks that are always filthy" with homosexual overtones. When he tries to rid himself of such thoughts, equally dirty rhymes replace them.

Obsessions about homosexual behavior in heterosexuals are quite common. I recall the report of an O-C bachelor who led an active sex life with various women. All at once he became obsessed with the notion that his current girl friend, despite her curvaceous female body, might have internal testicles rather than ovaries. He was appalled. In effect, then, he would be making love to a man. This would label him a homosexual. Such obsessions are particularly mortifying to a heterosexual, male or female, when, within the obsession, the homosexual acts are conceived of as enjoyable.

Self-Image

I still recall the anguish of a furniture salesman about his self-image. "I wake up in the morning and start to shave. I look in the mirror and I don't know who the fuck I am. There's no me. If I look to the right I see a prick. On the left side I can shave okay. I'm a good-looking guy, but why do I see this prick? Not every day, but most. Sometimes I laugh about it, but it's not funny. If I shave fast I can ignore it, but then I cut myself. Been going on for ten years now."

Many obsessionals suffer with equally distorted or low self-images. This is usually referred to as a *complex*, which further entrenches feelings of inferiority and can be self-destructive. Typically, self-image obsessions center about height, weight, age or body parts. Most concern the size or shape of the nose, chin, hairline, neck, breasts, ears, legs, buttocks, muscular development or other parts of the anatomy.

If you are considering plastic surgery, realize that this does not always erase your obsessionalism. For example, a young man told me, "I had a real complex about my big nose until I was eighteen. Then I went for a plastic. I stopped feeling so ugly but I began to worry like hell when I heard that rhinoplasty can leave a blood clot on the brain."

Complex About Youth. We are all familiar with the person who sees the ages of 29, 39, 49, 59, or even 69 years—those birthday "jumps"—as doomtime. In a culture that lays heavy emphasis on youth, obsessions abound, concerning skin tone, hair color, weight, eye bags and lines—all of which, to you, emblazon your age. Frantic to stave it off, you "live" in beauty salons and undergo face lifts. ("You must start by age forty and every six months, a nip here, a tuck there. Staying young isn't that easy.")

Men too become obsessed with wanting to look as if in their springtime. You are the attorney I know who spends three hours each morning at your toilet. This includes face exercises, massage, creams and ointments, hair tints, "the works," all meant to assure a triumph of continuing youth.

Status, Role and Careers

Ego function, as most people understand this psychologic term, also corresponds with your social identity and economic status. As a maladaptive obsessional secretly lacking ego strength, you may thrust egregiously for the top status role. This obsession to succeed appears in many vocations and was the theme of *What Makes Sammy Run*. Whether you yearn to be the financial, social or political power who Holds the Supreme Truth, or are racing toward world renown in the performing arts, or are determined to overshadow the Pasteurs and Salks of medical research, the same dynamic applies. You have become obsessed with riding out the glory road to fame.

In operating this way, you reckon only into the future, obsessively activating each nerve ending to fuel the tasks of success. I recall a stockbroker dying to reach his first million before age thirty-five; and you, another obsessed young man in the fashion industry, were set on outdoing the Diors and Halstons in haute couture within five years. Because your maladaptations prevented you both from succeeding, you acquired ulcers, colitis, migraine headaches or high blood pressure. Now, fractured in spirit, you drink away your defeats or live on tranquilizers.

RUMINATIONS

Ruminations are obsessional mind intruders that force you to squander your cerebration on nothings. "You chew the cud," firing anger, fears, worry, frustrations or distrust.

To meditate at times about ideas of the past, present or future or life's imponderables is acceptable enough. But ruminative thoughts can weigh you down with so many *why* and *what* questions that they serve only to draw you into a vacuum. For example, you will brood: What did that "funny" look your friend gave you indicate when you said "hello"? Why did that saleswoman make that mumbled remark? What is your coworker doing wearing that odd brown and black checkered tie today? Why did your boss speak in a hoarse whisper to your deskmate?

A full-scale rumination on a particular subject may continue for days. One young girl, a receptionist in a dental office, was asked by her date to come back to his apartment and keep him company that night. He had been overworking and said that he just wanted her in his arms for comfort but was too tired for lovemaking. In bed he held her and drowsed off. Unable to accept the simple reality of his behavior, her mind tumbled with one ruminative thought after the other over the next few days. What had he *really* meant? Was it a bet that he could sleep with her, hands off? Did he love her too much for casual sex? Wasn't she sensual enough? Maybe she was his mother figure and he felt guilty . . . or had he been planning a new sexual experiment for next time? Did he think she was too sure of him? And when he fell asleep, was that meant to arouse her to aggressiveness? She wrote most of these thoughts to him in a note. There was never a reply.

When ruminating bores in on critical frustrations, such as finding the right job, paying off a mortgage, moving to a better neighborhood or completing a long-range task, your thoughts tend to pessimism. In anticipating the worst you demonstrate lack of faith in yourself and potentials. (Ruminations may also emerge as phobias. See next chapter.)

Rumination Leads to Ideas of Reference

Adaptive people generally try to discriminate between the objective facts and their view of them. But when you are obsessional, you equate "facts" with your own neurotic outlook. Rumination twists and distorts your judgments. Such obsessional thinking may border on *ideas of reference*, i.e., you believe that people, including friends and family, are talking against you. You were the attractive young art editor who had been ruminating about the men at the bus stop who stared at you so "lecherously" every day. "I'm sure they feel me with their eyes and discuss me that way." Unless the bus came along, you feared they might accost you. At school you neglected your classes while you went from one to another person, indignantly decrying these episodes. You were a comely young woman; that men noticed you was natural. But your ruminations about their lusts engorged your thinking. After a time you began to assume that everyone was gossiping about you. You had no surcease because your ruminations pummeled you constantly.

Another insecure obsessional, you always try to penetrate the other's mind, fearing that any reference to you must be derogatory. Skepticism of people becomes an intense part of your social life. Often, even when you know that the other person holds flattering concepts about you and you trust him, you are still suspended in ruminative thoughts because *doubts* have supervened.

DOUBTS

No one is exempt from indecision at times. Doubts may arise which can deter you from an impulsive move that would affect your welfare. But doubts obsessionally conceived immobilize you from making even small decisions. Doubts start in little ways. Which tie do I wear? Is this tip enough? Should I walk or take the bus? Ought I to call Edith now or later? Shall I buy a new shirt or do with the old? Thus, to you, no risk means no threat of anything.

Indecision: Roadblock to Living

You are the college graduate so severely obsessional and over-powered by doubts that you cannot really converse because you must take three to five minutes in deciding whether to respond to a question or to make a comment. "I get hung up in my mind on a single phrase and then I can't go on. I forget what I wanted to say. The same with writing. I never finish a note. That gets me angry and down." Telling me just this much took you ten minutes.

At home, you make up-and-down motions with your hand, holding a pill between your fingers for five minutes before you can place it in your mouth. You bob your hand over a hamper, grasping your laundry before letting it drop in. It may be twenty minutes before you can settle on whether to turn out the light at bedtime. Even on a travel tour with your sister your obsessional doubts were so malignant that you asked her to snap pictures of you in identifiable places such as road signs or landmark buildings, to be certain that you had really been there.

Such prolonged doubts and indecision read as *totally* maladaptive. Like a torn and wounded bird, you need unlimited tenderness and prolonged care.

Doubts and Confusion About Reality

In some cases, the most astringent symptom of obsessionalism may be doubts about existence. You are standing on the street with your wife and dog. Suddenly you wonder about your pet. "Is my dog really a dog? I'm not sure. Of course it's a dog and here I am walking it, but why am I uncertain? I know it's my dog . . . but is it really mine? Why should I doubt that it's a dog and that it *is* mine? I must be going nuts."

This uncertainty about people, things and situations can become a bed of thorns. No longer do you trust your judgment, memory or orientation to reality. When such doubts persist, you think your mind is going. You have exhausted your ability to cope and are acutely depressed.

INSIGHTS TO HELP THE MALADAPTIVE WITH DISTURBED THOUGHTS

Obsessional ideas aggravate your ambivalence. You clutch at your obsessions because they help you shut out other conflicting thoughts. At the same time you pant to throw off your obsessional yoke. It fetters your thinking control. This convinces you that "you are going round the bend." (See Part Four on treatment.)

Obsessions About Being Obsessional

Continued ambivalence causes an obsession to breed an obsession. You knew this when you wept to me: "Miserere! I am on a high cliff all my life with nothing below but a deep gorge. I have one obsession and always it leads to another. Now I want to jump to the next cliff. Is that, too, another obsession? To get away from the first? This is why I never wear blue, my unlucky color. Maybe it will pull me out of balance and throw me into the gorge."

As obsessional self-doubts and ambivalences chase each other in circles, you are forced to ruminate about every move. Indecision keeps you transfixed. You must beg of others, "Take care of me. Tell me what to do." Your obsessionalism will progress until you find the decisive person to bring you off your cliffs into the safety zone you need.

Obsessions Are Not Delusions. First, in your obsessional state, you *know* that you are taunted by intrusive thoughts and ambivalence regarding a person or situation central to your obsession. But you hesitate about the validity of it. "If I touch this chair my mother may die." Next, your doubts. "Would it really happen, though? No, it can't. That's nonsense. But then . . . maybe it might. Oh, it can't . . ." Back and forth it goes because the obsession is antipathetic to your values. You long to be set free of its force over you.

The *delusional* person, to the contrary, does not know that his thoughts are distorting reality and he has *no* doubts. He believes omnipotently in his ideas. "I am all-powerful. If I touch this chair my mother will die." If requested to touch it, he does so but explains that he is handling it in such a special way that his mother will be saved.

Second, you recognize your obsessional thoughts as handicaps which evoke noxious emotions, since some relate to contamination, violence, strange sexuality and onerous complexes. You cannot be indifferent to them but you try. You fail to eject them from your mind because they possess their own peculiar logic. For example, your fear of accidents is plausible, since accidents do occur. Or if obsessed with contamination, you can rationalize that germs are ever present and do cause infection; and is it not wise to avoid muggings on the street at night when they are such a commonplace?

But every hazard or peril lodges its own quantum. It is your excessiveness, not your logic, that is obsessional. Thus, the line between rational caution and obsessional fears, doubts and anxieties must be drawn with extreme care for each person *within his milieu*.

The delusional person also defends his beliefs, no matter how farfetched, but does not want to change or give them up. They do not embarrass him, and unlike you, the obsessional, he cannot be reasoned out of them. Totally illogical, he "knows" absolutely that someone is poisoning his drinking water or another is planning his death by a prearranged auto accident. Quite simply, his convictions do not accord with reality.

Thus, while your obsessions are painfully harsh, they manifest a type of maladaptive personality and mental function only. *They are not a psychotic disorder.* Demoralizing? Yes, but your reality orientation can come to your rescue.

> *Thinking odd thoughts through the gauze of the real,*
> *the quakes and the puzzles, the yes-no umbrulla*
> *that leave in their wake the mark of the weal*
> *with bubbles of rubble that frump the medulla . . .*
> *Better to slip on an orange peel.*

· 12 ·
Feeling Disturbances
in the Maladaptive

Unpleasant associations and memories of the past, suspense and pessimism about the future, and scalding angers at current stresses may keep your feelings at a low boil. But to create any real felicity in relationships, these emotions must be mitigated, reconciled with the rewards of old experiences and weighed against the merit of the new.

However, forebodings in the obsessed individual far exceed those of the average person. Indeed, when crises arise, your emotions fuse together into such an uptight condition that all hope and bounce are ruled out. This prodigal emotionality and the absence of pleasure that it leaves (apathy) are typical of the maladaptive O-C's feeling tones.

ANXIETY

None of us can evade anxiety. Nor should we. Anxiety is the protective danger signal to your physical and psychologic intactness and sends you an SOS to energize your body resources and counter any threat or stress condition. Your nervous responses increase certain hormones, raise the blood pressure, tense the muscles and step up your breathing. You are then in a ready-for-action state. But while useful briefly, such tensions must be dispelled as soon as possible, because the body will exhaust itself if it remains charged up too long. This return to normal is accomplished by eliminating the stress or by undertaking an action that conserves you and is also productive.

But as a maladaptive O-C you feel *constantly* threatened, and you cannot discharge any small or large anxiety with dispatch and quick resolve. This is true even when you understand the need to do so. You crackle with tension about yourself, fear of what will happen next, and whether you will survive in one piece.

Ever on the Alert

Vigilance, a needed attribute at times for survival, is used constantly in obsessionalism. You are ever "on guard." You turn on your personal alarm system and remain chronically attentive to every trifle in life as if it were a potential obstruction or threat. For instance: Will the repairman come on time before I fix lunch? Will the supermarket run out of shopping bags? I'll need one. Will I have to wait long for the bus? Maybe it will get stuck in traffic. And can I get a seat on it? Will I be able to set my hair right for tonight's bridge group? In short, for every movement, your *anticipatory anxiety* keeps you uptight and at calamity's edge.

The Anxious Maladaptive Is a Professional Worrier. You are forever dysphoric with worry. As an obsessional "single," you wonder whether you will ever have another date. Should you pull yourself together for an invitation to a weekend party, you watch for rain and already feel a cold coming on. If you do capture a partner on your weekend, you will then begin to worry about your sexual allure. Your need will be to prove yourself desirable. You can never be sure of your charms and whether you are liked and accepted. This will intensify your anxiety and virtually guarantee social failure. In fact, you anticipate rejection or criticism. No matter what your plans you always fret for hours or days in advance about all the pitfalls that await you, whether it be sports, dancing or your social skills.

In another situation you are the executive who has never addressed an audience. When you are assigned the honor of making presentation speeches at a series of conferences, you almost fall apart. You reach for extra martinis at lunch and sleeping pills at night. Instead of learning how to speak publicly you think of quitting the job. "And I know why," you say gloomily. "I tear myself down and I can't dismiss any negative comment. It keeps biting at me all the time."

The connection between anxiety and obsessionalism can sometimes be startling even to the doctor, when patients make frantic "emergency" calls. "Doctor, can I take my pill while I'm sitting on the toilet?" You were entirely serious because you were developing a new set of obsessional behaviors (see Rituals in Chapter 13), and unquestionably you had to check each item. Emergency is as emergency does.

PHOBIAS

Phobias are different from fears. Fear means that we perceive and react to some *real* threat. To be daunted while alone in a dark house at an isolated place, to feel terror when a man with a knife is running amok on the street, or to quake because of a fire in the building is justified. Fear of obvious dangers produces the adaptive response of caution. You "stop, look and listen," then proceed with extra awareness and all senses sharpened for protective measures.

A phobia, however, is a specific fear that is disproportionate to a tangible or potential threat. Riding in an elevator or automobile, entering a crowded auditorium or department store, sitting in a dimly lit room or touching familiar objects does not rationally correlate with fright, since these things or situations in themselves cannot really molest you physically. Rather, the phobic stimulus is related in some *symbolic* way to your cowardice of spirit, regardless of the fear's origin.

Phobias Mean Loss of Control

The allusive symbols of a phobia frequently come out of the blue and intrude as the gnawing parasites of your obsessional thinking. Phobias persist even when you know that they are senseless. Like many other obsessional traits, they lead to avoidance behavior.

Sometimes called a "no-no compulsion," a phobia may be rationalized obsessively as prudence. Still, you recognize that you overdo it but you are loath to admit to this and you go to garrulous lengths to avoid its disclosure. In your job as a traveling salesman who shrinks from riding in an airplane you will blather on about your preference for driving and viewing the countryside. Or, for vacationing, declaim that you do not see the glamour of faraway places when there are still so many nearby to explore.

One uptight phobic social worker denies clinging to her mother for emotional support but quails at shopping alone in a department store. She contends that "mother is delightful company and, anyway, it gives her something to do." Actually, mother has plenty to do. "I can't understand my daughter. I thought the present lifestyle was to reject mother—alienation, generation gap, all that—but there she is and I can't get rid of her."

Your timidity of crowded places symptomatizes agoraphobia (fear of spaces, from the Greek agora, an open meeting place). This alarm at being outside the home represents about one half the phobias in the uptight maladaptive. You also fear the thought of going to movie houses, banquets, or parades but explain: "Who likes to be pushed around by a bunch of people?" You may even feel so harried in such a situation that you choke with sobs and rush mindlessly home. You would rather not go out at all.

One woman shows her primary agoraphobia by growing agitated, faint and wobbly should she leave a bus at an open plaza. "The buildings are like giant tombstones that seem to be falling on me." She leaves the bus at an earlier stop unless she can hang on to a companion tightly.

You may be the phobic who cannot write in another's presence.

143

You are afraid to endorse a check, pencil a note, or sign a charge slip in public. You also tremble at making change. This forces you to delegate your purchases to someone else. You boast: "My darling husband buys all my clothes for me." You add, "But he likes it."

Other phobias relate to bridges and tunnels; going to the hairdresser or barber shop; heights; standing near an open window; rain, thunder or lightning; animals, birds, the sound of crickets; or being touched or stared at in public.

Phobias About Illness. Are you one of many phobics who is a body watcher? A health worrier, you note every small variation in your body functions. You brood about each pimple, bruise or bump. One small drop of blood conjures up cancer, anemia, shock or emergency hospitalization. If you think you are "coming down with something" (a sneeze could augur a cold, a cough portend pneumonia or a slight befuddled spell in a stuffy bus mean heart failure), you need constant assurance that you will not die, will not "go off the rails," and will not pass on a bad inheritance to your children. You grab at this assurance because you do not want to believe that you are ill. But if no sneezes or coughs occur, then you read something in the paper or hear of a rare disease on TV, just discovered, and sure enough that is what you must have.

Yet when you discover that you are wrong, are you satisfied? No. Again you feel your discomforts because your body kicks up a fuss at what your phobias are doing to it. In this way your disquiets over possible symptoms and the ensuing anxiety symptoms feed on each other. Cause and effect continue to spiral.

Illness phobias are quite different from hypochondriasis (see Chapter 14). The hypochondriac truly believes that he is ill and has a compulsion to be ill, whereas you realize instinctively that behind your complaints a phobia exists, that you are not physically ill but afraid that you *might* be.

Phobophobias. At a time when most people in the United States were thrust into an economic (and emotional) depression, Franklin D. Roosevelt brought world attention to a unique kind of phobia—the fear of fear itself. It is called *phobophobia* and can prostrate the obsessionals, especially because all good sense seems to leave them and they feel sucked into a vortex from which there is no pullout.

ANGER

Like anxiety, anger is an emotion that energizes us to fight back when integrity and survival are at stake. However, anger also denotes the least civilized emotion in our biologic makeup; dehumanizing the person, it smashes social cooperativeness, cultural growth and the glow of personal charity.

You may be an angry obsessional possessed by utter frustration, the psychologic outcome of your tendency to uptight aloneness. You vent your anger either in single impulsive outbursts or in low-keyed artful sermons. The explosive pattern debilitates you, and you are left with the empty shell of remorse because you were unable to exercise control. But in spite of guilt you feel relieved. In the second pattern your anger is manifest in biting words or in a look of cold forbearance or contempt that conveys your acid hostility without further comment.

Anger Can Lead to Paranoia

Whether man or woman, as an angry maladaptive O-C or obsessional, you may remove yourself from the traditional friendships of your community. Instead you feed on distrust and suspicion, hyperalert to dissent, always ready for battle with others, with the environment and in defense of your own mistakes.

Automatically, you blame someone else for any mishaps that befall you. If your automobile comes to a dead stop in traffic, you accuse your wife; when driving it last she "did something" to the car. You shut out the fact that you noticed a defect a while ago but neglected to correct it. Your wife says: "It isn't so much that he always wins but that we both lose—each other."

Progressively you grow more aggressive, authoritarian or just nasty; and you withdraw into paranoia. In ruminating on the inequities that you see in everything, you perpetually taste the bile of your own bitter humors. But still and all, to understand you is to commiserate with the torture of your self-punishment—you suffer the most from your angers.

DEPRESSION

I have referred to the O-C maladaptive as the inevitable quarry of depression. Moreover, the feeling of depression is so usual a complication to maladaptation that most of my colleagues agree that it is integral to the obsessional syndrome. This relevance is apparent. Your nervous system, including the brain, is not immune from the assault of those surplus body chemicals that your maladaptations produce.

In my previous book *Up from Depression*, I discuss in detail the concept that persons cannot live indefinitely with chronic anxiety, fear, hostility or a superfluity of any annihilative feelings. Your nervous system will not bear with the surfeit of neurohumors, enzymes, hormones and other chemicals that are produced when you are uptight. The sensitive tissues and circuits of the brain wear down with this chemical imbalance in much the same way that your other organs (kidneys, heart, liver) exhaust themselves when strained too drastically.

Exhaustion of Adaptive Reserve

We can liken the exhaustion of nervous energy required for adaptation at any age to the drained battery of a machine. Everything comes to a halt. You are used up, tired, too tired to care. One may call it neurotic depression, depressive neurosis, nervous breakdown, or mental depression. I name it simply *an exhaustion of adaptive reserve.*

If you are a maladaptive uptight O-C, unable to compromise with your rigidities, tightly watchful and without the ability to modify outside pressures, your breaking point may come upon you suddenly. To be sure, we all live with horribly oppressive events today, anything from politics to pollution, which may erode our electrochemical energy systems. But you, as an obsessional, arrive at this erosion state sooner. You say it yourself. "I've had it" or "It's too much for me. I can't cope anymore." Translated, you have already exhausted most of your adaptive reserve. The stresses have become your personalized agonies. An added one and your last store of energy goes. You collapse into a full-scale depression.

The character of your feeling tones now changes. Rather than anxiety and fears, it is depression that is crushing you. Your anger is transmuted to agitation. The emphasis has shifted to physical morbidity and a strangulating hopelessness. Death entices you as a relief from your mind's anguish. But you fear it and are shaken. Ambivalence persists. You are afraid to die. But you are also afraid to live.

Symptoms of Depression in the Maladaptive

Whether we say it is poor coping, maladaptation or bad adjustment, the net result is either a retarded (slowed down) depression or an agitated (irritable) depression.

The Retarded Type of Depression.   A kind of boredom or nothingness settles over you which in itself can be painful. Apathy replaces your previous interest in being a neat, orderly perfectionist. "When I'm depressed I couldn't care less how I look. Nothing is important." Sleep is fitful and you have bad dreams. Your appetite for food and sex is lost. (Men often become impotent while depressed. Potency returns with recovery.) Your day sometimes starts on a note of optimism, but as each hour drags by, weariness and pessimism supplant the morning euphoria along with psychosomatic aches and pains. Pleasure in living is gone. You have spells of tears. Your attention span is nil for reading or listening.

The Agitated Type of Depression. Developing over a period of several weeks in the uptight O-C person, this kind of depression lets you become distraught easily and heedless of your personal hygiene or your home. You weep and complain of edgy nerves, feelings of tightness or burning in your head. You cry out, "If only I could get a good night's sleep, I would be myself again." You do awaken at about five A.M. or earlier, tired and miserable, sure that "I'm no good. I wish I were dead." You snap at everyone and accuse them of indifference and purposely upsetting you. You peck at food, lose weight, refuse to leave the house and believe that your memory is slipping. The thought of sex or any pleasure depresses you further. Sleeping medications and tranquilizers prescribed by the doctor seldom help.

Depression May Lead to Suicide

If the depression is mild, the symptoms are less dramatic. But as an uptight, let us say in your early sixties, your depression shows up when you start pushing for retirement prematurely. "I'm too old for work." If you are younger you believe that your job is causing your morose feelings. You look for something "easier." If married, the children are too much or you may leave your spouse. If you are a work addict you try to drown in more and more work, or if a teenager you may push for escape into alcohol or drugs. In all of the foregoing conditions, obsessionalism with depression presents a crisis state that should tell you of your need for help in order to stay alive, and not to let the Lorelei of suicide tempt you as the ultimate answer to your mental pain.

INSIGHTS TO HELP THE MALADAPTIVE WITH DISTURBED FEELINGS

Obsessionalism establishes you as a worrier, a phobic or a ruminator who may be demanding, sometimes bombastic and bossy. In your ambivalence you are famished for affection and love, but in your O-C maladaptations you are unable to dispense it and dare not accept its sensitizing auras of closeness. Unable to resolve your problem you may start subsisting on tranquilizers and go progressively downhill.

Obsessionals Are Angry with Themselves

Anger is more common in the obsessional man than in the woman (just as phobias are more common in maladaptive women than in men). In many kinds of neurotic personalities, anger is the powder barrel of your aggression. If you but knew it, your harsh front is your defense for having gone "over the line" into obsessionalism. You were unable to achieve the perfection that your O-C traits demanded; you were frustrated by inhibited sexual desires and other joys. Even when carping at the rest of the world, you were really blaring out your intolerance of yourself.

Over and over one hears the poignant refrain: "I'm constantly discontented with me. I always fight with people. Maybe a good relaxed life isn't really meant for a jerk like myself."

Another obsessional neurotic, in a burst of honesty, may say: "I guess I do nag and bicker when people won't accept my ways. But why do I get in a huff when they don't? I know I'm rigid, but I oughtn't to make them be, and still I do."

It is true that you are always off on a sally of gripes at service people, coworkers and friends. Exceptionally, you sometimes suppress your rages as counterproductive in your quest to get along. But your angry spirit is then pressed into the dangerous confinement of your obsession; you must watch every move with greater vigilance than ever.

Some Obsessionals Learn from Their Depressions

Many who live through an episode of depression gain something from it. You, for example, may have discovered that grudges do not pay. You reject your ruminations and realize that your phobias and fears can be cast off. You can go out and possibly travel. You mellow, learn how to give and accept more handsomely. You repair the edifice of yourself and feel more significant.

Nevertheless, you may still be far from an easy adaptation. Suppleness can still elude you or new difficulties arise. When life refuses to act like a perfectly balanced ledger with all the arithmetic in correct columns, a relapse of depression may occur. In Part Four we will discuss treatment of this condition and how its chain can be broken.

> You feel with your smoothing hands
> I feel with scrambled antennae
> of gray cobwebbed floating strands
> that skein me down into deeps
> so fearsome, so tearsome, they give me the creeps.
> Let me rise up into lands
> where joyance can freely chase through my glands.

· 13 ·
Behavior Disturbances in the Maladaptive

The embarrassing behavior of your maladaptations takes place because an inner force impels you to act this way. Rationally, you want to resist your nonsense deeds since they offend your sense of decorum—as much when you are alone as when observed. But with the hellions of your obsessional neurosis egging you on, you must execute the actions. Otherwise, you suffer frantic tension and worse, the sense of a sword held over you.

As noted in Chapter 1, compulsive behavior is welded to obsessional thoughts and emotions. However, the single "irresistible impulse," when merely occasional or rare, does not in itself earmark you as an obsessional. It is only when impulsive behavior is repeated often and continually, motivated by anxious persistence, that we call it obsessional and maladaptive.

The most common emergents of compulsive behavior within obsessions are rituals, checking, avoidance, and repetition.

RITUALS

Many ritual behaviors invented by the culture have been ingrained into your daily movements. Usually regarded as mild superstitions (see Chapter 8), they may consist of placing the middle finger over the index finger, crossing the heart, or muttering a "God willing"—all for good luck. They are not obsessional since they represent general beliefs, some quasi-religious, which we note all about us.

However, carrying out stereotyped and formalized designs of behavior that you must consummate before you can move ahead with living is maladaptive and an outright sign of obsessionalism. A woman says: "I have to touch the venetian blinds four times and then all the objets d'art in the vestibule five times. That prevents harm to my older brother. When he comes home safely it's proof that my ritual works. Maybe some people think it's stupid, but if I don't go through with it I start to stutter."

Another young lady, petite, adorable, but wearing a permanent frown, told me, "I go everywhere with my two shopping bags. I like to lug around pictures of my family, some old letters, my passport and birth certificate and the deed to our house. Maybe it's a bunch of goofiness to you, but they make me feel safe. So please don't bug me, and let me haul them in peace."

An abundance of rituals appear in different obsessional neurotics. The following are samples of those seen most often:

Washing Rituals

These compulsions are part and parcel of contamination fears (which also lead to checking and avoidance behavior). Perhaps it is your helpless need to wash your face seven times with seven different wash cloths in the morning. Otherwise you cannot leave the house. Or maybe you must sterilize glasses and eating utensils even when used by no one else; two cycles in the dishwasher usually satisfy the obsession. Clothes, especially underwear, receive special attention with many extra soapings and soakings. Washing one's hands up to fifty or more times a day is a universal compulsion, often noticed.

Less recognized are ritualistic mouth rinsings (after kissing and sexual contacts); multiple showers or baths with hair-washing and body-scrubbing; repeated daily enemas and vaginal douching; the heavy use of deodorants for the underarms, feet and genital areas; and such obsessions as face picking and ritualistic sunbathing on the front of the body, back and sides, clocked to the exact time and never an instant of unplanned exposure.

Bowel and Bladder Rituals

For the seclusive obsessional, waste elimination creates problems. For example, you cannot void in a wall urinal unless you are alone in the place. If you are a fussy woman you will never use a public toilet facility but rather suffer "on the road" until you reach home.

A fifty-year-old postal clerk whom I treated for severe agitated depression described his three-hour morning ritual for moving his bowels. "I don't like to monopolize the bathroom so I get up at five and drink a glass of hot water with lemon juice. I then do twenty knee bends, followed by a variety of body manipulations. After that a low enema is repeated twice with some abdominal exercises in between. Finally, I have my bowel movement."

Not much doubt that you are "tight-assed" and cannot relax your rectal sphincter; obsessionalism is constipating you. Your rituals, accompanied by your belief in them to "regularize" you, put you right in tune with the advertisements that admonish us constantly on this theme.

Counting Rituals

The compulsion to count, perform complex arithmetical routines or retain statistics mentally characterizes many obsessionals. This is not surprising since numbers and data fascinate people as the incontrovertible facts of life. Among O-Cs, thousands like you are walking encyclopedias of sports statistics. You recall accurately all batting averages, scores and league standings of major baseball players and games for the past twenty-five years. In addition, you remember all the significant dates in your family's lives, including birthdays, weddings, deaths, European trips, graduations, and so on.

You also multiply, divide and add special dates in your memory, then reflexively juggle them in some numerical sequence and bring forth the final answer as an even number under thirty. Should it not result that way you must repeat the entire computation until you obtain the "correct" number. Then you beam.

Napoleon too had a counting obsession. His immediate concern on entering any town that he captured was its fenestration. He counted all the windows in every house and building, the totals of which were then noted and filed.

At one time I knew the chief of a prestigious detective agency. His formidable intelligence, intuition and ability to reach for the jugular of any problem contributed to his success. He was attached, however, to an extensive counting and numbering obsession. The following is a partial extract from a statement in which he described it:

"I count the number of letters in the words spoken to me in any conversation, and I can tell you instantaneously the exact total of letters up to 350 or so. When you say, 'Good morning, John,' I make an immediate mental note that the phrase has 15 letters. When you asked me, 'Does your counting obsession interfere in your conversations with people?' I answered, 'Not really,' but before I answered I noted that your question contained 63 letters.

"I also must count the number of letters on every street sign. That does interfere sometimes, especially when I'm in a hurry to get somewhere in a car and there are lots of signs on the street. If there are three numbers on a house or store window I must multiply them. For example, I see 275 on a building. I then multiply 2 times 7 times 5. Of course, I do it very rapidly. It equals 70."

He once became obsessed with the number 1824. Whenever a difficult situation arose, the same number popped into his mind. This obsession no longer occurs, but it has taken a different slant. Should he become embroiled in an argument with his wife or partner, or if other unpleasant difficulties assail him, he picks an odd number such as 57 or 23 and mentally counts forward or backward until the bad thought and number disappear. The trouble is, it now takes him longer and longer. Very time-consuming. That worries him.

Some obsessive counting may dictate the mobility of a person and in that case prove an obstacle in living. One woman could not enter a room in her own home or elsewhere until she first counted the number of legs on all the furniture. Other obsessionals must count their fingers repeatedly or keep a record of the blondes or brunettes they encounter on the street. The auburn and gray-haired are excluded.

When such distracting rituals go on interminably the energies of the obsessional sometimes dwindle away into almost total exhaustion.

Bedtime Rituals

At night, you and many others must effectuate certain rituals that will permit sleep. "The blankets on my bed must be arranged in a certain way. If the yellow one is on the bottom I'm afraid of ending up in a coffin." You put the water glass three inches away on the night table, the sleeping pill to the left of it. You reset the chairs and dressers, tighten the sheets, examine the pillows to see that each corner fits snugly into the pillowcase, then don the eye mask and ear plugs. You are the obsessional at your busiest, ensuring your security at the most vulnerable moments of your twenty-four-hour period, sleeptime.

CHECKING BEHAVIOR

Everyone can easily recall situations where a check and a double-check saved aggravation and money, even disaster. Thus, a rationale for checking behavior does exist. However, if you are obsessional you must triple- and quadruple-check—in leaving the house or office, in preparing for a trip, in setting the table for guests or in making many surveys of your dress and personal conduct for faultlessness.

Rechecking

Back in my college days, you were the classmate who assumed that when you locked your car you had to check four times to be certain. You would walk away after parking and securing the car the first time. A few steps and doubts would hit you. "Did the lock click?" You returned, tested it and left. Again uncertain that you had heard the click, back you went. And once more you were unsure. After the fourth check your doubts were assuaged.

Today, you have condensed the ritual of returning for the four checks. You go through the business of searching over, under and around the car, then peering inside while you surreptitiously test the door handle in between each one of these maneuvers. This now seems to satisfy you. Even so, your wife voiced her impatience, part in fun, part in puzzlement and part in commiseration at your "crackpot" testing. Recently, she divorced you.

You are the fortyish woman who enlarges your small daily tasks into major obstacles as you try to get through the day. When, for example, you doubt that you signed a bank draft after you have sealed the envelope, you must open it to check on yourself. Resealing it, you are again besieged by doubts. "Did I really see my signature? Perhaps I'd better look . . ." It may now take two, three or more checkups to satisfy you.

Some kind of maladaptive checking behavior is incorporated into almost every obsession. In leaving the house, gas burners, lights, refrigerator, toilets, ashtrays, and window locks are the most regular items to be checked out several or more times. At the office, too, you who are the inventory manager cannot start work until you check the contents of your desk drawers several times, count and recount the stamps in the roll and shuffle your papers into perfect order several times. It is noon before you really get to your work.

Social Checking. The compulsion of a parent to call children excessively or, in reverse, of an adult child to telephone mother repeatedly can be obsessional. You may restrict your vacations to places where a telephone is easily on tap for conversations with your mother two to four times a day. Such urgent "checking in" renders holidays abroad or similar trips out of the question. Mother's severe admonitions when you were a child "always to be within reach and let us know" has been fixed. Now, to violate this long-standing symbol of devotion would stab you to the quick, with the sense of duty outraged.

AVOIDANCE BEHAVIOR

One way to deal with a conflicting situation or a disquieting stimulus is to avoid it. How many times have we detoured from a chosen path in order to circumvent a road under construction? Or crossed the street when we spied a friend whom we have neglected? Or dived into a coffee shop until an outpouring of obstreperous schoolchildren had dispersed? Also, as we saw in Chapter 8, people who maintain lifelong habits of superstitious belief will step wide to avoid an open ladder, or blow out a match rather than light three cigarettes with it. Such trifling avoidance behavior does not clog your day, touch you with chagrin or offend others, however.

But when you are an obsessional living on tenterhooks, you discover that you avoid countless persons, objects and situations. We have noted the avoidance maneuvers associated with dread of flying, driving or similar phobias. You may be the obsessional who would rather walk many flights of steps in order to avoid riding in an elevator. If you have contamination fears, the action follows the thought; you avoid anything "infectious," even bringing your own "sanitized" plastic cups to a cocktail party.

The avoidance behavior of contamination phobics can appear to be quite eccentric. I once observed such behavior in a public lavatory. A man entered and headed for the toilet booth. He pushed the swinging door in with his hips. No hands. On emerging he kicked the door out with his foot, then washed his hands thoroughly with paper towelling and soap and dried them on another towel. With a third paper towel he closed the water tap and covered the knob of the exit door. When he was halfway through, he held the door with his shoulder and tossed the towel into the receptacle.

His efficient manipulations were those of a surgeon in a scrub room. His hands never touched a single object in the lavatory.

Avoidance Behavior Shuts You In

When you quiver at losing self-control, you keep away from church or the theater because of a presentiment that you will yell "Fire!" and cause a riot. You stay home. If you anticipate vertigo in attending a sports event where there is a "mob," you will find an excuse not to go. In a more extreme case you were the research worker who, prior to my meeting with you, had to walk around and around the block every time a particular thought that contained the name Jerry or Frank occupied your mind. (Every known psychiatric technique had been utilized to establish the psychologic linkage with these names. No association could be made.) Since this obsessive thought recurred often, you were forced to make the wearisome trek around the same block almost perpetually. Finally you stayed home to become a recluse.

REPETITION BEHAVIOR

We learn by repetition. Hearing the same song over and over, the words and tune insinuate themselves into our memory banks. From language to multiplication tables, almost everything we want or need to know can be learned with repetition and practice. Such repetition contains fierce intent, and as any musician knows, great virtuosity is built on the hard practice of repetitive learning.

However, for the obsessional, repetitions in speech and other behavior produce only fatigue and merely augment the neuroticism.

Repetition behavior takes many forms. You may be anxious and stutter on consonants. In its own way, this habit represents a phobic avoidance of words. You are being too careful about the content of your speech in the expectation of making blunders. Your enunciations reflect your tense feelings.

When you must read memoranda, letters or instructions three

or more times, or say "hello, hello, hello" in rapid succession, you are also exhibiting repetition behavior. Or you may put a question several times. If you inquire about bus transportation you will ask your friend: "Do I take the M bus south?" "Yes." A moment passes. "It is the M bus that I must take?" Answer: "Yes." You think it over and a third time you ask, "You did say I should take the M bus?" Now the "yes" answer contains a note of annoyance and puzzlement.

The daughter of one of my patients says: "My mother raises the same questions over and over. If I don't answer each time, she yells, 'Where are your manners?' If I do answer she still asks again and claims that she didn't hear me the first two times. And really, there's nothing wrong with her hearing at all—when she wants to use it."

In reverse, you may be the obsessional who must repeat your instructions twice or more. For the third or nth time, you say, "Now, are you sure you've got it right? Let me tell it to you again."

Repetition behavior can be disabling. If you are on the street you may have to pause at every corner, readjust your coat, cuffs and trousers (or dress) and repeat the entire routine at the next corner. You may retrace certain steps prior to entering your front door, then go down and climb the stairs two or more times. After that you do it all over again twice or thrice. Obviously, the day is never-ending. Nothing else is completed and you are little better off than if bedridden.

INSIGHTS TO HELP THE MALADAPTIVE WITH DISTURBED BEHAVIOR

Rituals and other obsessional behavior described in this chapter do often relieve your anxiety. For example, you may believe, in all sincerity, that so long as you perform your ritual you will not collapse, explode, die or infect yourself or another. The gremlins will be appeased and will prevent all harm. You substitute a sym-

bolic behaviorism such as a hand-washing ritual to displace the anxiety of your conflicts.

As the postal clerk with the evacuation ritual, you let preoccupation with your spastic bowel displace your worries, perhaps in your case because of an obscure emotional clash about your sexual identity and a hazy awareness of a preference for homosexual love. You are determined to suppress this and act the role of a normal heterosexual.

The bedtime rituals that we discussed earlier are not devoid of a reasonable premise. Much as we all want to sleep in peace we do not, unlike the animals of the wild, possess sensory mechanisms that alert us to danger while asleep. Thus, without knowing why, we may gather security symbols for bedtime. In childhood, a doll or teddy bear, a special shirt or blanket may do. In adulthood, a night-light or an extra doorlock puts your mind (anxieties) at rest. But with obsessionally limited self-confidence, you need lots more assurance. Rituals provide you with it as the final measure, after you have taken all of your other precautions. Only then can you release into sleep.

Although *checking behavior* (and repetition too) begins with doubts, it can also stem from other mental processes. We know that in reaction formation, one functions on the principle that the best way to evade the hateful is to run from it in the opposite direction, actually or symbolically. Let us say that you repeatedly check on the health of a parent, sister or aunt whom you subconsciously dislike but to whom you could never hint of this distaste. You would then go to the other extreme, in your reaction formation, conveying a solicitude that hyperbolizes (and almost mocks) a love you never truly feel. But it wipes out your self-reproach and guilt for being unable to feel the affection that you think is expected of you.

Avoidance behavior was sharply exemplified by the problem that impelled you to walk around the block each time the name Jerry or Frank came to mind. Actually, though, this may have been your way of eluding any chance of reaching whatever goals had been marked out for you. Immobilized, you simply had to stay put, and this closed the issue. You thus avoided the unbearable responsibility of goal confrontation.

You are not the only obsessional who evades goal-oriented behavior. One woman has a faculty for winding herself into confusion at every stimulus. She may start to make the bed. Routine enough? But then she notices a tear in the seam of the spread's ruffle and starts to repair it. On her way for needle and thread she spots a smear on a mirror that she had just cleaned so she must rush for a cloth to give the mirror a swipe. However, the cloths are all dirty and she reproves herself. But she suddenly recalls that a worn bed sheet will do and in reaching for it she stops to make a note of her other linen supplies. On go the detours. By the end of the day she is enervated with her backing and filling. Little has been accomplished but she has avoided her more important tasks of cleaning, shopping and preparing meals. And the bed has not been made.

In *repetition behavior*, you may, for example, telephone repeatedly for instructions about medication. If asked why you must repeat your questions when the answers have been written out for you, your reply makes sense to you. "I feel safer when I *hear* the answer a number of times." Yes, repetition does strengthen security in your case.

Obsessional Behavior May Intensify

In an attempt to abolish your anxiety totally, you often elaborate on your obsessions. Now you cannot just cheat on your rituals occasionally, but you must increase their complexity. They become your masters and you feel powerless to resist them. Aware that others cannot understand your ritualism, and equally loathing yourself as your rituals' puppet, your discontent reaches a penultimate in dysphoria, uptight tension and irritability. As an obsessional, you are fast becoming a model of poor and unproductive function. Is there form to your life? Minimally. And very little substance.

You have now become maladaptive because your energy reserve has been squandered and requires attention. Half the battle to get well will be in recognizing your illness as obsessional. The other half must come from the empathic aid that is brought to your rescue.

My actions may thunder my thoughts and my feelings
and ritual lightning may strike
As I double-check detours and leave through the ceiling
for nineteen rides on my bike
. . . to stroke out the bumps of my psych.

· 14 ·

Psychosomatic Symptoms in the Maladaptive

Physical symptoms expose a maladaptive loss of vitality. They register your personality's turbulence as it infiltrates all receptors of the body process. They adulterate your health and usurp your right to flourish.

Do not think that such functional discomforts are "imaginary." Rather, they are caused by uneven or surcharged body chemistry in your adaptive progression. You have no physical derangement of any organ; medical examinations show up invariably as negative. The authentic illness is planted in the *modus operandi* of the living *process* (thus, functional), and not in an organic *defect* (hence, not physical). Although the symptoms are potentially reversible, the pressure that is generating them must be removed; or if it is a psychologic tempest, it must be settled.

Every O-C at some stage has endured several or many classical psychosomatic symptoms which telegraph the existence of an up-tight state. These O-Cs are the *complainers* (see The Health Conscious in Chapter 4).

GASTROINTESTINAL COMPLAINTS

Within uptight maladaptation, the most common problem is *constipation*. (In Freudian theory, the "anal character" is a retentive person whose money holdings represent anal fixation. Money symbolizes feces. Unable to give up money or his feces, he is a

163

constipated compulsive. One confused analysand mumbled, "Funny place to keep your money.")

Possibly, diarrhea alternating with constipation has beset you for years, an illness often named *chronic colitis* or *irritable colon*. As a spastic condition of the bowels, it coincides with tightness and cramps in other body parts. When spasticity knots your stomach, you also suffer indigestion, flatulence, and periodically the pains and heartburn of gastric ulcers.

An uptight schoolteacher was afflicted with diarrhea and constipation to the point of toxicity. Her tension rose because she was never sure of leaving the classroom fast enough to avoid an "accident." "I know I have colitis. I just can't eat the usual foods. And sometimes I feel I must have cancer. Yet the doctors refuse to tell me the truth and I don't know why." (Note the additional symptoms: cancerophobia and paranoia.)

MY HEAD AND NECK FEEL WRONG

Here your most pronounced symptom is headache, varying from tolerably dull pressure in the frontal areas to splitting pains at the temples, simulating migraine. A sickening nausea may also accompany them.

Between these extremes, an assortment of pressures, aches and shooting twinges in the head, face and neck have been described pitifully by my patients. You may refer to "this tensional headache that I have, a sort of squeezing inside my skull. Sometimes I could go wild with it. Or else the top burns, and other days it's like a tight rubber band all around and it throbs at the back of my head."

Face pains, often mistaken for sinusitis, are rather general too. Sometimes you feel them in the jaw or deep in the throat. If you are the taut and angry O-C who grinds your teeth during sleep or constantly clenches your jaws, your condition is called bruxism or temporomandibular syndrome. Or you may simply be the uptight woman who develops neck pains *after* you nap. Why? You lie rigid instead of resting because you cannot bear to muss the bed.

You would be better off napping in a chair until you decide to modify your orderliness.

MY ACHING BODY

The tightness of your obsessional neurosis obliges your muscles to work overtime, never letting go. This is why you are forever exhausted even though you have done little physical work. A spastic muscle is the same as a chronic charleyhorse. No wonder, then, that your abused body complains of cramps or stiffness across the shoulders with severe backache. You feel discomfort whether you sit, lie flat or curl on your side.

Persistent muscle tension, especially when the occasion calls for a carefree ease, puts extraordinary pressure on each bone joint. Test it yourself. Make a tight fist and press the knuckles of one hand against the other for a minute or so and see how the joints hurt. (When you are tensional, you are pulling your muscles and compressing your joints cruelly like this every second of the day. The results show in the unmistakable aches that wear you down.) Now let your hand muscles go slack and enjoy the dramatic relief.

MY CHEST CLOSES IN

The chest wall (rib cage) and the organs that it protects are also not spared from your uptightness. A TV sound engineer described a typical attack. "I got this feeling of constriction just behind the breastbone. It went up and down the center of my chest and it nauseated me besides." One woman told of the stabbing pains over her heart area which sometimes radiated into the left arm. This can suggest, and may in fact be, a symptom of cardiac insufficiency. Call it a heart attack, if you will, but uptight patients of mine have had a number of electrocardiograms when this symptom appeared, with all tracings normal. However, for a tensional neurotic, such symptoms could also be your saving grace. Because of your cardiac fears, you are coerced into rest and relaxation, forcing you, at least temporarily, to a slowdown of tension.

At times, those muscles that bind the rib cage become spastic and produce neuralgic pains in the chest. Such spasms also fix the rib cage in one position with subsequent sighing respiration and shortness of breath. Only in learning to calm yourself will this condition go.

THE TELLTALE SKIN

Offhand, one does not think of the skin as an organ of the body. It is—and at that, the largest. It responds psychosomatically to every feeling tone, blushing with embarrassment, turning red in rage and paling in fear; or it sweats, itches, ulcerates, wheals, dries, and so on.

As with many obsessionals, your skin may be sensitive to your fluctuating responses, developing prickly sensations, mild rashes and urticaria. Thus, the skin can be used somewhat as a barometer of emotional storms. I have reported that most maladaptive O-C women evidence a pink-red, irregular flush on the skin of their throat that sometimes extends to the jaw and side of the neck. This phenomenon, called *Cammer's sign*, seems to be specific for those women who go defensive at the slightest reference to any O-C trait. If you think you are an uptight woman, look in the mirror right now and see for yourself.

HYPERTENSION

One of the most ominous signals of anger or tension in the maladaptive O-C is a persistent rise in blood pressure. Obsessionals who cannot deal with frustration often say: "It makes my blood boil." The blood does not boil but the pressure does go up and leads to irritability, insomnia and pounding headaches.

This type of hypertension is readily treated with relaxation methods in behavior therapy (see Chapter 18). You may have noted the fluctuation of your blood pressure: it lowers when you are at peace and you can then deal better with your day-to-day tasks; it rises even when you try to veil your furies with crisp low-keyed language. One's heart may be wrung to see you in these blind mistakes of wrath, but whether you are mercifully forgiven or condemned for your tempers, you should know that your hypertension and its causes, if not eliminated, may destroy you.

INSOMNIA

If we add the number of prescriptions written for sedatives to the sale of over-the-counter drugs for offering sleep, then insomnia must be the most universal symptom that affects our uptight population. Like most maladaptive O-Cs, you swarm with ruminations in your nighttime thoughts. Unable to sacrifice control, you delay release into sleep or merely allow an uptight superficial drowsiness. You may be an obsessional who sleeps fitfully but near morning drops into a slumber so heavy that when you do awaken, you are groggy, not refreshed. Insomnia exasperates you, not so much because of its ensuing fatigue, but at the thought and dread all day of a repeat that night.

A friend of mine told me of her grandmother's recipe for this condition, one that often works: Close your eyes and visualize a pitch-black window shade slowly unrolling downwards. Printed on it in huge and even blacker letters is the word "SLEEP." In your mind's eye you concentrate on the shade as it gradually winds down. And so do you. Before it reaches the bottom you should be happily in dreamland.

GENITAL AND URINARY COMPLAINTS

Psychosomatic symptoms that suggest sexual dysfunction in the maladaptive O-C are many and diversified. Gynecologists can recite at length the discomforts that such women complain of: swelling, rawness and itching in and around a congested vulva, chronic infections, spasms and nebulous pains and distress in the pelvic area.

When your laments continue despite proper treatment, it is then that sexual difficulties become suspect. Even with gentle, stimulating caresses of all erogenous areas, you never lubricate enough. You may be so spastic and tight that penetration is almost impossible. Intercourse, when effected, is painful most times; the vagina is overly dry or too moist and irritated because of some discharge—never "right." The mere prospect of sexual intercourse that night might cause you to double over with backache and cramps in your lower abdomen and you wonder about possible trouble with your ovaries or perhaps "adhesions" from previous surgery flaring up. The next day you rush for emergency medical consultation.

Urologists are equally familiar with the sexually maladaptive man who complains of backache, pain in the testicles or groin, itching and swelling in the pelvic area, and so on. One man clearly saw the relationship of his symptoms to the demand for sexual performance. "I get burning sensations after sex and I think there's a urethral discharge. My penis draws with sticking pains. Maybe impotence would be easier to take." Yes, for obsessionalism's sake, you might indeed deny your sexual blessings and become a joyless epicene—unless you can be saved from yourself. However, most men do not want to forgo sex but O-C anxieties dominate their performance and they suffer from premature ejaculation, inability to ejaculate or total impotence.

Many internists have learned to recognize you as the "neurasthenic" maladaptive who talks of vague chest pains, sweating, dizzy spells, chills and weakness in the thighs, palpitations, and so on. Full examinations testify that your heart is normal, the blood pressure fine and your blood chemistry, hormones and metabolism all that they should be. What the physician also knows is that you are afraid of adult relationships but masturbate a great deal and feel guilty. Your symptoms will improve only when you gain the sociosexual skills that define maturity.

Psychologic Complaints of Sexual Conflict

The internist and his gynecologic consultant are familiar with the young matron who wails about her pressing fatigue and insomia, how she must bear with awful premenstrual tension and exhausting, prolonged bouts of menses. Moreover, she seems to respond adversely to birth control pills and intrauterine devices or any other contraceptive procedures. No physical, metabolic or technical reasons can be found for these dysfunctions.

Actually, playing two roles, a controlling houseproud and the devoted wife, you are snared in the conflict of your anorgasmic lovemaking and your inability to face the fact. In consulting me the hidden core of meaning in your complaints came to light. Admitting to being unfulfilled, what you really wanted was to manipulate the situation so that the onus of your unhappiness would fall on your husband for "not making a woman of me."

Uptight men, more than women, hate admitting to sexual inadequacies or related psychosomatic troubles, much less discussing them with a psychiatrist, psychologist or even the family physician. But the problems are ongoing, usually from bad to worse, and require professional help.

THE HYPOCHONDRIAC

Unlike the worrying, anxiety-ridden body watcher previously mentioned, you are the hypochondriac obsessed with health and body care, possessively interested in your malfunction. Your convictions, strong and irrevocable, say that your fancied ailments are spectacularly real. You are not necessarily perturbed about your illnesses. More importantly, you want to be sure that one and all, especially the doctor, acknowledge them to be gravely valid and understand the fragility of your constitution, that everyone will accept your symptoms, pay homage to them, court your medical

em, and even love you for them. Hypochondriasis is
vie, much as compulsive eating or physical culture is
others. To reinforce your obsession you must always be in the
throes of some illness, any illness, in the same way that a person
obsessed about safety must constantly check on all protective
devices.

The Compulsion to Be Ill

You are encompassed in a *specific compulsion to be ill*. To prove
your condition, you bait every doctor into doing more and more
tests. You accept the discomfort of the tests with a plumed
bravura. If they are negative it means the diagnosis is wrong. If, by
chance, some minor test result is positive—then *there*, you were
right. You are supremely justified, and apocalyptically you know
how terribly you are yet to suffer. Since you need the illness to
satisfy your obsessional anxieties, you will rarely follow a treatment
program, particularly when only a small aberration is at issue.
Should treatment be recommended, you inform the doctor that
you have tried "that prescription" given by a previous doctor and
it did not work.

It comes down to this. *You must not be cured.* In effect, you are
telling your physician: "You can't win with me. I'll go right on
complaining because I've *got* to be sick. That's me." The doctor
is so baffled that he accuses you of fakery. You in turn accuse him
of either failing to recognize your illness or, worse, not caring. You
then start happily on the next round to find another doctor's ear.

With it all (or despite it), some hypochondriacs are sweet and
appealing persons, if one can overlook their "illnesses."

The Hypochondriac Is Not Malingering. If once you are diag-
nosed properly and made to recognize the obsessionalism of your
complaints, family and friends dismiss their annoyance and tolerate
your health fussiness more compassionately. You pursue your obsession to be ill with all the zeal of a houseproud woman pluckily

chasing dirt; by good fortune, it is always there for both of you to worry about.

INSIGHTS TO HELP THE MALADAPTIVE'S PSYCHOSOMATIC SYMPTOMS

The family doctor would like to help maladaptives but finds them too difficult if not impossible. When he prescribes a diet for you, respite from stress, and medication, this is "old stuff." Rest? "Impossible. I'm too busy." Pills? Even if they give some relief, "They're only a crutch, and who wants that?" Just an antacid to ease a heartburn is refused. You stop visiting doctors for a while, convinced none of them have any desire or ability to help you. But as your tensions, fears and pains continue, you may look to Christian Science or perhaps the more exotic treatment of our new "therapy culture." Mostly, you devise your own nutritional regimen and intensify your orderliness because it gives you a structured base and softens your aggravations briefly. Yet overall, you remain uptight, and further limit your activities, including your sex life. Thus, you conclude that you are magnificently controlled and "doing all right."

But your maladaptive constrictions tighten into a disastrous vise, and at infrequent clear-sighted moments, you feel that you are the world's orphan.

> Why must I hurt
> with aches and pain
> I'd be more euphoric
> should good Fate deign
> never to let me be grieforic
> or know again a minute's strain
> But hell itself's no more caloric
> Than fears and nerves, my body's bane.

PART THREE

Sexual Maladaptation

· 15 ·
Sexual Behavior in the Maladaptive

Human sexual behavior is a biologically determined activity which includes social felicity, courtship and mating. Thus, every conceivable form of psychologic play and body contact expresses a covenant of ardor and vibrant love between two sexually ripened persons.

In this joining of pleasure and commitment, much of the gratification is culturally conditioned. It will vary within different value systems. To illustrate: One couple in a traditional setting may be fully pledged to a devoted marriage, wherein neither could do well without the other; a second pair may live radiantly as sexual playmates; a third couple, barely introduced, lose themselves in an intense bedroom adventure over a weekend. Yet all three couples savor to the full their intimacies and consider them normal and richly compensating.

The wide swing in norms of physical, social and psychologic outlooks within sexual activity is noted when a love nip for one woman becomes a sadistic hurt to someone else, when intense erogenous stimulation for another turns bliss to pain. One couple might veto oral intercourse as perverse; another would feel sensually deprived if their sexual menu lacked it. Initial stimulation may be superfluous for the woman who loves a fast "flyer" because she achieves orgasm rapidly with deep penetration. Spread-eagled on the bed, she sings out: "I'm ready whenever you are, hon." Another might think this so crude that the libido would go into reverse.

Like everyone else, you, too, decide what determines deviant or perverse sexual behavior. You see yourself as normal, except perhaps for a few little hangups, some inhibitions, one or two unique fantasies or occasional difficulties in performing. If you are a maladaptive O-C, you often teeter between following the convention of the "right thing" in sex as opposed to your desires to do as you please and to hell with whether it's the "wrong thing."

We can start with the most distinct maladaptive sexual trait, *basic inhibition*. (But again, a reminder: Not all of these inhibitions appear in every maladaptive; the following simply describe the broad spectrum.)

BASIC INHIBITIONS

If your last date was a repressed, unresponsive individual, you probably hit a stone wall of inhibited sexual maladaptation. If you were the discomfited woman you might reflect of him: "A real insipid item, no sap in it." As the thwarted man you would sigh: "A cold tomato, not the kind you want to squeeze." No matter what the visible social graces, this sort of person probably abides by some or all of the following mandates:

Sex is the biologic animal in us and basically dirty.
Sexual impulses should be laundered and contained.
Masturbation destroys physical and mental health.
Any touching is to be absolutely ruled out.
Homosexuality is loathsome.
Intercourse, other than in the missionary position, is perverse.
Loose social behavior (dancing, hugging) leads to licentious-
ness.
Exposing one's "intimate parts" is revolting and forbidden.
Thoughts and feelings about sex are unfit for conversation.

We are, of course, describing the obsessional prude, male or female, who cannot accommodate to the old and ordinary, much less to the startlingly new culture of today. Movies and TV programs that show nudity as a commonplace bring forth the specious protest: "I hate nudes anyway. I've seen them all, Rubens, Goya, Renoir, with those big backsides . . . Why look at a naked body when you can admire it covered up with a beautiful gown?"

The Conflicts of Inhibition

As an obsessional young man, doubtful of enough assertiveness to ensure potency, you will reject sex, thereby reinforcing self-doubts of your masculine image. If you resolve your conflict by marrying a passive woman, you end up in an almost sexless union. If you succumb to a stronger female, the sexual rapport seems good for a time but soon you resent her dominance. Or you may have chosen a skittish minx who loves a good frolic.

"Sweetie, let's make love differently tonight."

"Like how?"

"We'll have a pillow fight. I win, then you chase me and when you catch up you pretend to rape me."

You are thrown by the unpremeditated. How to play a simple game without being confused and a penis going flaccid at this new idea?

You are the obsessional woman who also harbors inhibiting conflicts. With the right man, you feel that of course you could be as sexually competent as any professional mistress. But how amazing, the many faults you can find in the man who is totally eligible. You would like to be passive and dependent—"feminine." Yet he leaves you unresponsive because actually you would want to control him. But if you could, you would not respect him.

Thus, each obsessional dreams of being the more sophisticated and powerful of the two, while equally craving to be innocent and curled into the pocket of the other. Each also knows that the true delights of sexual intercourse mean sacrificing cerebral control for the emotional distillations of abandonment. Back and forth they shuttle, frustrated within ambivalence and inhibition. The divergent tracks never meet.

Intimacy

Intimacy implies exposure. But you shun it. Halt! So far, no further. You may have been married for decades and never have seen your spouse's body. Nudity is taboo. The wife of a dental technician, you speak of it: "I hardly ever show myself to my husband. It arouses him and I don't want sex that much. I know he likes to look at my breasts, so I let him sometimes for a special treat." If your husband is the obsessional and you are freer about your body, he may bark: "Cover up and don't act like a tramp." A too sensuous mate may be an embarrassment of riches.

It is the obsessional of the pair who delimits intimacy. Darkness. Night clothes. An uncreaking bed. Love words in romantic euphemisms. The earthy language of sex repels. "Oh baby, you're screwing me in all its glory," or "Wow! What a great piece of ass," can inhibit the other. The vagina goes dry or the penis collapses. Psychobiologic freedom of intimate behavior violates the sensibilities to extinction.

As the uptight inhibited man, you avoid pleasuring your mate with the kisses that her libido craves—on her inner thighs perhaps, toes, breasts and the sweet hidden crevices that should call to you. But no, you reject these endearments. Such attentions might invite similar ones, or she might think you disgusting. If she rationalized her inhibitions aloud she would say, "I don't want that all-over lovemaking. I'm too fat," or "I'm ashamed of that scar on my stomach." Neither one of you can believe that to a beloved, your flesh is a sensuous magnet, inviting to the touch, to be handled and heated with love. You see only repulsion and imperfections that destroy the eroticism of sexual union.

Even the small intimacy of exploratory tip-of-the-tongue kisses may be excluded—a starting behavior that can lead to the flareup of intense desire. But to the uptight, just the wisp of such a fancy seems a threat.

Certainly, you would never accept the heightened bond of casual sex in unlikely settings or "quickies" at odd times. He: "Lovey, right now on the back porch . . . just feel that swelling." Or she: "I've had the hots all day, honey. Come on, let's do it here in the kitchen. Dinner can wait." Not for you though. You refuse to allow the intimacy of sex any space in your daily allowance of emotion, let alone surrender to the upsurge of a raunchy approach.

"It's just a body function," one uptight executive says, lapsing into the sternly intellectual. "Let's face it, intercourse is a clumsy procedure, nature's worst gaffe. Penetration destroys the sense of being a separate self. Needed to procreate? Ye-es, but why not as expeditiously as possible?"

Dissimilarly, the perfectionist obsessional takes a thorough start-to-finish view. The sexual act is choreographed ritually. As in the tango, with leading pressures, he indicates now this, now that. In observing all the rules of the sex manual, he is performing dutifully to his spouse. Thus, the act is completed when he ejaculates, with no exultance for either one. Or if he is a tidy-clean, he must jump up and wash instantly. One woman said, "And if he has a cold and feels like sex, he ties handkerchiefs over both our mouths." In such relationships, no more intimacy flourishes from sexual activity than if it had never taken place.

Shame

Sensation is a danger signal to the O-C obsessional. Really to love would cause you to quiver with fright. You desire what quickens you and smells delicious. Your palms are moist with wanting. But you are ashamed. At times, you may deliberately concentrate on a business problem to diffuse these excitements. At a social event, you risk a foreignism with panache and kiss your hostess' hand. One would never know that shame and aloofness dictated this impersonal elegance of maleness. If a woman, you turn a queenly cheek for a kiss, not on your lips. The conditioned embarrassment of body contact leaves you removed in greetings on any occasion.

To feel excruciating shame is common enough in the intimacy of the O-C woman's bed who endures frustration because she cannot ask to be stimulated where the sensation is especially delectable.

179

Too timid to say, "a little to the left, faster . . . now press hard
. . . oh, that's heaven, more!" And fearful of being condemned for
a joyous outcry at the moment of climactic intensity, she suppresses
herself. "My God, he'd think I was a real tart." It is even possible
that your O-C traits will distract you from orgasm totally by the use
of turnoff ruminations. "Did I finish my shopping list for tomorrow?
And I mustn't forget to add memo pads."

The woman who is not afraid of orgasm is also the shameless
wench who will reach out for a quick honeyed feel of her man's
crotch, just as he likes to nuzzle her breasts or squeeze her backside,
clothed or not.

If you are too fearful to initiate a sexual encounter, to moan with
ecstasy as he tongues your labia with long strokes in foreplay; if you
won't ask for some variants of your usual sex act such as, "Let's
watch ourselves doing it in the mirror"; if you reject the role of a
pulsating and eager sexmate, preferring that of a passive, uninvolved
partner, then you are reinforcing the conflicts of your inhibition and
shame.

Secrecy

As a way of survival, secrecy has been learned grimly by people
living in police states. You, however, churn up your own police
state, ever afraid that your personal aspirations and dreams of sensual thrills might be revealed. Secrecy thus allows you the con-
venience of the denial mechanism. Top-drawer hush can almost
obliterate the memory of an "immoral" act. It seems never to have
happened.

But though shame looks on in disapproval, the inhibited do acquire outlets, such as collections of pornographic "art," which they
pore over in secret. The wife of an obsessional finance executive
once asked me why her husband had to hide his "girlie mags," especially since she came upon them so easily. "If those sex pictures
excite him, that's okay. He doesn't get horny enough anyhow. I've
always wished he weren't so uptight about sex." Another wife felt
hurt. "I can't see the reason for Joe to use those photos for helping

him have an erection. I've got a come-and-get-it body and I know how to give him a good time. Why is he so loused up about sex?" (See Chapter 18.)

Or if you are the woman (any age) who buries yourself in romantic and gothic novels, your clitoris tingles and your pelvic muscles tighten while you envision the lascivious intimacies so pruriently sketched in. But you would deny this, pointing out the book's social and historical merit just as you would blandly overlook the "smutty" parts of a sex-oriented film.

Thus, having explored the facts of physical emotion secondhand (and for the present satisfied your needs), you expound on sex as dirty, romanticism unreal, and purity the only guide to a decent life. However, curiosity is still there and desire too. When sexual impulses again rampage through your body and you burn for a man who would mount you and funnel his organ into your throbbing vagina, you resort to another kind of gratification—fantasies of sex.

Fantasy Life

Sexual fantasies integrate themselves into growth and development starting around puberty or even before. In this text, however, we will be concerned only with the fantasy patterns of the maladaptive O-C. As a woman of this category, the lover in your passive-aggressive fantasies appears as mature, affectionate and tender. He can anticipate your most extravagant urges. While he arouses you with gentleness, he can also be masterful when you clamor for sexual turmoil in climax. He satiates all your femaleness.

Some women also have fantasies of rape, although this is not so universal as most men believe. Rather, you picture yourself engaging in group sex, lesbian love, seduction of older men or young boys, or exhibitionism—anything from sexual sport in a mirrored room to fornication with an army general in the presence of his entire division. You may also be a mesmerized crotchwatcher. Your fantasies about the fullness of the penis and its pleasure potentials are no less vivid than the man's hot image of you in a tight blouse and pants.

Some of your most exciting fantasies center about sex play with men who are "morally" unavailable—your husband's best friend or your best friend's husband. And incest? Why not? In fantasy, barriers of coupling with a close family member are easily crossed. Equally, the inhibitions that preclude all the orgastic subtleties of a voluptuary can be improvised and enjoyed without conditioned moral restraints. But with your maladaptive inhibitions you could never act upon your fantasy life. Reality is ever there, forbidding any kind of crossover.

Now let us suppose that you are the maladaptive man who revels in fantasies of yourself as an aggressive lover. You see yourself playing the satyr in orgiastic rites, ravishing one woman after another at will, saturating them with lust and debauchment. Or you may be another who enjoys the fantasy of a passive male role. Here you are being seduced by a wanton whose delights you were always warned against. Waves of sensation pour through your body. She purrs and exudes an alluring scent. And through the entire fantasy you remain quiescent as her fingers, mouth and tongue explore you and caress your penis and scrotum until that moment when you break through into an explosive convulsion of a true orgasm. Only a wish-dream? To be sure. But in it you can soar to any heights of delirious thrill.

The alternative is blankness. Occasionally you may stare into space, caught up in a fancy of sexual pleasure with a real-life love partner. Briefly, it enfolds you. Then you grow cold in the bleak knowledge that it will never happen that way. You feel as if you have been bludgeoned.

Emotional Confusion

Many O-Cs in sexual conflict are angry people, unaware of being hostile toward themselves for their perfectionism, constrictions and inhibitions. Hence, they convert the bedroom into a showcase for exhibiting super self-control in order to crowd out their self-hate.

However, if you are the O-C man who has mastered yourself with such overcontrol in order to resolve your emotional conflicts about sex, chances are that control has now conquered you.

In Chapter 14 we discussed the spastic nature of uptight symptoms: constipation, muscle tension, general "tightness" (or perhaps difficulty in starting a urinary flow). In sex, this spasticity appears as retarded ejaculations. Thus, while you are proud of your superb erections, you cannot ejaculate and experience release. You penetrate and thrust interminably, satisfying your mate with multiple orgasms, but psychologically your overcontrol does not allow you to let go. Finally you stop intercourse from sheer fatigue and the apathy of "What's the use?"

Actually, you fear committing the self because you have strangled your emotional freedoms with distrust of a mate's true love. You feed on abysmal deprivation, knowing unhappily that you are a mere implement without completion, unshared and a divided man. Despite the triumphs of erectile competence, you cannot yield your semen burst. Though release and ejaculation might be effected in the giving of your love, you are terrified of it. This might put the other in possession of your ego identity.

In the opposite condition, when anxiety about creditable erections dominates sexual adaptiveness, you may be the man who suffers premature ejaculations or impotence. Inhibited to the core, you cannot be sensualized for lengthy intervals by fondling a woman's body, kissing her breasts and nipples, savoring the taste and delicacy of her genitals; you are equally unable to feast with slow enthrallment on the sweet languor of licking kisses when you are petted from head to toe. Instead you rise to rapid arousal and immediate ejaculation. Indeed, you may "pop off" before you penetrate or within seconds afterward.

There is also the ruinous situation of the woman who deliberately induces prematurity in an anxious O-C by encouraging him to "get it over with fast." Her emphasis is on O-C dysfunction rather than sexual enjoyment. As an inhibited O-C she may succeed in emasculating her husband (see Chapter 3, Control). She feels comfortable with an impotent man and is relieved that she does not have to go through the motions of participating in sexual pleasure. She fosters this dysfunction with a show of the heroic: "I love you, dear, despite it." This detaches her from "his" problem, and she avoids any effort to encourage improvement or to cooperate in sex therapy.

I also recall the emotional confusion of the compulsive wife who deliberately inhibited her own sexual drives and channeled them into duty-bound maladaptation. The husband, a manufacturer, whose kind and devoted ambitions centered on giving his family "everything," was nevertheless blind to the fact that essentially you, his wife, were not receiving the most important happiness of your union—and by your own option.

You had early been traumatized by your parents' divorce. Misguided and blundering your way through life, you carried the corpse of the broken marriage on your back, vowing that you would never be a divorced woman, no matter what. Insecure and perpetually frightened, you were dulled to sensuous or erotic stimulation and, of course, orgasm. One motivating thought, only, guided you—to provide pleasure for your husband. Feverishly one-sided in serving his sexual needs, you became adept in learning vaginal muscularity, all the tongue and lip skills of oral stimulation and the pretense of climax.

To yourself, you would admit: "I enjoy sex just knowing that I satisfy him, watching him quiver and groan with delight, and then hit the ceiling and explode." This fed his ego and male complacency; he was unaware that you were not sharing his sexual pleasures. Knowing of your possessiveness, a friend asked curiously, "Doesn't it make you jealous when he goes to Paris and those other places on his business trips with all those women around to take him to bed?" You would smile. "It doesn't matter what he does with his dingus there. As long as he brings it back to me." True, there were times when you felt the tension of no release, but these were compensated for by the thrills you could lavish on him. By now, you know that you are cheating yourself but will do nothing about it. Occasionally you masturbate, but you do not enjoy it because you shut out any fantasy images of yourself in the throes of sexual ecstasy that should go with it.

Another kind of confusion about sexual rapport was making a misery of life for an obsessive young man, an assistant art curator. He disclosed, "It's my misfortune to be married to a beautiful woman. I know that sounds funny because I love beauty, but it scares me in a woman and I can't handle it. . . . I get inferior feelings of being puny and lumpish. I just don't feel entitled to share sex with her." The very exquisiteness of your wife overwhelmed you and became a turnoff. You were terrified of making any love advances, looking upon her with the same awe and reverence you accorded a work of art in your galleries, not to be touched by a mere clod of a man. "No, she's not cold. She really tries to get me going. But I move away. I keep thinking—suppose I scratched or bruised her. I'd never forgive myself for spoiling all that perfection." Inevitably she divorced him, and when he married a woman who was plain but empathic to him, his warmth was aroused and for the first time he was sexually and socially happy and at ease.

SOCIOSEXUAL MANEUVERS OF THE MALADAPTIVE

So much has been said, printed, and shown about sex today that it might almost be considered as a write-off, just another jaded ploy of life, overexposed, depersonalized, simply a performance of copulation. So the maladaptive sees it. "What's the fun, really? Where do I fit into the picture? What are my priorities in the go-around of pleasure?"

Thus, you keep a constant vigil over your sociosexual transactions for some kind of safe foothold on life. This, in turn, delineates your neuroticism and its quelling effects upon you.

Sexuality to Bind the Marriage

You are the maladaptive woman who begins to sense that the ties with your husband are fraying. Having exhausted your other O-C traits as marital binders (perfectionism in housekeeping, admirable budgeting, and so on), you return to sex, guided by your friends' advice or magazine articles on how to invigorate your spouse's interest. The X-rated films (skin flicks), serious publications and the like tell you that a sex revolution has been blowing up and perhaps "instead of fighting it, join it." You smoke pot several times a week to disinhibit yourself as the others do. You offer sexual novelties that you would customarily avoid or refuse—a quick extra while the kids are visiting with the neighbors, oral sex ("both of us to each other"), capering about in a black lace bra, sex when staying at your parents' home (the guilt-ridden ground), or a swinging night of a threesome in bed for a sybaritic romp.

You are really testing your self-confidence and you resent stooping to this role. It names you a failure. Your husband detects your anxious sexual performance as you ask repeatedly whether you have satisfied all his wants; he senses your own response as mechanical and concludes that you are more of a nag and burden than a glad mate in bed.

And you are puzzled. "So why is it that when I go out with my husband's partner I can shoot to the moon with him? He doesn't even have to ask. . . . I do everything we both love. When we meet at a motel his pecker is poking right out at me as soon as I walk in. I turn on like a fire alarm. I'm wet even before I can get my panties off. And do I go wild with him." Yes, drunk on the wine of disinhibition.

Sometimes Is Not Enough. The uptight man may also want to bind a marriage to avoid the social brankruptcy implied in separation or divorce. For instance, your wife demands more frequent and satisfying sexual release. In effect, she is saying: "If you love me, dammit, prove it in the hay." You cannot ignore the challenge and you cannot always deliver. "Does she think it's a battery-operated toy? Where I push a button and make it stand up for her?" Thus, gradually, coitus activated by obligatory motives in either man or woman loses its bloom. You both retreat and soon you are back in your inhibited stalemate.

Avoidance of Sexual Intercourse

Some maladaptive O-C men and women, suppressed and non-orgasmic, try to avoid sex completely. You may plead a headache to your husband's advances, but if it is unconvincing you use other gambits. "I put my hair in curlers and wait until I hear him snore. And if he lays a hand on me, even accidentally in his sleep, I tiptoe into the living room." Or you may be the woman who makes a fright of yourself with face creams, girdles and lip salves. If your husband still insists on wooing you with what you call his rapacious demands, you lie passive, no give, no fun, no canoodling, and if you had your way, no semen. "It's so mucky. Ugh!"

One man who saw through the trickery was furious. "Why should I have to go somewhere else for it? I've got a beautiful wife. Why can't she put out for me? I'm a loving man and I want to show her I am."

Or you are the maladaptive O-C man who wants to avoid intercourse. You purposely drain your energies through compulsive work schedules and hobbies. With a reduced libidinous drive to start with ("I have a low sexual profile"), you are as adept as a woman in inventing fatigue, indigestion or backache. One time you insisted that your young daughter come with you and your wife on a long holiday weekend and because of the budget you would all share the same room—the better to make sure that sex would be excluded.

Trying for the Second Honeymoon

Suppressed sexuality can sometimes be disinhibited for short periods of time—whether with pot, a bar night on the town, doubling with another couple or in other ways.

I remember when you made a conscious attempt to recapture the sensual voltage of your marriage by a "second honeymoon" with your wife. You told me that you wanted to get away from your systems job and your inhibited self. You planned your first real vacation for a tour through the Caribbean Islands. In a cavalier moment you announced that you would "go sexual" in every room of every hotel you stayed in. Carried away by your own audacity as a dashing lover, you felt vibrant and carefree. Your wife too was caught up in it. On the trip you met your own challenge, and astonished at your sexual prowess you declared that bathrooms (both tubs and shower stalls) were to be regarded as separate rooms for fulfilling your goals. Both of you were intoxicated with the adventure. Never were you tense or uptight for a moment.

You reveled in every sexual maneuver and position—in bed, your wife riding you on top, face to face and tightly embraced in the bathtub, mutual masturbation in the shower, and in coital union over the edge of the breakfast table. You even made love on the balcony chaise of that Hilton hotel, totally nude, warmed by semitropical breezes and the evening stars for your canopy, recklessly oblivious of any possible voyeurs.

However, back in your own milieu and settled down again, your inhibitions progressively returned. You sank into the doldrums of your old routine, which relegated sex only to sporadic intervals of your obsessional, orderly life (see Operant Conditioning in Chapter 18), with an occasional sneaky feel down the open-necked dress of your spouse or a lingering pat on her behind to remind you nostalgically of your Caribbean fling.

The second honeymoon is an affair in masquerade. Projected into the role of lovers amidst romantic settings, a couple can disregard all other commitments. But should the O-C maladaptive be unable to dismiss them repeatedly for such love interludes with his mate back at home, then a real affair with another person may often substitute for the marriage bind.

Lovers at Work

Lacking experience and the boldness for carrying on an affair, you take uptight precautions to avoid discovery. You slope around corners with over-the-shoulder glances, opéra bouffe style, you meet clandestinely in horrible offbeat restaurants, you communicate with each other in code, and you use a general post-office box as the letter drop.

In all of this, one can well sympathize with your anxieties and fears. You are "caught in the web of your own deceit," not so much by your conduct as by your own entrenched moral watchdogs. Inevitably, guilt feelings surface and you let the affair be discovered.

After the expected recriminations your marriage may be reconciled. Or it may be dissolved, followed by sole devotion to your loved one, without marriage.

In your new situation with a lusty mistress, life has changed miraculously. She meets you at the door, places your palm over her pubis, wiggling and winding around you. Later, as you undress each other, she leads you to the bed by your penis, then gives you a skin bath with hundreds of fast nipping kisses. Fully ablaze you return these attentions and go on to sexual excitements more steaming than any you had ever thought could exist.

Thus, having broken out of your prosaic and structured marital existence, you sense that remarrying will shut off your disinhibition and reawaken all the traits of O-C orderliness, propriety and drab sexual relations. You want these no longer. You want "moral" accountability to no one, least of all to yourself. You must remain single. (See Selective Reinforcement in Chapter 18.)

Escape into Promiscuity

Through compulsive promiscuity, you are an O-C maladaptive who is thumbing your nose at the culture, venting your contempt and anger because, uptight as you are, you cannot adjust to it. No tang or zest is offered. Reaction formation becomes your mechanism for evading the intimacies of a true love attachment. You seek safety in numbers. (One social worker seduced twelve different men in one month but did not experience orgasm once.) Promiscuous sexuality will not refresh your love feelings, nor will it totally liquidate your unease. The relish, such as it is, derives from your blackmail of the maladaptive in you. It shoves you into the conquest of "something new" (a temporary disinhibitor) which, for the sexual itinerant, has the power to attract and therefore make it worthwhile. Thus, you demonstrate your reward in some relief from tension. Your search for continuing gratification continues. You are, at least for a while, mildly euphoric.

Typically, as a maladaptive O-C man or woman, single or married, you may find yourself at a resort where you slip into an episode that is sexually active. After your partner leaves, neither one of you retains fond memories of the other. You chalk off the experience as a letdown. With only a fuzzed dreary recollection of it, you are despondent without knowing why. To blot it out and with your appetite still whetted, you go to bed with one of the hotel employees. A surgeon bachelor summed it up. "Eventually, you find that you're just moving on from one pelvis to another. It gets to be dull. Even the anticipation of a new date turns sour."

Flirtation and Teasing

Many maladaptive O-C women cherish the role of a tease. To attract men and satisfy your confidence as a charmer is almost enough sexual expression for you. You really do not want to be put to the test. When read correctly, your body language says: "The flag's up but don't touch. I'm not available . . . for the whole bit." One divorcée, eyes glistening, described her elation with the flirting game. "It's the most gorgeous thing to arouse a man. I can have an orgasm just baiting him, no matter where we are."

You have become an artist at titillating dalliance. Your perfectionism is also an effective tool when you dress with studied décolletage for that air of sexual emanation. On most dates you allow small privileges at first, brushed kisses and tentative embraces. When you catch fire, soul kisses, breast and genital fondling follow, and ultimately mutual masturbation to orgasm, the farthest sexual indulgence.

However, since there are no absolutes, at rare intervals, you jump the flirtation fence for an afternoon or weekend of bawdy larking in bed. But whether it is hanky-panky or "going all out," the finale is always the best part for you—those after-moments of cuddling, just being held and "loved." It was all worth it for this alone.

SOCIOSEXUAL IDENTITY

We have seen that as a maladaptive single O-C, regardless of other traits, you tend to be a secretive rather than an outgoing person. Whether divorced, separated or widowed, you are stamped unmistakably as "a single." However, you do not always live singly. Many of you do, but others couple up in one establishment.

There are combinations of parent and son or daughter, two sisters, two brothers, or brother and sister. Apart from such family unions, maladaptive O-C friends, with or without homosexuality, may also live together. *The Odd Couple*, dramatized in the theater and on TV, shows the perfectionist O-C (Felix), living with his noncompulsive psychologic opposite, the sloppy Oscar. Finally, there is the married couple, each malignantly O-C and obsessional, who live asexually as companions.

The conduct of these persons alternates between adaptive and maladaptive, depending on how they deal with their ambivalences and their identities from time to time.

The Single Man

You are the confirmed bachelor, generally familiar to most. The word "confirmed" tells us immediately that you are unbending about your single status. This attitude usually extends to your judgments and O-C convictions in other matters as well. Your friends and relatives have given up trying to marry you off to that "ideal" woman. Your coterie sees you as sensitive, a bit aloof, but they always call upon you when they need that extra man at a party. In this role you are delightful.

You probably retain an emotional attachment to your mother or to a sister. Basically maladaptive, you are not intensely oriented to sex but your need to masturbate annoys you. Perhaps you maintain one or several long-standing heterosexual affairs more for the purpose of dating than loving.

At an evening entertainment you may light up with genuine interest when a girl draws you into a dance. But your ambivalence intervenes. The man in you loves her cheek-to-cheek blandishments. The prig in you feels torn. Which to be? Let yourself go and enjoy it as you feel your penis harden and your skin tingle? Or move back from the promise of her breasts as they gently nudge for your male response? Suddenly the scene fragments, and desolate "for no reason," you would like to tell everyone to go to hell and run out.

The Single Woman

Many young women implicated in today's liberation movements and other changing values seem to prefer a single status for psychosocial and economic reasons. They are adaptive persons.

As the female counterparts of the bachelor, others are O-Cs like yourself and stay single because of maladaptive traits. At my first meeting with you my impression was of a bright-eyed woman, winsome in gesture and speech. Then your picture unrolled as fastidious, disciplined and controlling.

Relatives and friends know your stated desire to marry as a sham. Your niece, an astute young girl, told me, "Aunt Sue? She says she'll marry sometime but I think she *likes* being single. I'll bet if she really wanted a guy of her own she'd know how to find him." She tells it correctly. You are meticulous about which Mr. Right will possess your vagina, but essentially the combined attributes you want do not exist. Your selectivity indicates your determination to remain single. You are amicable, in a calculated fashion, proper, sometimes involved with liberal activists; rarely do you utter any kind of brash statement, but somehow you must always have it "my way."

You cannot ditch your sexual drives entirely any more than the bachelor can. Your dates are usually with someone "safe," except when you are drawn into a major sexual experience—on which you trip. Invariably, it is a disaster. Inwardly repelled by your sweating hairy lover, his male odor and the whole "squalid" nature of sex, your flattened affects make you less than an inspiring bed partner. You prefer to sip at a cocktail glass rather than flavor your mouth with his lips and flesh and phallus, and all the other rewards that his body offers.

Eventually, the emotional demands of the affair threaten your privacy. You end it with any palatable excuse. It has served its purpose and certified you as female. You are ready to return to your unbothered state.

Limitations on the Single Woman. If you have not accepted yourself as a "single," your social life may be emptier and more irritating than that of the maladaptive bachelor. Since single women outnumber men, you are not in demand as a fill-in at your married friends' dinner parties, and you are thus aggrieved by social neglect. True, your income may afford freedom of movement to go to a restaurant, movie or theater, but your aloneness makes you exquisitely sensitive to its social nuances. To be out with another couple is no better. You feel "like a third wheel." Insecurity and frustration settle in as you try to adjust to a "coupled" society. A chronic depressive state may overtake you.

When an Active Sex Life Is Cut Off. Some single women, especially if they are widowed but have experienced satisfactory sex lives in their marriage, feel utterly lost when they seek social contacts with no success, and are ultimately forced to suppress all sexual impulses. I think of a South American woman I met, fun-loving and gregarious, who asked piteously, "Tell me, how do you combinate in this country?"

Odd Couples

Earlier, I spoke of the many single maladaptives, unable to live alone, who dilute their anxieties by dwelling together in some kind of neurotically enforced relationship. You may be one of such couples. The common denominator of these compacts, whether composed of kin or others, is the psychosocial security obtained, reinforced by a one-to-one devotion. Having failed to mature and unable to provide for your psychologic selfhood, you compensate by keeping occupied with uptight concern for the health and welfare of your companion. You are always available to any beck or call. In fact, each of you, as maladaptive O-Cs or obsessionals, makes in-

numerable demands upon the other for which you patiently interrupt work and outside interests. Occasionally, one of you may
demur, but in your need to lean, it is in a whisper, not a shout.

You therefore live together with reasonable harmony and economic sharing, each according to your talents and abilities. Your
social, cultural and work interests may have nothing in common,
and your secret lives, fantasies and sexual habits vaguely approxi-
mate those of the maladaptive bachelor or single woman. But let no
outsider interfere between you because as time goes on, such ties
may become more possessive and indivisible than those of any
marital relationship.

Married Couples Who Live as Single Persons

Rather often, an O-C man marries an equally rigid woman. I
previously mentioned that such unions may decompensate into an
asexual détente, frequent enough in the lives of such inhibited
persons.

However, some social variants in these pairings need special mention. Yours may be the matter of children. Neither of you really
wants offspring but each must prove your social obligations. On
balance, you settle for one child. After that, married life may become more devoid of sex with each passing month. Should psychosomatic difficulties arise, they provide just the right coat of white-
wash for suppressing your sexual drive. Content to live as brother
and sister, you will never consult Masters and Johnson.

Another variant in obsessional couples concerns you who have
the same all-consuming work addiction. It leaves you no energy for
social mingling or a sex life. Affectional exchanges are simply part of
your civilities rather than expressions of libido. We find this condition in the many Ma and Pa businesses of franchised enterprises.
Small motels, roadside diners, novelty shops and hundreds of other
eked-out ventures are run by such hard-driven, self-sacrificing couples as yourselves, drudging through impossibly long hours to assure
a continuing income, but with no joy, no laughter, no altitudes of

cheer. Family gatherings are your only social life. You do not have friends, only customers.

Homosexuals

This discussion of homosexuality is not meant to cover the entire subject. It will be limited to your related maladaptive O-C traits.

Many of you, male and female, are O-Cs with varying obsessional traits. It is my impression that these traits predominate in you because of the greater struggle with your social status. In an unenlightened society the insecurity of your sexual identity and partnerships can be staggering, especially where it counts—on the job. You are often forced to camouflage your identity and role. While you struggle with many of the usual conflicts of sexual preference, your discontents and instabilities are reinforced to a large degree by a hostile culture.

You resolve some of your conflicts and allay a good deal of your agitation when you regiment yourself as an O-C, i.e., stick to your convictions undeviatingly, maintain a neat and tidy home, give your possessions indefatigable care, sometimes in the best houseproud tradition, and live a private life. Much of your fussiness (in men) is not the effeminate side of you. It is your uptight need to be compulsively just-so, exact, and obsessively alert to society's acceptance or rejection of you.

Knowing about hurt, firsthand, you are also more tender and sensitive as homosexual lovers than most heterosexuals. You will burst with pride about even a minor achievement of your sweetheart or ache with sympathy over a cut finger. However, you may also be as contumacious as the heterosexual and as domineering in your own sociosexual proclivities.

Summing up, I believe that homosexuals and heterosexuals are equally uptight and unstable when obsessionalism about sexual release, compulsive promiscuity and other maladaptive O-C traits intrude, and thus require help for these personality disturbances.

SEXUAL PERVERSIONS

According to one dictionary definition, perversion means a turning away from that which is considered generally to be "right or good." It also implies a corruption of values and an opposition to what is admissible to the culture. Such definition is all-encompassing and vague enough to satisfy the censorious. Psychiatrically, perversions are abnormal and generally refer to deviant sexual practices.

Within the obsessional neurosis, perversions are translated as "irresistible behavior," similar to rituals and the single manias. Many perversions are minor or of trifling intensity and are kept secret for a lifetime. They scarcely matter in the person's social adaptations. It is when they offend the social order overtly that the individual, unable to change, is penalized for them.

Normal Versus Perverse

Biosocially, we can say that every kind of sensual stimulation (touch, taste, smell, sight, hearing) and all sexual practices are normal provided they occur with the consent and conscious participation of the other adult person(s) involved.

Based on this principle, stimulation and function of sex become obsessional and perverse when you can be aroused by one form of sensory excitation only and/or can achieve sexual satisfaction solely from one kind of act. For example, masturbation is an appropriate release for sexual tension when other means are not readily available. But compulsive masturbation is considered perverse when you reject all other outlets and use it as your exclusive sexual practice.

Visual stimulation is also normal for ultimately bringing you to orgasm. However, if you are a *voyeur* (Peeping Tom) who achieves full stimulation *solely* from looking at whatever inflames you erotically to a climax with masturbation, this is considered perverse. *Exhibitionism* is similarly classified as perverse when you are wholly and orgasmically gratified simply by exposing your body or genitals to the full view of others.

There is also the *satyr*, fixed on the adolescent practice of *scoring*, who compulsively stalks and pursues new conquests. You may be his female counterpart, the *nymphomaniac*, whose frequency of orgasm constitutes the satisfying element. However, the promiscuous is usually motivated by self-depreciation and a frenetic quest for acceptance and favor. Many promiscuous women fail repeatedly to achieve orgasm and do not enjoy sex. Nymphomaniacs do.

Sadism refers to the sexual enjoyment of inflicting cruelty. Its name derives from the Marquis de Sade, who wrote many books extolling sexual orgies in which physical and psychologic abuse are imposed on the victim whose pain arouses the sadist to sexual fervor.

Masochism describes the orgasmic sexual response in the person who is being hurt. It is named after Count Leopold von Sacher-Masoch, a novelist whose characters found sexual ecstasy in the torments of physical and emotional violence such as being whipped, beaten and degraded.

Coprophemia is the perverse act of uttering obscene words to women. Coprophemic men make telephone calls to a woman hoping that she will respond to their foul language. They are then stimulated to ejaculation.

Sodomy, as a perversion, refers to anal intercourse. According to the Bible, the Palestinian cities of Sodom, Admah and Gomorrah were destroyed by fire from heaven because of this carnal practice. Today, the term sodomy is used in law as referring to any unnatural sexual relations between humans, meaning oral and anal intercourse as well as *bestiality* (relations with animals).

Fetishism is a unique kind of perverse obsession. A fetish is an idol or some other object believed to have magical powers. Applied to perverse sexual stimulation, it may be a glove, scarf or similar personal item that symbolizes or is associated with the loved one. Possessing, handling and, in some cases, fantasizing the fetish, usually with masturbation, is enough to bring the fetishist to orgasm.

One well-dressed older man in a department store approached a young lady who had just sneezed. "I have allergies like that too." He added abruptly, "Take off your shoes and let me look at them." Dumbfounded, she obeyed. He then licked the sole of each shoe from toe to heel and immediately walked away to the men's room.

Transvestism is the compulsion, most common in certain obsessional men, to cross-dress in women's clothes. It is their perversion and they usually keep it a secret by limiting it to undergarments. A young waitress came home unexpectedly one day to find her brother, a plumber, lounging in her bedroom chair reading a book, smoking a cigar and wearing her panties and bra. She ran out, screeching, "Mom, come quick. Joey's out of his head. He thinks he's me. And they're my best lace undies too." He was quite irritated with her stupid objections.

Periodically and in secret, a transvestite dresses completely as a woman and may even go shopping or visit socially. Some have capitalized on this compulsion by earning a livelihood as female impersonators. Most famous of all recent transvestites is the character of Klinger in TV's *M*A*S*H*. Perverse and incredible? Well yes. But loved and dear to everyone.

INSIGHTS TO HELP THE SEXUAL MALADAPTIVE

As an O-C maladaptive, your ambivalence begs to be resolved. It pulls you in contrary directions and attenuates your natural flow of sensual energy.

The misfortune here is that within, you may hide the dulcet tones of love, elation and gaiety. But you are too inhibited, over-regulated and devoid of words to show your feelings on your sleeve. You dampen your own libido.

Even if you express the language of a tender mate, your anxiety belies conviction. This puts you doubly at a loss. Every cell of you struggles to open up your feelings because you still believe that, "in my own way," you can really care for someone. Yet you cannot say it. The emotional tools you require have rusted into partial decay.

The Confusion of Needs

Thus, as O-Cs and obsessionals, your psychosexual defenses preclude a healthy union (marital or nonmarital). Yet separation does not free you for rewarding social encounters. You are the girl who says, "After the third date, if it goes that far with him, any him, I have to decide how much to get involved to hold his interest." In your maladaptive O-C rationale, you are explaining that you want the rapport to develop bindingly without sex taking over. You refuse to be "conquered" into bed because you want to know that you are liked and loved for your own identity.

That the sensual you is also your identity, that you might learn to become a more equal participant in the pact of reaching for heights of transport and climax, does not occur to you. You add, "I realize that I can either be miserably lonely or play the sexual game and get uptight doing it. But I'm not the kind who wiggles. I don't douse on perfume or use four-color eyeshadow or wear tight sweaters to show off my boobs for every man to stare at. And I won't enter the rat race at resorts or the 'meet' market in cocktail bars and laugh at their jokes like a hyena. It's all so one-sided. They want what they want and that's the answer, I guess. So how do I attract a man just as a friend and keep it that way?"

The chances are that you will not, so you decide to forgo the chore of seductive role-playing. You accept loneliness as the lesser evil.

In the male arena, you are the maladaptive O-C who continues for a while to make the rounds in your perfunctory search for bed partners if only to assure yourself of your masculinity. But you too are confused. "I don't know what these women want or how far I can go. I don't get their message. It almost seems better just to stay home." How much of this you can tolerate without despair will depend on the way you adapt overall to your O-C traits.

Frigidity and Impotence

When you are a maladaptive O-C woman you tend to be frigid, that is, sexually unresponsive. Your cynicism about any particular male often masks a basic truth—hostility toward all males. You put it this way: "I know what they're after and I freeze. They feel the icy draft too and move away."

But frigidity is more than blunted feelings about sex or an absence of libido. You are emotionally repelled at the thought of sensuous or erotic stimuli. Mostly, your frigidity is a total kind of negativism to your female role despite pretty dresses and other allurements which you adopt. Your anger, a bitter rage at your own inhibitions, is predominant. For this you throw the guilt at the man. You feel, oh yes, he's ready enough to be "on the make," but why doesn't he know how to break down my defenses against enjoying sex? After all, isn't that *his* job? You thus absolve yourself of all responsibility or commitment for making a success of any love relationship.*

As for the maladaptive man, you have felt the vindictive stings of women (perhaps your spouse)—their unspoken accusations that you are not a lover to be cherished but rather an adversary on all levels whose ego must be vanquished until you are brought humbly to your knees. Though not actually impotent, you now start behaving as if you were. "I can live without it." But not as a happy person because this unfulfilled mode of life drives you to other defensive maneuvers, from work addiction to arrogance, intolerance and righteousness.

You thus keep at a distance from women and develop functional impotence. Your loss of ability to erect does not mean that you do not hunger for sexual pleasures. But you have begun to suppress them. On the occasions when you are desperate to "try again" as a

* Vaginismus also occurs in some women who are not frigid but who have developed a reflexic spasm to penile ingress, a condition in which the vagina clamps down so that penetration is impossible. Similar to the gag reflex of the throat, it is easily and successfully treated with behavioral therapy. See Chapter 18.

man, your anxiety brings defeat. You do not trust your partner to help desensitize your fear of failure and the embarrassment of your "inadequacies." Like the frigid woman, you secretly condemn her for not understanding your plight, without realizing that you have never taken the trouble to bring it into the open and explain it. You maintain your O-C defenses.

One mourns this waste of life's gifts as we see such men and women end up vitiated by total sex maladaptation, along with other uptight disturbances of thoughts, feelings and behavior. They try to carry off their roles, but one hears the eerie note of the hollow and forsaken. All day they live in the dark of deficiency and shrunken spirit, unable to pluck out the why of it.

Intimacy Can Be Your Lifeline

Intimacy with a mate is the organism's wisdom of lips, limbs, hearts and thoughts in a continuum of closeness. Intimacy reinforces your sensate focus. Each one of you is yourself and each one is the other.

Intimacy demands the use of a singularly human behavior, nature's gift of speech. Intimacy brings you out of your anatomical shell to reveal your thoughts. When you verbalize whatever threatens you, your loyal champion closes ranks and helps you withstand it.

Intimacy lets you know your priceless worth to your mate. It gives you courage and fortitude. It expands your ego.

Intimacy reconciles differing likes, efforts, talents and concepts.

Intimacy eddies out and touches others with the lambency of your love.

Intimacy contains no forbidden grounds. Intimacy gives you completion.

> To take possession of one to one
> and find thrilled foci of heat in flesh,
> And blood so hot you could but mesh
> to guard the tenancy you won.

With no iota cased in gyve,
and leaping heart in thrall of flame
you did most swiftly make your claim
to gain free ease, to be alive.

So out of the mal
and into the peace,
is it not love that's sought?
Sings the madrigal of sweet release . . .
for no coin,
can it be bought.

· 16 ·
Rating Scale for the Obsessional Neurotic

Obsessional neurotics include 60 percent of obsessive-compulsive personalities (O-Cs) who have swung over from adaptive to maladaptive, i.e., neurotic. Here, decompensation into obsessionalism interferes with the pursuit of your goals and desires, inhibits your sexual activity, deprives you of pleasure and generates tension to a marked degree.

These impairments produce distressing psychosomatic symptoms. Your social relationships are impoverished and lacerated, and you cannot settle into a productive role and place in society, even though you may achieve partial success in some areas.

More worrisome, you may have gone further and become almost wholly immobilized by multiple fears, doubts, perplexities or angers, and by time-consuming and mortifying rituals which dominate your waking hours. These make such simple functions as dressing or leaving the house insurmountable for you. Enjoyment disappears utterly as you castigate yourself for falling victim to this malignant neurosis.

The strictures of your obsessionalism may be viewed as an overadaptation to anxiety and insecurities. Just as the "overqualified" worker often may not find employment, so the overadaptive becomes maladaptive. Your obsessional thoughts, nervously attuned feelings, combustible sensitivities and driving behavior are intemperate; one may say "hyper." They are packed with excess and exhaust your nervous system to a depressive state. Now you are too receptive to other stresses which potentiate your anxieties and add to your ambivalence, morbidity and fears. How intense this plight is, as it shows in your neurotic patterns, can be measured by you with the following self-rating scale. (See Chapter 9 for suggestions about the use of this testing procedure.)

Self-Rating
Obsessional Neurotic Scale

Circle appropriate number for each of the following statements. Total your score.	None or a little of the time	Some of the time	Good part of the time	Most or all of the time
1. Unpleasant, frightening or unwanted thoughts keep coming into my head.	1	2	3	4
2. I am preoccupied with silly thoughts about nonsensical things.	1	2	3	4
3. I question myself, or have doubts about things I must do.	1	2	3	4
4. It is hard for me to make decisions.	1	2	3	4
5. I am tense or nervous.	1	2	3	4
6. I worry over stupid little things.	1	2	3	4
7. I panic easily.	1	2	3	4
8. I live with many fears and phobias.	1	2	3	4
9. I think that I'm getting fed up with the way people are.	1	2	3	4
10. I think that I just don't enjoy life enough.	1	2	3	4
11. I must arrange, or do things in special ways for no particular reason.	1	2	3	4
12. Ritualistic habits tend to dominate my life.	1	2	3	4
13. I check and recheck gas knobs, windows, doors, lights, etc. when leaving the house.	1	2	3	4
14. After completing a task I review my work over and over again.	1	2	3	4
15. It bothers me when I brush against people or am touched.	1	2	3	4
16. I avoid the slightest contact with body secretions or dirty things like waste receptacles.	1	2	3	4
17. I dislike using glasses or silverware unless I know that they are dishwasher clean.	1	2	3	4
18. I think that lately I've been avoiding sexual relations.	1	2	3	4

Circle appropriate number for each of the following statements. Total your score.	None or a little of the time	Some of the time	Good part of the time	Most or all of the time
19. I think too much about what people say.	1	2	3	4
20. I do certain things over and over even though I know it is foolish to do them.	1	2	3	4
21. I find myself thinking about the past or trying to anticipate the future more than I like to.	1	2	3	4
22. My daily activities tire me out.	1	2	3	4
23. I worry too much about everything.	1	2	3	4
24. I feel that I cannot go on this way much longer.	1	2	3	4
25. I think that I am almost losing my mind.	1	2	3	4

COLUMN TOTALS

TOTAL SCORE

Scoring

25–45. You are nonobsessional and adaptive.

46–55. You are mildly obsessional but reasonably adaptive. However, a lack of self-confidence is evident.

56–70. You are moderately obsessional and socially maladaptive. You are prone to depression and cannot always meet your expectations. Professional help might be indicated.

71–100. You are severely obsessional and depressed. Your surroundings agitate you. You feel closed in and can see no way out. You require professional help.

PART FOUR

Changing Yourself

· 17 ·
How You Can Change

Although you still appear to be adaptive, your eyes are now opened to the inroads of the uptight compulsiveness that spoils your camaraderies, kinships, sexual savor and occupational output. Each day, you feel more strung up on wires. Your sensory receptors, like sharp pinpoints, quiver at the slightest stir, and maladaptation quashes the very composure and security that you grope for. You wish sometimes that you could shed your O-C traits to feel lighter and more carefree.

If you are an obsessional neurotic, you are defeated by your rituals, phobias and panic; you exasperate your household and put them to flight. What is your choice? To drag along in your own troubled way? To remove yourself? Or perhaps to make a definite gesture that will bring you into social harmony?

MUST MY TOTAL PERSONALITY BE REMADE?

No. *First*, to think of overriding your successful adaptations with arbitrary goals toward which you must strive would be like writing rules in water. Whether you are a perfectionist air-traffic controller, a conscience-ridden completer, a precise and exacting doctor of dentistry, or whatever, you would resist destroying your useful adaptations and undermine change because you know that your *adaptive* compulsions profit you.

Second, you could not be remade entirely. The story of your growth will never be known in full because it began with the genetic potentials that helped determine your constitutional, social and psychologic strengths and weaknesses. Such multiple causes of O-C behavior or an obsessional state would be impossible to dig out. Thus, the reasons for your disorder can be educed only from the sum of your life experiences and how you are now adjusting to them.

Third, personality is always a process in the making. Its history is continuous and transitional, influenced by every current event and stress that befall you. Whatever the impacts and conditionings of the past may have been, nothing can transform them. They are over, forever imprinted in your brain circuits and cannot be undone. The supremely decisive fact is what is happening to you now, in your uptight way of life. In remodeling your harmful traits, you move toward a more benign and comfortable personality function for the now and for the future.

Working Toward Practical Change

What you are seeking is an alteration in your functioning traits whose strictures have brought you to a major damage crunch. To begin with, you have the problem of learning to see the person you are as others see you. This must be met head on. For instance: Will you study this book to understand yourself? After that, if you decide that you do want a more serene existence, how will you go about it? Can family and friends, or you alone, or professional help support your decision?

Before you answer, you should know first that *motivation* for change is paramount and your responsibility; that your *expectations* of change in yourself must coordinate with those of your family, your psychiatrist and society, too; finally, that *goals* in treatment will be specific for you.

MOTIVATION FOR TREATMENT OR CHANGE

Comprehending your adaptations and maladaptive devices is more than a matter of knowledge, education, intelligence or even value judgments. You may be one of many who has said at some time: "Oh, I understand my emotional hangups intellectually, but I just can't do anything about them." Yes, your value judgments have tricked you into snubbing your insights before you were motivated to heed them. You are also suggesting that your maladaptive behavior does not distress you enough, as yet, to want to change.

Motivation implies a will and need to scale the walls of your psychologic defenses. To modify, you may have to be defined professionally because your tendency, unless you are caught in a maladaptive crisis, is to retreat. "There's nothing really wrong with me. It's just everything that's happening. Besides, you can't change human nature." Your conception of a "judgmental" encounter with a professional critic makes you cringe. You do not want your ego smacked in the face, and you tremble at the thought of a psychologic diagnosis that might imply irrational or abnormal behavior. Your defenses say: "Don't go." Your need cries: "Go."

You Are Motivated When You Hurt

As a rule, you and others are motivated to change when you feel the threat of social exclusion, physical pain, sexual failure, conjugal hazards, your job slipping away, or constant psychologic pangs. Your maladaptive traits say that you are a loser, and suddenly you want to be set right as decisively as you would want a malignant tumor excised or an infection cleared up.

You are really asking yourself: How long have I been hurting without admitting it? The ball is now in your court.

We will suppose that you are the perfectionist stenographer who is feverishly compelled to type your letters with no corrections or erasures. Each page must be pure. You throw out every one that seems blemished and you redo it. The other stenos type twenty or more letters a day to your four or five and you are fired. Perfect work was a worthy bent—until it lost you one job after the other in rapid succession. You have a mother to support and a job is essential. You are hurting. When you finally grasp the fact that lack of flexibility is a gravestone, you decide that you must mend yourself or see a mender.

You are the beautiful chic O-C widow of a colleague of mine. For over two years you were still mourning your loss. You blamed your depressed feelings on the selfishness of old friends. "They never invite me anymore. There's no room in the world for a single person." But you forget that you have bitched at everyone, vented your egocentricity, demanded that they stroke your emotional wounds, made yourself selective and ungiving. Even loyal intimates began to bypass you. Only when your married daughter summoned the courage to tell you, "Mother, you're destroying yourself. It's got to stop," did you know how dreadfully you were hurting and agree to professional help.

Ordinarily, a wife might be the person to motivate change in a bad-tempered and controlling sixty-year-old husband who allowed her no tangible assets in her name and even delayed probate to forestall an inheritance due her. She begged him to consider psychiatric evaluation. He blew sky high and left her, consoling his bruised feelings with a careless sexual liaison. Not until his girl friend rebelled at his bossiness and uptight tantrums did he submit to going for advice. Now he was hurting very badly indeed. Frantic to terminate the affair, he wanted to renew his marriage. The original problem was complicated by this new domestic predicament.

Wouldn't-You-Thinkisms of Motivation. If you are an intolerant houseproud woman you admit that you want to throw things when delivery boys track dirt into the vestibule, the handyman leaves his muck behind him, or your husband isn't punctual to the split second for dinner, especially since you make sure the food is hot, the way he likes it. "Yes, I won't deny that these things upset me. But that doesn't mean I need psychiatry. If people behaved the way they should, I'd be all right." A tranquilizer to quiet your nerves? "Rubbish. Pills are a fad." *Wouldn't you think* that recognition would dawn? That the world will not change to suit you? That you need a heightened tolerance for others? That you require an authoritative source to teach you that everything cannot run your way? You are not motivated because you are still not aware that it is your uptightness getting the better of you, not other people.

An O-C stationery salesman, you shudder at the heap of new burdens that promotion to sales manager would mean. You say, "Sure I want to earn more money, but when I get a large order for pens I begin to worry that the pens might leak. Then I can't keep my mind on the customer, so I lose the sale. And if I were manager I'd be the one called to account when somebody else's sales go down. It's bad enough just when it's my own foul-up." Wouldn't you think that a need to modify your obsessional doubts and anxieties might strike you one of these days?

You recall the schoolteacher with colitis whom I described in Chapter 14. Angry, prudish and uptight, she is given to cutting remarks and caustic cynicisms. She haunts the offices of the gastroenterologist. When told that her symptoms are probably psychosomatic, she is furious. "I'm not crazy. If you'll only straighten out my bowels I'll be okay." Her assistant principal suggests that she consult a psychiatrist. "You're so hostile," he says, "that you're really crapping on the whole world. That's why you're obsessed with your bowels." He is probably right. Wouldn't you think that she would take her friend's advice and consider the psychosomatic reality?

Motivation and Willpower

Everyone makes decisions and in doing so uses willpower to generate adaptive behavior. Your will must also support your motivation in treatment. But if previously it was joined to faulty decisions and failures in life, it may have deteriorated. Free-floating anxiety, nourished by inaction, often enfeebles willpower. However, supported by positive actions, yours can be energized. Most decisions to change require a conditioning process for stimulating the will. In Chapter 18 you will see that every maladaptive person benefits from strong rewards for each small exertion of the will to encourage getting well.

YOUR EXPECTATIONS OF CHANGE

At the beginning of this chapter I indicated that as an adaptive person you would like to improve on your faults and not touch the good traits. But what happens when a difference of opinion arises as to what constitutes a good or a bad trait in you?

Any trait may be interpreted as a healthy or faulty defense against the same anxiety, depending on the point of view. As an adaptive O-C you are, to your business partner, a perfectionist worker; to your neighbors, an amiable acquaintance; to your wife, the man she leans on; to your friends, a domineering compulsive; to a psychologist, an obsessed individual. Which of these opinions will decide your expectations for change?

Of primary import, however, which is the hurting trait? Because of your hidden insecurities you become a compulsive worker. You consider this a good trait, "since you get out only as much as you put in." This overreaction to your fearfulness brings forth attitudes of authoritative expertise which to others sound like arrogance and egotism. You wish you could change this trait. At bottom, you are kindly and sociable and you see that you are estranging friends.

Your wife, though, declares that you simply do not take off enough time to mingle with people. She wants your work addiction modified but not your "superiority." To her this is a personality strength (which she lacks). "Nobody can push my husband around. He's no weakling and I don't want him to seem like one." Who is right, you or she? You long to have your friends like you and to regard you as a "good guy and great fun." Will your expectations (to modify your overbearance) be undercut by your wife's demand that only your work habits (which you are convinced you need) be changed?

Another dissenting view was raised in regard to a man whose wife had implored him to see me. As a worker in the arts she turned to her craft for a word sketch of him before he arrived. "I've always been afraid to criticize him—he's so uptight in that purple mantle of imperial righteousness, with that silver-white nimbus of honor around his head, and that fancied scepter he carries for shooting off his crimson shafts of intellect. But one day I saw that it was all just a mirage of his own self-love. He's not regal. He's a dun-colored trickie-dickie painted on a very small canvas. So how do you get him off that pedestal and make him into someone affectionate and lovable?"

The husband admitted that fond thoughts for her often swirled through his mind, but somehow he could not nail them down into words and actions. He also conceded that maybe he should try to unbend some to please her, but asserted unequivocally that he felt entitled to be put back on his Olympian heights. Which expectations can here be met in treatment?

Or you may simply be an adaptive O-C who would like to "get rid of thoughts in my head that don't belong there," and perhaps change some sexual hangups that frustrate you and your mate. These expectations are for limited modification of particular complaints only, all other personality traits to be excluded.

Unspoken Expectations: The Call for Professional Help

Like every uptight O-C person and obsessional neurotic, you bring your ambivalences to any program for change. You complain: "I seem not to want to be married, yet I love my wife. I'm also afraid to live alone." A married woman will say: "I'm in a bind. I want to be able to do what I want to do. But I'm unhappy doing my own thing." In both cases, you know that you are inhibited by anxieties, self-doubts and vague fears. And you cannot formulate your desires and ambitions.

Fundamentally, each of you wants to loosen up. You would like to be made anew into a relaxed, sensuous and mature person, able to effect your own decisions and to be responsive to life's benefices. That is your *real* need.

On the other hand, you want utter safety, the freedom to maintain your defenses and to set your own (unattainable) standards. The expectation here is to be rid of symptoms that unhinge your life, preferably with magic ("Maybe I can just be hypnotized and change over quick?"). Or you hope that a psychiatrist, like a good angel, will offer you love and approval, applaud your efforts, overlook your deficiencies, accept you uncritically and, in some mystical way, make everything work out. This is your *felt* need.

The Psychiatrist's Expectations of Treatment

We know there is no magic and that only a handful believe in miracles. We do have an accumulated scientific and clinical stock of knowledge about human performance and of experience with certain methods for changing O-C and obsessional function, which methods have proven to be highly therapeutic. Add to this the psychiatrist's authority and personality for improving your condition. His expectations then are based on utilizing the art of his professional skills to the full, in order to derive a maximum improvement, *consistent with the expectations that you have disclosed.*

The general psychiatrist, most broadly qualified of the practitioners who diagnose, treat, and prognosticate in the wide spectrum of mental and personality disorders, is faced with two important questions: Are your goals short or longer range? Which therapies will work best for you in order to achieve them? His expectations are now inherent in the goals that will be set for you.

GOALS IN TREATMENT

Ideally, the goal of rational treatment is to rid you of hurt and ache, to remove the immediate cause of your abnormal process—that is, to render it inoperative—and to repair the ravages of your disorder.

Rarely, though, do we attain all these goals in dealing with most illnesses, whether they are purely physical or psychologic, because few specific treatments exist which can wipe out the full cause of an illness. Among these specifics in clinical medicine, antibiotics do eliminate an infection. In preventive medicine, safety devices and inoculations against typhoid, smallpox, poliomyelitis, and so on, may also be considered ammunition aimed directly against the cause of a disorder. However, there are no specifics in psychiatric practice, largely because a single treatable cause for personality or mental disorder is yet to be discovered.

As was pointed out, compulsive behavior or obsessionalism is not always a direct consequence of a particular event, evoked thought or distressful emotion. The interconnections between your ritual behavior, phobias, doubts, ruminations and lack of self-confidence are often lost in the past and too complex to unravel. Nor does the unraveling process help change you. *Each symptom is handled best as a separate part-disturbance in your life.* Treatment of all diseases and discomforts, mental or physical, except for the few specifics mentioned, is empirical or *symptomatic.*

Of all psychiatric disorders the most difficult to treat is the obsessional neurosis. It is so complicated an illness that Freud gave up on it, indicating that analysis was useful only in a certain few of such cases. Today we know more about behavior modification, and the astute clinician can evaluate this puzzler, conclude whether your function is adaptive or maladaptive, and treat it as such. The goal therefore is to deal with the behavioral function as it now presents itself overtly, and switch it over to a better track in the present and for the future.

In accordance with the P.E.G. standard that I presented in Chapter 1, goals in treatment are set (1) to help you realize your *potentials* fully by improving and strengthening your biologic, intellectual, social and psychologic assets; (2) to develop your *effectiveness* as a contributing member of society; and (3) to educate you to *gratification*, put plainly, to enjoy life. Toward this purpose a comprehensive treatment program uses all validated psychologic, behavioral, social and biomedical procedures in any combination that is therapeutic. Synthesis and integrated function in the present and for the future, rather than a dismantling of the past, are the key to treatment of the maladaptive O-C or obsessional.

Measuring therapeutic results by the P.E.G. standard as each *maladaptive symptom is overcome* gives you a grip on the reality of facts. This information alone can help bring you the relief you need and a promise of the good that lies ahead.

· 18 ·

Behavior Therapy

Traditionally, psychiatry and medicine teach that internal events of the body and external forces on the body influence the "mind." Actually, the mind is brain function which produces thoughts, feelings and behavior simultaneously for a total response. Thinking, unaccompanied by an emotion or action, can no more exist than a one-sided triangle. The behaviorist, for utilitarian purposes, considers actions to be the essential fact of the O-C's adaptive personality or maladaptive neurosis and believes that the most effective therapeutic techniques are those that modify behavior directly in large strides or small progressive steps until the desired level of adaptation is acquired.

MODIFYING BEHAVIOR

Behavior therapy, based on learning and conditioning principles, consists of many pragmatic techniques which systematically improve on maladaptive personality limitations. As we saw in Chapter 17, the physician and the patient must both know exactly what symptom complex is to be modified and, in treatment, which principle applies and what changes may be expected. The goals are explicit: for example, to erase the fear of driving a car, to reduce high blood pressure, to break a particular ritual, to stop kleptomania, to interrupt obsessions about contamination, or to expunge any number of other destructive traits.

The end result of behavior modification should be a decrease in tensions caused by your excessive O-C traits and unwanted thoughts with uptight feelings, i.e., a change in your maladaptive and inappropriate behavior. Always, of course, the general goal awaits you at the end of the trail. This may be called "relating better to people," "gaining in self-confidence," "enjoying life more," or simply "getting well."

Behavior therapy corresponds with relearning to play a musical instrument. Here the instrument is your own mind and body and requires your faithful and correct practice at home. Naturally, in personality and sexual disorders that create marital conflict and friction, the active involvement of the mate is essential.

Multifaceted in form and substance, behavior therapy is rooted in the common sense of man's will to survive. Indeed, one can say that every parent who ever hoped to educate his child into maximum fulfillment or perhaps to mold it into "a chip off the old block" used many of the principles, some as old as the hills, that are now theorized and employed by behaviorists but which you can apply on your own.

Mind Control

With behavior therapy you can reestablish personal mind control for your actions, feelings or thoughts (a control you lost when you became maladaptive). We know that, pragmatically, maladaptive behavior may be stopped, redirected, reinforced or modified in many ways. Paralleling this, the anxiety-vigilance-fear-anger complex of uptightness can also be conditioned and altered for emotional control. Thought stopping is one of the techniques in behavior therapy for ideational control. It is a strong influence in eliminating or reducing the distress of obsessions, ruminations and doubts.

Expansion of Treatment. Behavior therapy has broadened rapidly in the past decade. It is still being assessed as it accumulates data; and its principles and applications are being refined constantly, which will improve treatment results. The reader who explores this subject will find that many new words are born which describe essentially the same procedures. No matter. It is reassuring to know that you, as well as the behaviorist, can always test results objectively, by evaluating changes as they occur in you from week to week. As previously indicated, your total improvement can also be measured according to the P.E.G. standard.

We can now examine behavior modification under three main categories: relaxation procedures, learning procedures and exposure procedures. Many techniques fit into two or all three of these categories. I will call attention to the overlaps where they arise.

RELAXATION PROCEDURES

Almost every O-C, adaptive or maladaptive, is unable to relax. You may not realize that the concept of a relaxation response in behavior theory means *all body systems are at rest*. It also denotes mind rest from ponderings, worries and malign thoughts.

Probably you have never thought that you must *learn* how to rest your body. The fact is, because you never developed this faculty as a natural skill, a good night's sleep does not relax you automatically. You may wake up tired as a result of excessive mental activity while asleep. In the next sections I will discuss some relaxation methods which are always in your control and can be applied by you under many conditions of stress. However, you must learn how to execute them. At first glance, they may appear to be simplistic, but for best results, your whole efforts must be given them in persistent and disciplined practice.

Progressive Relaxation

This technique, initially developed by Dr. Edmund Jacobson for work-addicted executives in the 1930s (and since modified), emphasizes deep muscle relaxation to achieve a calm state under stress conditions.

RELAXATION AND EMOTIONAL CONTROL LOG

NAME __R. E._____ LOG TIME FROM __Feb. 2__ TO __Feb. 8__

This record will help you gain control of your emotions (anxiety, worry, fear, anger, frustration, tension, aggravation and so on) as you learn how to relax. Rate yourself every evening. Total all the checked squares and watch the score become less each week. You will feel best when you score between 25 and 30.

I. RATE TODAY'S EMOTIONAL LEVEL

	very relaxed			somewhat relaxed			somewhat tense			very tense	COMMENT: What stress caused you to become tense? What helped you to relax?
	1	2	3	4	5	6	7	8	9	10		
DAY 1.										✓	Mother bugged me all day about not going out more.
DAY 2.			✓								Accomplished a lot today.
DAY 3.								✓			Usual tension. Expected girl friend.
DAY 4.					✓						My boss gave me a big compliment.
DAY 5.							✓				Blind date.
DAY 6.						✓					Blind date called back.
DAY 7.						✓					Good day. Mother not on my back.

THIS WEEK'S SCORE __45__ LAST WEEK'S SCORE __52__

II. RATE YOUR SUCCESS WITH YOUR RELAXATION EXERCISES

	very beneficial			somewhat beneficial			not beneficial				COMMENT
	1	2	3	4	5	6	7	8	9	10	
DAY 1.									✓		Kept thinking "why am I such a jerk?"
DAY 2.			✓								TM helped me fall asleep easier.
DAY 3.							✓				Stomach bothered me today
DAY 4.		✓									Felt encouraged - Meditation a welcome relief -
DAY 5.								✓			Worried about blind date.
DAY 6.								✓			Couldn't concentrate. Bad thoughts persist.
DAY 7.					✓						Felt I could get better.

THIS WEEK'S SCORE __44__ LAST WEEK'S SCORE __50__

Training begins by sitting in a comfortable armchair. You are instructed to tense, and then relax immediately, certain muscle groups. Make a tight fist (as you were directed in an earlier section), hold it for about ten seconds and then let go slowly. Notice now how limp your arms and hands feel. Starting there, you progress to the head and face muscles, chest, back, thighs, legs and down to the toes. Although the therapist guides you into total relaxation, you may acquire this skill with practice at your own pace. Do not be disappointed if it takes you two or three months of daily effort to become proficient. However, as your tensions dissolve, you will gain new self-confidence and become master of your body.

Autogenic Training

Devised by Dr. Wolfgang Luthe, autogenic training means self-generated relaxation through your own power of subconscious suggestion. Using passive concentration you create an inner sense of warmth, heaviness and tranquility. One may call it a form of "self-hypnosis" as you shut out all other stimuli and imagine a state of restful inertia or ease, or you concentrate on the word "calm." Amazingly, you *feel* calm. Similar to progressive relaxation, this requires methodical training and, again, daily performance to obtain the self-control you are after.

Meditation

Meditative techniques for deep relaxation stem from ancient Eastern practices of body and mind control. Some are incorporated into Yoga, Zen Buddhism, Japanese morita therapy and other philosophic-physiologic practices, but the crux of the psychologic concept is the single-minded need to set aside time in order to relax mentally by shutting out disturbing, anxious or obsessional thoughts. As an uptight perfectionist or turbulent and frustrated O-C you can experience pleasant self-immersions which permit a quiet tolerance of your disturbing thoughts or emotions after going through these procedures.

Transcendental Meditation (TM). Currently popular in the United States, TM is an informal, effortless measure. Twice a day for fifteen to twenty minutes you sit composed in a quiet room with your eyes shut. You contemplate silently a one-syllable word or sound, called your "mantra" (or sacred formula). The same word is always used—*om, one, balm* or any other that you choose initially. In effect, you attempt to stop all other thoughts and learn to concentrate only on your mantra. You will not float through space or experience mystical auras, and you are not required to change your faith or life-style. You merely follow this simple procedure regularly with no variation in technique. Your blood pressure will drop and your pulse slow down as you relax progressively.

Temporary release (or relaxation) can be achieved for uptightness in mild crises with relaxing postures, breathing exercises, or living in slow time (letting people and events pass you by, being lulled by the mental image of a greensward with delicately swaying trees and blossoms). Or you can use the emotional catharses of screaming, shouting obscenities, making fists at imagined foes, and so on, privately or with others whose chief virtue is tolerance.

Relaxation, including meditation, does not extinguish obsessional thoughts. These thoughts may persist but they are attenuated by control of anxiety and are no longer a baleful force.

Biofeedback Training

You have heard of the lie detector (polygraph), a package of many instruments in one, which records several physiologic responses to pointed questions or other provocations. Most polygraphs record the heart rate (pulse), frequency and amplitude of breathing, muscle tone, brain-wave pattern, skin temperature, electrical skin resistance and blood pressure. More sophisticated instruments measure differences in voice sounds, nail-bed capillaries, pupillary dilation, eye movements, and numerous other physiologic responses to tension and relaxation.

Biofeedback training today employs similar instruments which monitor brain-wave patterns (EEG for electroencephalograph), muscle tone (EMG for electromyograph), electrical skin resistance (GSR for galvanic skin reflex), skin temperature, blood pressure and pulse. These instruments feed back information about the duration and intensity of your internal responses to any kind of tension or uptightness. Dials, lights, buzzers, or automatic graphs on moving paper provide audio or visual records of your adaptive (physiologic) responses to every movement, thought, and pleasant or unpleasant stimulus in your environment:

Noises: symphonic music or gossipy nattering
Objects: a marble sculpture or a bristling cactus
Lights: softly shaded lamps or flickering neons
Odors: a flower scent or a garbage pile
Tastes: salad dressing or a bitter tonic.

You also learn immediately of your emotional response to people from words, attitudes and directives: "Do that!" instead of "Would you mind doing that for me?" "Hey you!" instead of "Won't you please come here?" Or your startled response to the unexpected (your spouse in the arms of your neighbor), as well as your reactions to TV watching or table conversation. Most importantly, biofeedback reports your reactions to your fantasies and hidden thoughts. These two last stimuli become especially significant for systematic desensitization, which we will take up later in detail.

As an adaptive O-C you may always appear cool and imperturbable. But when your nervous function is monitored with biofeedback instruments in vivo (real life situations), you, like everyone else, disclose the strains of fears and wraths that arise with pressures that goad you into disrepair. You are much more a storm of nerves than you thought.

With instantaneous feedback information on the intensity of your thoughts, angers, and anxieties, you are now equipped to practice control of your internal energies (many of which you thought previously were uncontrollable) and to condition yourself to relax.

Relaxation Techniques with Biofeedback. Deep relaxation can be gained with structured exercises such as those described, provided that you do not use shortcuts which will weaken your control. At least one month is needed for the average adaptive O-C to learn the skill of progressive relaxation, assisted by biofeedback instruments and supervised once a week by a trained therapist. Tape-recorded instructions and inexpensive GSR units or other biofeedback devices to guide home practice (a minimum of half an hour daily) are available to you in a well-directed program.

Relaxation and Behavior Therapy. Relaxation is only one facet, but a major one, of behavioral change. Used alone, it is an excellent counterconditioner to anxiety. It effectively diminishes or eradicates psychosomatic symptoms such as tensional and migraine headaches, high blood pressure, muscle spasms, colitis, chest pains and stomach upsets. Angers that explode if you are a controlling, righteous and intolerant O-C subside, and you can think clearly of more constructive solutions to your problems. Also, this skill in obsessionals removes discomfort in provocative situations. You discover that, once relaxed, you can rely on your own decisions and actions.

Reporting to Yourself

The advantage of a direct behavioral approach to the stress generated by your perfectionism, the obdurate need to be punctual, clean and tidy, or any of the other traits described in this book can be appraised quickly by keeping records of your day-to-day behavior. Such a record is called a log or flow chart. Like the ship captain or air pilot who logs his bearings, you too can report yourself to yourself, and discover exactly where "you are at" by daily entries.

On page 222 is a Relaxation and Emotional Control Log. Any variation of it can be devised or adapted easily to measure your weekly progress in learning how to relax with whatever technique suits you as you face stresses.

Relaxation is integrated with learning and exposure procedures in which anxiety is to be kept at a low level. This is especially true for

226

adaptive and maladaptive O-Cs with sexual dysfunctions, habit and speech disorders, work addiction, some phobias, panic states or social dilemmas.

LEARNING PROCEDURES

The dos and don'ts of social commingling are an intrinsic part of a continual learning experience. For example, you know that you learn to smoke in many cultures but that learning *not* to smoke becomes a new learning (perhaps more worthwhile than the first one). Therapy thus suggests that you can, practicing the right technique, learn adaptive behaviors and let the maladaptive ones decay.

It is never too late "for salvation" if you are motivated to change. However, learning is an intricate process, and for reasons not fully understood, some people learn faster and better than others.

Operant Conditioning: Learning Through Rewards and Penalties*

Much as Molière's M. Jourdain, of *Le Bourgeois Gentilhomme*, was delighted to discover from his Philosophy Master that "for more than forty years I've been talking prose without any idea of it," you, as a parent, will also be amazed to realize that you have often used the learning principle of *operant conditioning* and never been aware of it.

Yet we should all know that praise, money, gifts or special treats reinforce a desired behavior and reward efforts (if generously offered) to persist with it. " 'Tis better to give praise than to have praised prised from one." In applying operant conditioning for "good" behavior, you have given your child love, cookies, toys and other rewards. We call this *positive selective reinforcement* or *contingent rewarding*.

* In this book I substitute the word "penalty" for "punishment." Although the latter is the word most commonly used in the lexicon of behavior therapy, to me, "punishment" is a brutal, inhumane concept and should have no place in the therapeutic armamentarium. We are doctors (*primum non nocere*—first of all, do no harm), not inflicters.

The dropping (and ultimate disappearance) of unwanted behavior can also be augmented by aversive conditioning or *negative reinforcement*. Here, penalties are paired with "bad" behavior. (Using this principle cruelly, some mothers have burned their children's fingers "so they'll never play with matches again." Not recommended. The child will learn to hate you.)

In treatment, too, ways are found to reinforce your adaptive traits positively with contingent rewards or, when indicated, aversive techniques. Contingent rewards and penalties with operant procedures can help you modify your compulsive behavior, sociosexual inadequacies, phobias and many O-C traits that keep you careworn and perpetually on the anxious seat. At times, positive and negative reinforcements are used concurrently; as we accept the good (adaptive) at the same time we set out to eliminate the bad (maladaptive).

Selective Reinforcement. I noted in Chapter 17 that O-C men and women are fraught with a *real*, not just *felt*, need for love and the enjoyment of life that goes beyond material things, and the routine exchange of marital services or the grunted acknowledgment of favors or attentions. Change is effected most patently in O-Cs who are rewarded with expressed endearments and lavish words of esteem. Even a sweet pinch on the behind can give you that sense of a desired and desiring mate. Everyone is always hungry for recognition and reward. No exceptions here.

I once listened to you (a hardworking tradesman) complain bitterly about your uptight emasculating wife. "She'll never change." I asked you what you had ever done to help her do so. Had you scraped her raw with criticism or ever noticed and rewarded anything that pleased you? One thing was apparent: anger with her offending traits had hardened your alienation. In my office your demands for extensive change in her burst out of you. She was aghast. "I can't ever change *that* much." However, when you were taught to encourage her every small daily effort as she learned how to be more flexible, life improved considerably. You began to compliment her in many ways. Even so, you must still keep alert not to criticize when she regresses to her occasional cold intolerances and tries to run your home like a barracks; and certainly never tell her, "You're right where you started." She will simply give up and revert to type completely.

The principles of selective reinforcement were clearly demonstrated (Chapter 15) when you, a married man, disinhibited your uptight sexual moralities by having an affair. Divorced, and freed by your romance from your monotonous, orderly and proper routine, you jubilated in the sauce of your adventure. You knew these rewards would go on only if you continued the excitement of escape and *remained unmarried*.

Aversive Conditioning.   In operant conditioning (mentioned earlier) a painful aversive stimulus, coupled with a detrimental behavior, inhibits the latter. The behavior may ultimately stop merely because the pain is anticipated. For example, you were the exhibitionist who exposed yourself to little girls in parks and became embroiled with the police. You were desperate to conquer this maladaptation. In treatment, you were shown pictures of young girls and the moment you felt the urge to zip open your pants, you received a painful electric shock on the tip of your finger. You were taught to give yourself this faradic charge with a pocket-sized electronic device each time you even *thought* about your compulsion. The desire finally diminished to an occasional fugitive thought, then fell into desuetude. You had learned through negative reinforcement with the painful penalizer how *not* to behave maladaptively.

THE RUBBER BAND.   Another simple aversive conditioner that I have used with marked success is for those of you who want to abolish your kleptomania. For example, a rubber band of good quality is placed on your wrist. You are asked to close your eyes and imagine yourself shoplifting. I then snap the band so that it produces a sharp, painful sting. Your thought breaks off and you shift to the reality. "Ouch! No shoplifting for me." You must then visit your favorite department store every day, and as you approach the merchandise that tempts you, zing! you snap the band forcibly and keep snapping until your hankering goes away. The sting is a negative reinforcer. After a short time, simply *staring* at the rubber band will keep you from shoplifting again.

Aversive conditioning has been used to advantage for many obsessional thoughts and actions, especially to reduce "appetitive" behavior such as compulsive gambling, voyeurism, alcohol addiction (by using the drug antabuse) and so on. It has also been applied to inhibit child molesting, child abuse and homosexuality (in the last-named, only for those who want to change their pleasure in this kind of love). However, it is not effective for any such behavior unless you are willing to subject yourself to the aversive stimulus over an extended time.

SCARE TACTICS.   Unwanted behavior can be inhibited by *covert sensitization.* Let us say that you toy with the idea of embezzling some money, but you bracket this thought with the consequences of being caught. Nothing new about this. From ancient times all societies, cultures and religions have used negative reinforcement and aversive tactics to keep you away from a specific behavior so that neither the devil nor the policeman would "ketch yuh doin' what you're not supposed to do." It may have been only a violation of a minor religious ban, but if you were sensitized to the horrors of sin at an early age, you covertly stayed on the safe side.

Negative Reinforcement.   Negative conditioning of O-C traits can sometimes be accomplished when you consciously withhold praise or rewards for an O-C trait that you want eliminated. This is called *extinction.* Casting a fish-eye at your martinet wife for being silly and aimless in her orderly routine can deprive her of its joys, and she may gradually feel punished and forgo her compulsive immaculacy. Oppositely you reward her if you make your approval plain when she does *not* fluff up your chair cushions forbiddingly, leaves the record on the turntable to be played again and keeps hands off your unfinished book on the coffee stand. Thus, should you impetuously insist that you both hie off to a movie with another couple, make it clear that you will love her all the more if she does not change clothes from head to foot and leaves the heels of your shoes unshined, you are giving her praise for being resilient.

Unwittingly, parents often selectively reinforce maladaptive behavior and negate adaptive behavior. For instance, you may pour attention on your child when it sulks and whines. The child continues this way because its behavior is being rewarded by gaining your full concentration. But when the youngster plays happily, does its homework, or completes a chore and you take it for granted with no praise, your failure to reward it strips the child of needed encouragement.

You are operating backwards. The whining child should be admonished to stop its attention-gathering: "If you must fuss go to your room until you're fit company again." This is called "time out." When its behavior is constructive you should applaud the child. "You practiced the piano well. I enjoyed it." Or, "Your homework is done on time and well prepared. That was good planning." Psychotherapists, too, who allow O-C patients unlimited freedom to spill out their tirades at life are, in effect, bolstering righteousness, intolerance, and all sorts of obsessionalism because the patient can now wallow in past hurts, relish them, add details, some distorted, and bathe in bathos.

In my experience when patients are prompted to "bury the past" and to change in the present, their thriving adaptation is the reward, and their associations vanish. The past dies.

Directive Therapy

Adaptive O-Cs are not amenable to directive therapy except when caught in a crisis. However, obsessional or chronically maladaptive O-C persons are thrown by ambiguity and must often be told exactly what to do and how to do it. Did you ever hear an immobilized person say to someone close by: "Don't just sit there. Do something." Immediate action to reduce the panic is cried for and must be supplied. Long-term change, however, in social skills, assertiveness and communication requires week-to-week improvement, usually with some form of directive therapy such as shaping (as well as interpersonal reaction therapy, which we call encounters. See Chapter 19).

Shaping. It is not probable that you would reach the top rung of a ladder unless you took only one or two rungs at a time. The means of reaching a desired goal by breaking it into smaller steps and following a consistent program to achieve the end goal is called *shaping.*

In Part One, I indicated that if you are overconscientious or compulsive about your privacy and distrustful of everyone, your behavior should be reshaped for a more adaptive accommodation, and I suggested some of the ways to do this. I also described an O-C mother who ordered her children to bed the moment the clock struck the preordained hour. She too needed to reshape her behavior. Yes, you were the thirty-two-year-old married suburbanite who declared that the crumbs your children (ages three, five and eight) dropped when eating "drive me crazy. I don't care what they eat but they mustn't make dirt." You screeched at them whenever any of your schedules were disarranged. You expected them to be superclean, noiseless, and never dawdling when summoned. You had other similar traits, such as attempting to bridle your husband with your controlling reins.

Screaming at your children was one thing, but when you started beating them too, even you were so shocked that you agreed to therapy. Your motivation was furthered because your husband had stopped coming home for dinner until the kids were asleep. The hassles had been too much for him. And often now he was indifferent to any lovemaking.

PUTTING THE PIECES TOGETHER. A program for reshaping your behavior consisted of step-by-step instructions in relating to your family. This involved some detailed insights into your anger at yourself for your inability to give affection, your frenzied priorities for the care of your possessions above the care of your family, and your compulsion to live by the clock.

The first lesson was to learn the essentials of mothering. However, you showed such strained disquiet to your parenthood that assignments were given for changing only small behaviors at first: for example, to let some crumbs fall while the children ate and clear them up later; to lengthen the time allowed for their dressing; to permit them to play in the den, not only in their own rooms; at the same time to increase your interest in each child. Rewards came fairly quickly. With less yelling and disapproval you were not worn to a frazzle at the day's end; your husband began to come home for dinner.

You too experimented. When you prepared foods he especially liked and, later, enticed him into some active bedding at an earlier hour, relations with him improved. More assignments from the therapist followed. You bathed the younger ones instead of leaving this to the eldest child. You were encouraged to hold the children, blow them kisses at their play; to listen to their "ess-siting" experiences; to forgo your backgammon and be home when they returned from school and to invite their friends in. Today, rather than keeping them on a leash with a lookout for bad behavior, you can laugh with them, overlook the muss and enjoy the fascinating subtleties of their growth. Everyone is happier.

Shaping behavior is also part of systematic desensitization, which we will take up in a later section. Through these procedures, many O-Cs have overcome such disabling traits as shyness, grudge-bearing, playing the martyr or following strict schedules (the silver must be polished every Thursday afternoon). Small variations in activities gradually disintegrate O-C routines and, in the aggregate, build into a major personality change.

Modeling. People learn by mimicking those whom they respect. Parents and teachers set examples or demonstrate skills by *modeling.* "See, this is how I tie a shoelace." Or, "Look, I'm not afraid to paddle a rowboat."

Your parents modeled social deportment for you (manners, speech and habits) as well as anxieties, fears and angers. Behavior therapists often cause change in their patients, not necessarily because of what is said, but by what the therapist does.

I combined this principle with *in vivo* desensitization in helping my wife overcome her morbid horror of snakes. Late one summer a three-foot harmless field snake was sunning itself on our patio. My wife shrieked for me, then ran inside and clanged the dinner bell. As I approached, the snake raised its head, decided I was no threat and resumed its partially coiled rest. I called my wife. "See? He's really saying, 'I'm not bothering you, so why do you bother me?'" Apprehensive but with my assurance, she advanced slowly toward the snake. Again it raised its head and eyed us as its friends. Finally, I handled it, letting it wind around my arm. My wife watched breathlessly. After that, the snake returned again and again to its favorite sunning spot. Each time as I assured my wife and touched the snake she was less afraid. Today, she takes it in stride, and she pets it and tries to coax it around her wrist.

The learning of adaptive behavior by imitation is based on assurance through identification with the model. While it requires patience on both sides, and repetition, it usually pays off when combined with shaping or hierarchic step-by-step procedures.

Modeling is effective in overcoming avoidance behavior, many phobias and contamination fears and is also a component of flooding. To accept the advice and suggestion of another person who models a more adaptive behavior for you is to show strength, not weakness. You are being discerning and absorptive.

Assertive Training

Countless books and magazine articles have been written for the shy person. There are also special schools and therapies through which you can learn to improve your social skills. You may be a humbled person who lives with terrible doubts of your natural assets and innate worth. You wish you had the guts to assert yourself.

In obsessionalism, this absence of self-sufficiency adds, in part, to your psychologic imprisonment. A mature person says, "I don't know about tomorrow, but however things turn out it will probably end up okay." You mean that no matter what happens you will handle it and, if it is favorable, enjoy it. If it goes wrong you will cope somehow and move on—or you will pay the piper and learn from your mistake. However, if you are an uptight O-C maladaptive you anticipate the worst, doubt that you will cope, grow angry if you fail and ruminate about why it "always" happens to you.

Act Out.   Obviously, you must study the art of optimism and, to support it, assert yourself. Humility is an estimable virtue but so is "speaking up" as its balance wheel. Practicing with attainable goals will help you fight your timidity and better your self-concept. For example, you are an inhibited O-C, uncertain of acceptance. Start by making eye contact whenever you talk with someone. Then consciously listen to your voice. Make certain that it is firm and clear. After practicing these two easy directives, your next step is to act out behavior in which you do as you want to, rather than avoid it with shyness. Go to the ladies' or men's room even if it means having 200 people at a banquet observe you. Ask your superior at work for permission to leave a half hour early. Request a special table in a restaurant or ask for better seats at the box office. Do not hesitate to return a defective item. Venture your opinion in a group. If your date turns you on, invite him (her) in.

For example, I recall you as a gawky, adolescent girl with many obsessions. Mostly you were mortified by a severe facial tic which lent itself to your classmates' mockery. I had you discipline the tic by selective reinforcement; you denied yourself dessert (which you adored) if you had a tic that day. In less than one month, after some craving deprivations, the tic subsided. Later, you learned to address the classroom and to talk with your peers more smoothly. You knew that you were not popular and never held class office, but on follow-up I found that you had become a more positive person and socially in demand. But have a care: learning to be assertive does not mean being aggressive and "coming on strong." Others bristle at this. Asserting yourself in a pleasant way invites respect and cordiality.

Feeling Talk. Now, start to communicate with "feeling talk." If someone puts you down, tell the person quietly that you *do not like it.* Equally, when complimented, *acknowledge it* with a smile and a positive, "Thank you. That makes me *feel* so good." Or, "I *loved* what you said about my dress." Take note of your impact on people. As an O-C you tend to discount the favors you do for others or their appreciation of your kindnesses. Change. Never dismiss a commendation as unmerited. You debase yourself.

Thus, to help you mitigate your self-depreciation, behavior therapists use modeling, shaping, systematic desensitization, role rehearsal and many of the other techniques described in this chapter.

Psychodynamics vs. Behavior Therapy

A colleague of mine who practices psychoanalysis reported a case history of an obsessional young man who would attempt to kiss his girl gingerly from behind her field of vision. He attributed this to his sense of inadequacy and certainty of rejection. This led to a discussion with the analyst of concealed hostility and aggressive impulses toward women. Hopefully, this antagonism would be resolved through the analysis, and the patient would learn to kiss the girl properly.

Presented with the same problem, a behaviorist would put aside the psychodynamic process in favor of a direct behavioral approach. He would instruct the young man to look at his girl, embrace her with a frontal approach and bestow a positive kiss on her mouth. Selective reinforcement, through gaining the kiss, would then further other pleasant intimacies, spur him on, and probably rout his shynesses.

Training in social skills and sexual behavior is a complex process, but then so is training for jobs, combat, home repair, or skills in survival. Regardless of any other psychologic support or insight, the need is to apply the self and develop know-how in order to become and remain adaptive.

Contracting

The reciprocity of every social or work relationship represents a spoken or unspoken contract to behave in some particular way with the other. Judicious compromises usually bring forth adaptive success. A small sample: "We'll make a bargain. I'll read you that new story if you'll go to bed by eight o'clock." Such contracting is used extensively today for many discordances and is one of the best ways of defusing your uptightness and teaching you how to make concessions, especially for intrafamily peace.

Contracting to improve behavior in relationships usually starts with eliminating minor irritants which are more easily negotiated. Subsequent contracts tackle more serious discords. Final contracts deal with the major sources of conflict that are ravaging the relationship. A gradual beginning also educates the participants to the responsibilities and cogency of the procedure. (With some of the more shattering traits, in a crisis it is advisable to initiate a rapid reduction of strain, with a fast reciprocal agreement.)

An example of a minor contingency contract: As a workaholic husband married to a perfectionist wife, you both acknowledge that certain traits in your personalities clash. You negotiate. "If you come home early enough to greet our guests when we entertain, then I won't put you in a fury by vacuuming the place right after they all leave."

You stick to this trading off of one negative behavior against another to enhance the relationship, and now you are inspired to make many contracts for positive ("giving") behavior. In surprisingly short order, you find that you gladden rather than anger each other. You even put humor into some of your contracts. Life is smoother and more pleasant. Your personalities are undergoing change.

Contracting Leads to Empathy. The rigidities of O-C and obsessional perfectionism create unrealistic expectations in uptight persons. To the extent that you cannot compromise or change, your

237

CONTRACTING AND EXCHANGE BEHAVIOR LOG

NAME _A.L. and R.L._ LOG TIME FROM **Feb. 2** TO **Feb. 28**

This record must be kept in order to avoid arguments about the terms of a negotiated contract and the obligations agreed upon. The first, or 'hurt' party determines the scoring or the degree to which the contract has been fulfilled. The first party may not shift his (her) promise or arbitrarily add new terms. The second party may not alter the scoring.

BEHAVIOR (point value) or (yes-no)	M	Tu	W	Th	F	S	S	WEEK'S SCORE
1. Husband will notify wife of whereabouts	Y.	-	N	N	N	-	-	1 Yes
when out on "after hours" business	N.	-	-	Y	Y	-	-	2 Yes
matters (Yes-No)	Y	-	Y	Y	-	-	-	3 Yes
	Y	-	Y	Y	-	Y	-	4 Yes
2. Husband will stop lecturing wife	5	6	6	2	5	10	10	44
as if she is a first-grader	6	4	4	1	7	10	6	38
(Wife scores 1-10)	6	3	4	3	5	7	3	31
	3	1	0	3	3	2	3	15
3.								

CONSEQUENCES 1. Wife will not smoke in car without opening window.
2. Wife will not smoke in bedroom if score is under 35

SIGNED _(Wife)_
(first party)

SIGNED _(Husband)_
(second party)

DATE _Jan. 29_

SOCIAL SKILL IMPROVEMENT LOG

NAME __S. I. L._____ LOG TIME FROM __Feb. 2_____ TO __Feb. 23__

This record is meant to help you assert yourself, improve your social (and/or sexual) performance and increase your constructive activities. An accurate tally of your positive behavior will allow you to monitor your progress and encourage you in achieving your goal.

BEHAVIORAL GOAL (specify)	SHAPING METHOD (specific assignments)	CHECK IF PURSUED METHOD: DOUBLE CHECK IF ACHIEVED GOAL						
		M	T	W	T	F	S	S
1. Public speaking	1. Select topic and present to class (club)			✓				
	2. Practice speech on tape recorder - listen to playback	✓	✓ ✓					✓
	3. Repeat weak parts		✓	✓				✓✓
	4. Have trusted friend listen and make corrections		✓					✓✓
	5. Give speech			✓✓				
2. Dating	1. Call 5 women for dates	✓		·✓				✓
		✓			✓			
	2. Make concrete plans for each date		✓					✓
	3. Buy a new sport coat			✓✓				
	4. Role play date in group therapy				✓✓			

COMMENT: _____

_____

_____

MEDICATION: __None_____

RITUAL OR HABIT REDUCTION LOG   Jan 29. to Feb. 4.
                                 Jan. 21   to Jan. 27
NAME V. J.   LOG TIME FROM Jan. 12   to Jan. 18

This record will help you reduce the number of maladaptive habits or rituals in your life. For each
countable behavior listed, record the number of times that you repeat it each day. Totaling the entries
at the end of the week will give you an accurate measure of your improvement. Compare totals with the
previous week.

SPECIFIC RITUAL OBSERVED		Mon	Tues	Wed	Thur	Fri	Sat	Sun	WEEK'S TOTAL
1. HANDWASHING	Jan 12-18	80	86	82	98	106	150	144	746
	Jan. 21-27	65	60	31	53	62	72	70	413
	Jan 29-Feb.4	63	57	25	48	51	44	76	364
2. THOUGHTS ABOUT DEATH	12-18	15	19	11	16	15	22	20	118
	21-27	11	20	6	10	12	16	18	93
	29-2/4	15	18	5	12	9	10	17	86
3. LENGTH OF SHOWERS	12-18	20min	20min	—	20min	20min	25min	20min	Av. 21 min
(CONTAMINATION)	21-27	—	20min	15min	15min	—	20min	25min	19 min
	29-2/4	20min	15min	—	15 min	15min	15min	15min	16min
4. MAKING WIFE WASH	12-18	5	3	5	2	0	6	8	29
HANDS.	21-27	2	0	0	1	0	2	2	7
	29-2/4	0	0	0	0	0	0	0	0
5. HAVE SEX W/O IMMEDIATE		—	0	0	1	1	1	1	4
SHOWER AND CHANGE ONLY TOP SHEET		0	0	—	1	0	1	0	2
		0	0	0	—	0	1	0	1

COMMENT: No alcohol of any kind. No pot.

MEDICATION: Valium - about 15 mgm a day (3 tablets)

demands stay unreasonable and set up destructive misunderstanding and failures in empathy. Contracting to change and sticking to it break the cycle of quarrels, rages or even physical abuse. "It behooves a prudent person to make trial of everything before arms," said Terence of Rome 2000 years ago. You are doing this on contract, but more—you are getting to know how the other person feels.

In a family affair, you are the arbitrary, autocratic O-C father who objects to the man your daughter is dating. "He's beneath you. Drop him before you get too smoochy." Your daughter refuses, there are heated words and you threaten to throw him out if he should call. No communication. In the brooding interim silence over the next few days, the dynamite level is almost reached. Mother negotiates a contract. Your daughter is to bring the young man for dinner and you are at least to pretend a welcome. The couple will leave shortly after the meal, to let your feelings cool off. Several such evenings of controlled behavior take place. You still believe the young man is not worthy enough, but you begin to see some of his good points. Generally, the surface is calm, respectful and friendly. At worst, it is not enthusiastic. Adaptiveness, through rough compromise, has replaced stubborn maladaptive responses.

The following brief examples of contingency contracting bring to mind some couples in which one or both partners were O-Cs.

FIRST CASE.   The man is a stingy hoarder, the woman a stubborn controller. *Contract:* He will discontinue nosing through the closets to make sure she's held on to all his old shirts and other worn-out garments that she was sending to the thrift shop and he will not mention how hard he works for every penny. She in return will not point out his mistakes in driving on the highway.

SECOND CASE.   *Contract:* The husband will stop his dinnertime squabbling with the children about their day's activities. The wife will refrain from criticizing his social manners.

THIRD CASE.   *Contract:* He will no longer ignore his wife's appearance as if she were a cipher and he will stop raving about the looks of every other woman they meet. She will no longer keep track of the frequency and duration of his visits with his mother in the same building.

FOURTH CASE. *Contract:* Instead of going their separate ways for diversion, the wife will watch her husband's game of tennis and show an interest in his skills. He will sit in on his wife's rehearsals at the local theater group and later make contributory suggestions.

FIFTH CASE. *Contract:* If he is feeling a bit randy but too inhibited to initiate a sexual advance, he will learn to speak up and tell her, rather than stay angry all next day because she could not read his sexual wants. She, in turn, agrees to enter the spirit of playing around for arousal before going to bed—wearing a blond wig and long dangling earrings while strutting before him naked in stilt-heel slippers, or innovating other turn-on games instead of cold-shouldering such ideas as "silly."

These last two contracts are the best kinds because they work toward positive acts rather than alleviating negative (undesirable) behavior.

Contingency contracting in which your actions depend on those of another no doubt offers one of the best therapeutic methods to O-Cs in helping you lose uptight needs which alienate others. It gets rid of stubborn resistance to change and substitutes rewards for shared effort in marital and other social quarters. As a behavioral approach, contracting has become widespread. It is really a sort of harmonious barter which corrects maladaptive sociosexual maneuvers, especially at the low thresholds of antagonistic couples wherein one or the other mate manipulates sexual arousal and intercourse into an incompatible design for love. (See Chapter 15.)

Defusing the Uptight: A Behavioral Approach. You are the married man whose compulsion it is to expedite whatever comes to your attention on the instant. Let your wife but mention that a kitchen shelf is cracked, then it must be fixed immediately, even if it displaces her as she prepares dinner. Or if a telephone call interrupts a meal, you will satisfy the caller and let the dinner spoil. Your wife has learned several tricks. She never mentions a broken anything except when you are puttering around looking for a "fix-it" project. (You are addicted to them and sometimes "improve" what your wife prefers unimproved.) She never gives you two projects at one time or you would complete both, even if it meant canceling a movie, not visiting friends or getting to bed very late. She answers the telephone herself now and arranges for you to call back later. For the summer months, on weekends in the country she contracts to let you work all day Saturday, but you must keep Sunday to be with her. Your adolescent son also negotiates on time schedules for various ground and basement chores; you can make suggestions but you must not "take over" for uncompleted jobs within the time schedule except by mutual consent.

Running Interference. Your wife knows that you are your own psychologic barometer. She described her "fielding" operation. "I know when he will relax and I let him make the most of it. I also feel when he's liable to blow his stack, so I keep the kids off him and delay mentioning anything unpleasant or situations that will upset him." She is a wise woman. She knows that, for better or worse, you have your O-C moments or days and you need someone to guard you from your own bullheadedness. Compromise works like a charm where intolerance would wreck your marriage.

Unplanned Contracts: Assurance. I once visited a couple in the country. The O-C husband, a brilliant banking expert, harbored a childish pride in his culinary talents on a hibachi. He had finished the steaks and brought them into the kitchen for his wife's inspection. Just inside the door he spilled some of his martini on the platter. "Oh, look what I did. They're spoiled." His wife gave a quick swipe to the inner side of the platter with a paper napkin. "No, honey," she said in a half-whisper, "whoever heard of some perfectly good gin hurting a steak? They're just fine." And then this big strong renowned man of the business world quavered: "Thank you for being so nice about it." It was a tender and touching moment of instantaneous assurance. He returned to the terrace with his usual jaunty bearing.

Thought Stopping

Intrusive, painful or objectionable thoughts and nighttime rumi-nations can be stopped. "Impossible," you may say. "I've already tried to put them out of my mind, but they keep coming back. They just run rampant. I get irritable and feel crowded inside." Yes, but you can learn how to exterminate them and quickly.

Have you ever decided of a sudden to tune out a conversation or TV program and retire to a private daydream? Or, in reverse, to shut out the daydream and set your mind on a reality? Such thought stopping is similar to the physical act of braking your car to an abrupt halt when you perceive a threat in continued motion, or the control of cutting off an emotional outburst that would cause you embarrassment. These skills are taught in a procedure called cogni-tive behavior therapy.

You came to see me one day, a badly bewildered woman of middle age, ailing with thoughts that you might injure or even kill your granddaughter, whom you really loved. You had avoided her because of this, much to everyone's dismay. Thought stopping helped you. In my office you were instructed to think of your ob-session. I clapped my hands together sharply and commanded, "Stop!" You were taken aback but responded instantly. The obses-sional thought went. You were then instructed in commanding yourself to "Stop" whenever the obnoxious thought came and to slide over quickly to thoughts of the young girl's lovable ways. With persistent practice over a few weeks, the obsession was gone and your anxiety too. Your twinkling smile proclaimed their disappear-ance.

Ritual Stopping

Maladaptive ritual behavior is something we must halt, just as we end a ruminative thought or a furious outburst or, for that matter, bring down a fever or interrupt a nightmare.

Ritual stopping is also called *apotrepic therapy*. Interference with

244

compulsive rituals may be accomplished by mild physical restraint (always and only with the patient's consent), with distracting activities, persuasion, contingent rewards, psychologic modeling, or contracting. Assurance is given the patient that nothing dire will ensue, even though the continuity of the ritual has been broken.

One very orthodox religious young man would stand in the doorway of his bathroom for two to six hours while some family member helped him recite prayers. He demanded that more and more of the family take part in the ritual each day. The time interval also lengthened because he had to repeat each prayer until it was letter perfect and every inflection carried the exact nuance he wanted. His ritual was throwing the entire household into turmoil. Beyond endurance, the family turned for help. They were instructed that the ritual was to be stopped at progressively shorter intervals with only one member present, a different one each morning. At a set time several of them were to remove him gently from the bathroom threshold. Eventually the ritual was weakened and it ceased. Life for the others became tolerable and normal.

Staying Clear of Rituals. When an O-C persists in his traits, or an obsessional browbeats a family by imposing a ritual on them, and they participate in it, they are in effect exacerbating the condition by reinforcing the maladaptive behavior. In a crisis, of course, compassion and assurance for the demoralized individual are the only recourse until professional help is obtained. But at no time should relatives involve themselves physically with the ritual. This simply strengthens the obsession, as we have just observed. It is the persistent diminution of ritualistic behavior that breaks the chain of enslavement-anxiety-ritual-enslavement, and so on. The more often a ritual is interrupted, the more the person tastes freedom from it.

Reporting to Yourself

Just as in relaxation, it is important to record the changes produced by your efforts in learning how to modify inappropriate or maladaptive behavior. You can and should do this with the logs such as the one shown earlier and those in the following pages. A "good report" on yourself will stimulate you to further and extended effort.

The notes on logs or flow charts, for example, reveal the reduced number of hours in work addiction; how quickly and positively you can turn away from your urge to kleptomania; the decrease, let us say, from fifty to five times a day of a hand-washing or other ritual; the degree to which you lessen a rumination about infanticide (and let it fade out) so that you can handle a knife without fear of killing your child; the amount of freedom gained from the impulse to gamble, to molest children or to engage in voyeurism; the development daily of self-assertion; or the stepped-up and variegated activity of more blissful sexual union.

Perhaps you are the young woman addicted to list making who wants to overcome this compulsion. You would start to count the number of items on your list every evening. Cross out five, the next evening six, then seven, and on down the line to none. Soon you will find rewards: Your tasks are accomplished because you have wasted no time in list making and you are actually improving your memory. Or you can try the cold turkey way (see Flooding, next section). Tear up every list you have even if it convulses you. And make no other ones. Amazingly, you will remember your main duties. If you overlook something, there's always the next day. But each evening record how much less your list making means in your life.

EXPOSURE PROCEDURES

The principle governing this behavioral technique is confrontation. You are challenged squarely by the object or situation (stimulus) that provokes your fear, anxiety or other symptoms.

Exposure to confrontation with a stimulus demands that you comprehend totally the procedure and agree to cooperate, even though you will undergo a certain amount of psychologic abrasion until you achieve the loss of your phobia, the end of a ritualistic practice, the resolution to a sexual dilemma or the change of whatever maladaptive characteristic you are trying to alter.

Exposure methods may be used gradually as in *systematic desensitization*, wherein anxiety is held at a low level, or rapidly as in *flooding*, in which high levels of anxiety are activated.

Suppose as a child you were afraid of the dog. Your parents let you just look at him and gave you quiet assurance as they brought the animal closer and closer. Your anxiety was constantly allayed as each move took place until at last you could touch him, hold his paw, and finally roll over on the ground with him and play together.

Had your parents forced you to pet the dog immediately, this would have been called *flooding*. No doubt, in situations from which you tended to retreat, they did expose you to flooding experiences, despite your anxieties. The stimulus may have been heights, new people, nursery school or whatever else caused you to draw back; but because of the circumstances involved, a quick adaptation to them on your part was necessary. You were therefore subjected to an all-at-once, totally immersing procedure.

Exposure can occur *in vivo* or in fantasy. In the latter, the patient imagines the feared stimulus or place. We can now discuss the two extremes of exposure, the gradual method and the intense flooding.

Systematic Desensitization

Suppose that you are oppressed by the common phobia of riding in a subway. The first step to desensitization would be to teach you how to relax, progressively assisted by biofeedback monitoring (although any technique that suits you best may be used). Relaxation, we noted earlier, is a first-rate counterconditioner to anxiety. When you can go limp at will, the therapist sets up a *hierarchy of fears*. This is a simple listing of behaviors ranked in the order of their power to create anxious feeling tones. You can also set your own hierarchy and pace yourself.

The first to be practiced should be the one you fear least. For your subway phobia this would consist of approaching the entrance to the subway. Then, while standing there, you call on your prior training and relax. The second step in the hierarchy is to descend to the bottom of the entrance stairs, and again you consciously relax. The next day you repeat this procedure, but now you approach the turnstile and make yourself deliberately at ease. And so on. The actual hierarchy is evolved in about the following order.

1. Approach the subway entrance. Relax.
2. Stop at the stairs. Relax.
3. Descend the stairs. Relax.
4. Approach the turnstile. Relax.
5. Pass through the turnstile. Relax.
6. Approach the platform. Relax.
7. Stand on the platform, allow trains to pass until you are fully relaxed.
8. Board the train and ride to one stop only. Relax.
9. Board the next train and ride two stops. Relax.

By this time you will feel brave enough to go on to your destination. This procedure may take several days. Or you can expose yourself at any point in the hierarchy as often as you wish, until you can manage the next step. It may be done in the company of someone who models for you, that is, precedes you in each stage of the hierarchy and demonstrates that "nothing happens." Different hierarchies can be worked out for any kind of phobia (elevators, animals, heights or airplanes, for example) and the phobia is overcome.

Desensitization in Fantasy. Sitting in an easychair, monitored by biofeedback instruments, you fantasize, i.e., visualize mentally the first step of the hierarchy of fears. The instruments will tell you whether you are staying relaxed. If the first step kicks off anxiety, you require further practice in deep relaxation. But if your ease remains constant, you go on mentally to the second, third, fourth steps, and on. You establish the time of your own gradations until you reach the last one, still fully relaxed. You then lose your phobia.

Fantasy is an effective instrument that is combined with masturbation and/or intercourse for men and women who are sexually overcontrolled. It is difficult to pinpoint such overcontrol in the O-C woman but not so in the O-C man. The latter suffers from retarded ejaculations (see Chapter 15). The goal here is for the man to release into orgasm. Vivid fantasies or the use of film strips which strengthen his fantasies are combined with masturbation, either on his own or by his mate, or with intercourse in a relaxed atmosphere. This procedure may ultimately bring about easier ejaculation.

Desensitization in Vivo. Desensitization in real life is generally more forceful than in fantasy and, for some conditions, a must. For example, you were the young man who came to see me, agitated about premature ejaculations. First, you learned to relax so that your great anxiety which was inducing a too rapid sexual climax would subside. In practice at home, your wife assisted you in this relaxation. Immediately following penetration and after each thrust of the penis, you stopped all motion to reduce your anxiety level and excitement. Then again the thrust . . . stopping . . . thrust . . . until optimal control was achieved and the pattern for future normal sexual intercourse was reestablished.

Some adjunctive techniques in desensitization of anxiety for premature ejaculation involve more active participation of the woman. She may slow ejaculation by squeezing the penis just below the glans, effectively subduing the leap to climax, or she may assume the female superior position and thus be in fuller control of all the sexual movements.

For women who develop vaginismus, desensitization *in vivo* with the use of a simple operant procedure is highly serviceable. While not a common dysfunction, vaginismus can be bothersome because the clamping spasm (see Chapter 15) prevents penetration and precludes intercourse. In a relaxed setting, the woman practices inserting dilators of progressively increasing size until she can easily tolerate one somewhat larger and wider than a man's penis. She then repeats this practice, but with her mate inserting the dilators. Next she practices inserting her fingers and finally her mate's fingers. At this point she will probably no longer be spastic and intercourse can take place.

However, if the vaginismus is part of frigidity or a phobic avoidance of sex, these aspects of her dysfunction must be treated first.

Desensitization for Other Sexual Dysfunctions. This procedure also helps frigid and nonorgastic women, especially those who are motivated to rise above this handicap but are inhibited by body exposure, stimulation or body contact.

As an extremely uptight woman, you may begin systematic desensitization with fantasy. The hierarchy of imagined events over a period of several weeks starts with your nude mirrored image, and you picture your unclothed mate at the far end of the room. You then visualize his gradual approach: you touch his hand; you permit him to caress your face, then your breasts and on to full body stimulation; finally, still in fantasy, to intercourse. Or the fantasy may start with you and your mate in close body contact but fully clothed. Then an entire sequence of undressing, of body stimulation, and finally intercourse. Here too you can establish your own hierarchy to accord with your anxiety levels. After such systematic desensitization in a "pretend" process, the hierarchy is repeated *in vivo* with your mate. (We will discuss this procedure further on as *role rehearsal*.)

Behavior therapists use films or still-life pictures as adjuncts to desensitization procedures and role rehearsal. These provide positive visual details about sexual stimulation and techniques for coitus and impassion the viewer with desire. The films show scenes of nudity, of couples in intimate embrace caressing each other's body parts and using a number of tantalizing positions for intercourse to suit individual needs—one couple astride an armless chair, front to front; another couple participating in a spontaneous quickie; and a third enjoying the subtleties of oral stimulation as they take possession of each other.

Thus, such films disinhibit as they effectively model seductive behavior and tempt the senses of those who may have long been repressed. The very aliveness and emphasis on the rapture of sex play and ultimate orgasm desensitize the anxious person and show the way to sensual and erotic liberation.

Flooding

In this behavioral exercise, you are exposed to an alarming stimulus all at once and remain exposed until you habituate to it. If you are a phobic person, you are directly confronted with the feared object, an elevator. Accompanied by a person who will model the behavior, you are taken directly into the elevator to ride up and down until you adapt without anxiety. *You get used to it.* Such intense immersions may go on for two to six or more hours; or they can be accomplished in divided doses with each session lasting from one-half to one hour. Experience has shown that single sessions of prolonged exposure work to better advantage than shorter, even though more frequent, exposures.

Maintaining High Anxiety Levels. Implosion is another term that refers to flooding while high anxiety levels are held. You must be motivated to tolerate this. You were the nurse's aide who developed an unreasoning fear of crossing streets even when the light was green. The presence of automobiles and trucks almost sent you into hysterics. With your permission, an instructor-model brought you to a heavily trafficked spot. You stood there trembling for several hours while the therapist intensified your anxiety by making you conscious of all the dangers. By the third session you were able to "take the scene" and cross the street, though with some trepidation. After several weeks you were free of the phobia and so collected that you could dodge the vehicles coming at you around the corners with the best of them.

Another case of implosive flooding: you may recall that in Part One I described the tidy-clean person. I asked one such woman to empty a full ashtray in the center of her living room rug and leave it there for forty-eight hours. At intervals she would return to glare at it. However, not only did the experience wither her dirt-chasing propensity, but afterward whenever she spotted something mussed or scummy, she would shrug, "Oh well, it can wait for another forty-eight hours if need be."

There was also the child who drew back from learning to dive into a pool. The instructor encouraged him to try it once, then had him dive repeatedly and continually for more than two hours. The child's fear went, and suddenly he felt so challenged to perform well that he wished he could learn the swan dive that very day. Adults too have become habituated to driving on narrow winding mountain roads with precipitous drops after prolonged exposure to such exploits. "You know it's not as bad as I thought it would be" is the verdict after the immersion.

Flooding in Avoidance Behavior.   Flooding with high anxiety levels does wonders for avoidance behavior. That young man in Part Two who was so phobic about being contaminated by ash cans and waste receptacles—remember him? And that he had to follow a zigzag course home to avoid the containers? I asked him to walk the streets in the company of his wife, to touch at first every lamppost, then fire hydrants, then to add ash cans and garbage containers to his project. The final instruction, after going through this process for several weeks, was to touch his wife and then to kiss her. The contamination threat was "disproved" and the avoidance behavior dwindled away.

Saturation.   This flooding technique is used involuntarily by many people. Have you ever gorged yourself on food that made your mouth water, whether steak, candy, cake, rice, nuts—but so steadily that you ended by being sick of them? Those with an "I want to see" obsession can also be supersaturated once they glut their curiosity. Saturation helps too with inhibited maladaptive anxieties. For example, as a bashful college student, you "wondered" about sexual acts all the time. You had never seen a nude female body. Forthwith, you were escorted to five X-rated films by the therapist in one day after which you had "had it." Soon afterward you met a girl, and now, with your ruminations gone, you felt more confident about the female of the species and what made her tick.

Prudes can sometimes be disinhibited and lose their obsessiveness with correct dress, deportment or "what the neighbors would think." I recall the phenomenal breakthrough of an exceedingly pretty but sexually uptight married woman who was flooded during a resort holiday with an unanticipated real-life situation.

At the beach with her husband, she suddenly found herself immersed in a wave of sensuality by the nakedness all around her—hundreds of bikini-clad men and women. As she watched them, fascinated, there came the first crack in her defensive armor and an overwhelming release from O-C constraints. Compelled beyond thought, she pulled her female impulses out of hibernation and flew off to buy a bikini for herself. She returned and, defiantly, she wore it. Her husband flipped. That brazen little woman wasn't such a cold piece after all, parading around and smiling at the lecherous stares of the other males. He flared up. What the hell! No other bull was going to charge into *his* pasture.

Aglow with all the attention thrust at her, she was demurely acquiescent when her husband said, "Come on," and dragged her to their room on the run. Her disinhibited mind sang, "Ready, willing and able." In bed, she could not wait for his hands and mouth to be all over her. When he kissed her breasts she felt urgent messages to her downtown area and directed him toward it. With a receptively moist vulva, she knew the lust and thrall of sexual enravishment, more exciting than any of the wildest fantasies she had ever conceived. The pleasure of her responses was so rewarding that it demanded more and more of the sauce in repeat performances, daytime and nights. For the first time in her life she felt like a woman desired and desiring, as she learned that sexual gratifications are second to none. All because of two little scraps of fabric.

Flooding in Psychotherapy and Learning. Encounter groups of various kinds, marathons in the nude, round-the-clock rap sessions, or labor-management all-night negotiations, as well as "total immersion" for learning a foreign language—all are basically behavior modification procedures using flooding techniques to achieve some specific goal in the shortest possible time. Flooding is not limited to maladaptive behavior.

However, this technique is especially good therapy when the

maladaptation results from phobias. The exception to the procedure is made when the anxiety level is so extraordinarily high that it might intensify the phobia. Flooding is immediately discontinued.

In vivo flooding is more effective than in fantasy, although for some obsessions, such as a fear of falling out of an airplane, it would be supererogatory to point out that here, reality would be impractical. Fantasy flooding for fears of flying may be augmented by placing the person in a mockup of a plane, or for other phobias by using movies in which he or she seems to be part of the action, with recorded sound effects of thunder, animals, crowds of people, whichever is appropriate, all meant to create exposure to the sights and sounds of the evocative stimuli.

Role Rehearsal. This composite technique brings exposure, learning procedures, shaping, modeling and counterconditioning in systematic desensitization together as they crisscross and interact for full benefit.

For instance, when you acted out a proposal to your fiancée in advance, became involved in make-believe games with your child or sexually with your spouse, or practiced your sales pitch for a promotion before a mirror, you applied the concept of role rehearsal, an excellent technique for learning new skills and peeling off the anxieties and inhibitions of social behavior and sexual revelry.

We know that unresolved anxiety about carrying through a certain role will usually ensure its failure. For example, you fear impotence. The thought dominates you when you attempt sexual intercourse. Blocked by anxiety, you cannot erect to your excitatory sensations and are now, in actual fact, functionally impotent. Thus, sexual (and other) skills are best achieved by progressive exposures to increasingly higher levels of anxiety stimuli. In sequence, the anxiety must be resolved at each level, as it impinges on you. Role rehearsal can bring this about, and finally resolve, the impotence.

The therapist suggests that you detour on direct sexual intercourse at first. Instead, you concentrate on your enjoyment of sexuality in an advancing sequence, first, kissing your mate, going on to body fondling, then progressing to genital stimulation. She collaborates and you are really rehearsing each step, skipping none. Now you are not only free of anxiety but in a deep glow of bliss at every stage of your sensual travels. At last, certain that you can respond with full erection, the penetrating thrust is beautifully accomplished because you have maintained the confidence earned in your rehearsed performance.

Masters and Johnson have used the preceding technique with encouraging success, along with an adjunctive measure. They ask their patients to stay in a nearby motel for two weeks, away from all social or work obligations, and with only ardent desire to occupy them. Free of extraneous pressures, the couple throw off the inhibitions of dysfunction quite rapidly. (See Selective Reinforcement earlier in this chapter.)

Role rehearsal *in vivo* nullifies the basic inhibitions expressed in shame, fear of intimacy and need of secrecy often alleged to be sexual shyness, as we saw in Chapter 15.

Sexual therapy combines role rehearsal with other behavior techniques for such dysfunctions as vaginismus, painful intercourse, failure to lubricate. *In vivo* role rehearsal is practiced in privacy and carefully paced in the proper setting with an enthusiastic and sensitive mate. Guided by instructions previously given by the therapist, this procedure will remove your inadequacies in a high percentage of cases.

Role rehearsal is used by many O-Cs and uptights on their own initiative. For example, you may practice your after-dinner speech to obviate stage fright, or even try out your entrances and exits for a social affair. Such behavior therapy rarely requires a therapist. One diffident young woman combined role rehearsal with operant conditioning (stimulus control). Because her hand shook in the stress of social situations, she practiced lifting a cup with an increasing amount of fluid each time until the tremor was gone.

Role Reversal. This is an interesting flooding procedure which can change certain behavior with almost lightning speed. A sixteen-year-old girl flatly refused her mother's request to help in the kitchen with a crass "Fuck you." Despite protest, she persisted in this reply to anything asked of her. The next time she did so, her mother answered quietly, without a sidelong glance, "Fuck you twice." The girl let out an appalled "Moth—err," and bolted from the kitchen, never to use this conversational gambit in the household again.

I suggested a role reversal to the married woman (Chapter 15), whose inhibited husband relied on surreptitious browsing through his collection of pornography for titillating arousal. One evening she confronted him with his film strips. She had set up the projector. "Okay, darling, you and I are going to watch these movies together. Why shouldn't I have some of the excitement too?" As the film unrolled, they reached out to each other. With each evening's film-watching, their sexual ardor was more and more invigorated to erotic intimacies. They began to shut off the projector earlier and with mutual accord make for the bedroom. Having discovered new ways of intercourse, sitting, lying, kneeling, they went on to elaborate and invent their own styles of lovemaking.

When their teen-age children were out, unable to wait, they would stop on the stairs for a bit of preliminary diddle. Once, while so engrossed in their sexual turbulence that nothing else existed, they rolled gently off the bed to the floor, still clasped tightly together, and so moved on to climax. Only when they realized where they were did they laugh at the absurdity. One thing was clear: they did not need the films anymore. The regression to play-mating and bedmating had renewed their youth with all its biology of wanting and needing.

In a different context of role reversal, you were the houseproud woman who tried to use the mechanism of denial to rationalize your perfectionist traits. "Yes, I do fuss about keeping my place spit and polish. But honestly, I'm not so bad. You should know my son . . . would you believe it? He moved out of our place because he said I was too sloppy for him. Me! SLOPPY!" You cried a bit. "And you should see his place. It's like a furniture showroom. He shudders if you walk around in it, so you start to tiptoe. Or if you sit in the wrong chair he looks like murder. Sometimes I think he's a real weirdo. . . ." She thought for a moment and suddenly broke out, "But maybe you think I am too. I wonder if that's the way I act sometimes. . . ." She continued to ruminate aloud in this vein, projecting herself into a role reversal that unexpectedly flooded her with some insight into herself. This episode, which had started as a complaint, became the impetus toward modifying her own perfectionism. Here, role reversal was combined with rational emotive therapy (RET), which ultimately brought forth a striking diminution of her houseproud obsession.

While role reversal can be contracted between two people, I sometimes ask the grudge-bearer, the righteous obsessional, or the controller to make a silent mental contract. You negotiate this bargain with another's weakness by changing one of your own personal traits which you suspect the other dislikes as much as you dislike that of your counterpart. Very often, it prompts you to objectify, to alter your grudge-bearing tendency and to diminish your intolerance and rigidity. One woman became so mischievously entranced by the game that when she gave full scope to her more amicable qualities, she completely mystified the "silent" partner in the contract, who began to ask herself what she had disliked in her friend in the first place.

Flooding Requires Cooperation. Patients who are willing to take a long hard look at themselves have been successfully desensitized to their obsessions about a body smell, their height or some other complex of inferiority. While full patient cooperation is essential for all behavior modification, it is especially so in exposure techniques, which require strong motivation to withstand the fear, anxiety or anger that may be engendered.

In the play *Cyrano de Bergerac,* Christian de Neuvillette taunts Cyrano in a long harangue about his enormously large nose. This scene exemplifies flooding at its most dramatic; Cyrano must control his anger because Christian is the beloved of Roxanne, who in turn is the object of Cyrano's own secret and hopeless passion. Until then, no one had ever dared mention Cyrano's nose without fear of being run through by his expert sword.

Here, the single episode of desensitization is not repeated or re-inforced, but the obsessional taboo is broken by overwhelming exposure plus Cyrano's firm motivation not to commit violence on the man Roxanne loves.

When the tendency to flee from objects or situations in a flooding technique causes panic or fear, or you want to lash out in anger or simply quit, then modeling by a therapist first, in or out of the office environment, can encourage you to imitation. Should this fail in the beginning, other behavior procedures are substituted.

Reporting to Yourself

Devise your own charts to record week-to-week improvement in overcoming your phobias, avoidance behavior, sexual dysfunctions and similar maladaptations. You may also want to record your less frequent need for a model in flooding techniques and the measurement of your increasing self-confidence levels.

Another gauge of your improvement is to retest yourself with the Obsssive-Compulsive Personality Inventory (Chapter 9) and the Obsessional Neurotic Scale (Chapter 16). A lowered score will encourage you to persist in mastering the disabling traits in your personality.

SELF-REGULATION

Behavior therapy can enrich your life only when you want to change your actions, thoughts and emotions. Let me say again—you cannot do this without practicing diligently.

Some of your homework may seem difficult because of the enormous obligation to counter your anxiety. You may try to evade an exposure technique, resist the removal of a phobia or retreat from the specifics of sexual therapy because of prior suppressions and conditioned sensitivities. Possibly you will attempt to wheedle the therapist into listening to a long recital of your woes, hoping that this will remove your uptightness. "My husband doesn't satisfy my needs." "I can't cope." "The children's jabber drives me up the wall." Your therapist will then make it clear that your desire to spend the session in complaints is a waste, whereas decisions and your determination to implement them will set a process in motion far more valuable to your mental health than all the gloomy pleasure of ventilation that you so dearly long for.

While effective for your O-C uptightness and maladaptations, behavior therapy may require adjunctive types of available treatment for a comprehensive approach toward raising your level on not only your flow charts and the O-C and ON scales but your P.E.G. index as well. In the next chapter an overview of these adjunctive therapies is presented.

· 19 ·
An Overview of Other Treatment Procedures

Psychotherapy, family therapy and biologic (physical) therapies combine for the maximum treatment of uptight O-Cs and maladaptive obsessionals. While behavior therapy offers the best prognosis for such people, nonetheless each individual presents multiple and diversified needs. The psychiatrist thereupon selects those methods familiar to him which will augment the total treatment program to the patient's best advantage for improvement.

PSYCHOTHERAPY

Many psychotherapies are at hand which are founded on psychologic theories of mental dysfunction and personality disorder. They are broadly based procedures in which relationships, words, directives and interactions are used therapeutically in the attempt to (1) influence you to exchange your distress for adaptive psychologic function, (2) retrieve your ego strength and self-confidence, (3) upgrade your communication, (4) give you significance and a lighter heart, (5) teach you to enjoy and be enjoyed, to love and be loved.

To bring off all these ideal ends quickly would be a daunting task to you. Hence, for the O-C and obsessional, goals for treatment that will bear fruit in a shorter time should be chosen cannily and pursued with immediate vigor.

The maze of therapeutic methods that I will attempt to define for you in an educative perspective comprises the more popular brands.

Psychoanalysis and Dynamic Psychotherapies

The fountainhead of dynamic psychotherapies is found in Freudian theory and treatment, whose purpose is to ransack your inner "unconscious" psychology. Through repeated analyses of transference phenomena and resistance to treatment, it is assumed that your defenses will be demolished; that this will happen because you clarify and interpret the psychic dynamic material of your free associations and dreams; and that over an extended period of time, your behavior will become adaptive involuntarily because the ingredients of your psyche will blend into a harmonious whole.

Psychoanalysis has not remedied O-C maladaptations or decompensations to any degree. This is mostly because the treatment, by its very nature, demands an ego so mighty that it can digest the oddities of all analytic ramifications. This would be counterproductive. Your damaged personality threads are so brittle to begin with that you cannot face such intimately shocking revelations about yourself. Reliving your emotions on the analytic couch becomes an exercise in ticking off otiose trivia from your past; it lets you ruminate and doubt at length. Swamped already in ambivalence and low self-esteem, you fear that you will be unable to emerge intact. Thus, change from maladaptation is rarely brought about; psychoanalysts themselves agree that obsessionals are not easy to treat successfully.

Eclectic Psychotherapies

The virtue of an electic approach lies in its capacity to bring rational shrewdness into the therapy of symptom complexes as they arise. If you are maladaptive and in a ferment of panic or hopeless despondency, the immediate therapeutic instrument is rocklike *support*, to provide you with assurance, or unquestioning *acceptance* because you feel spurned by the world and want to die. Or it may be *release* that you cry for, a listening ear that allows you catharsis of a real or fancied event that is splintering you with guilt. If you are an immobilized obsessional, *directive* psychotherapy will conduct you into new learning, arouse you from your inhibitions and propel you into motion swiftly.

Creativity may be applied to sublimate your frustrations. Painting, handicrafts, gardening or any other kind of personal industriousness (but not obligatory) may divert your anxieties and nourish your fruitfulness to battle your O-C traits. These tactics and expedients, plus such other strategy as manipulating the environment, counseling, emotive and insight therapy, hypnotherapy and psychodrama, figure in the equipment of the eclectic therapist.

Many psychotherapists are self-styled eclectics when in fact they mean this description to indicate mostly that they are not solely devoted to Freudian concepts. They do not, in fact, use varieties of psychologic procedures. The eclectic psychotherapist finds that his most effectual implement is himself. The trust you place in his human qualities (or those of any other healer) can, to be sure, inspire you to future promise of brighter skies. Your motivation to change and to search for higher altitudes of living will be as good as your rapport with him impels you to be.

Eclecticism in psychotherapy, however, should not be equated with the comprehensive and integrated treatment programs of the *general psychiatrist*. The latter combines various psychotherapies with family and biologic procedures to treat the person in his totality. We will discuss this further on.

Quasi-Religious Therapies

Large groups of people adopt Christian Science, Scientology, Reevaluation Counseling, the teachings of the Arica Institute or the Divine Light Mission and similar "therapies." These individuals want new inspiration or a metaphysical or religious concept of healing. Here programming (or structuring the belief) reinforces faith in the union of the individual with a sort of cosmic consciousness. It allows escape from the tyranny of an uptight ego by submerging individual strivings into the sublime abstraction of mind (or soul). For brief or long moments, obsessional ego trips can be terminated and tensions dramatically reduced, in the knowledge that we live on earth only transiently. New meaning in life may arise and the intuition that one is now well.

Self-Realization and Consciousness-Raising Therapies

If you are the chilly disaffected O-C or the meek obsessional who must learn to assert yourself, developing a new social adroitness takes priority. For this, many O-Cs use a shortcut out of their inhibitions and join encounter groups, nude marathons, screaming, touching and other such therapies.

However, when you acquire this new assertive resource, the awareness encounters that you have undergone may tend to exalt the self but to exploit the next person, who may be low on defenses. Thus, to feel strongly about "doing your own thing" at the expense of someone else means that you are failing overall, because along with awareness should go its twin, "share-ness." To break out of inhibition so that you can know love is one side of the equation. To invite and accept love is the other.

Self-Help and Peer Group Therapies

For you whose lives are dominated by a single ruinous trait (alcoholism, gambling, drug or child abuse) peer group therapies prove of enormous value. Alcoholics Anonymous, Gamblers Anonymous, Recovery, Inc., and many others are nationally known.

In more recent years *transactional analysis* and psychologic systems of self-help have given assistance in acquiring social stability, in losing weight (Weight Watchers), in dropping the smoking habit (Smoke Enders), and in learning compassion and adequacy. Self-help books are abundant, and for those who respond to the printed word, such *bibliotherapy* can be an influential force.

However, what is most affecting to watch is the impact of peer group activity among adolescents. Their rough-and-tumble behavior and emotionality bring full support and direction from each other. With adults they are off-balance, clumsy *and open to reproach*. In their own ranks they can latch on to a venture, announce their goals, get frightened, backslide *and still not be condemned*. Only normal adolescent behavior from their own will be seen, with an "I will do unto you as I would have you do unto me" philosophy. Until adolescents achieve their natural adult maturity, they receive only from their own kind the respect and liking that they need.

Group Therapies

Classical group pyschotherapy identifies the biosocial model of neurotic behavior as "sick," to be altered by some form of social interaction. Group therapy gives you a ready-made social setting in which, as a lonely O-C or a maladaptive obsessional, you find outlets for your inhibitions, group directives for modifying yourself, and support in many dilemmas.

FAMILY THERAPY

An uptight O-C or obsessional neurotic who is whipped by chronic anxieties, rituals, phobias and other maladaptive traits can harass an entire family circle into such schisms that intense clashes spring up out of nowhere. In Chapter 18 I indicated that family involvement is essential in the treatment of O-C uptights whose traits become excessive and maladaptive.

Thus, therapy means that the intrafamilial animosities triggered by you must be treated *with* you and the family, concomitantly. It makes no difference whether the family is for or against you as their troublemaker. It is crucial that they participate. If empathy, support, love and kindness emanate from them, the treatment gains for all will be apparent quickly.

Marital Therapy and Marital Counseling

These approaches usually refer to psychotherapy given to you and your mate in joint session. Any of the procedures just discussed are used. Contingency contracting, the main technique currently employed, was described in the previous chapter. Regardless of the techniques in marital therapy, the supportive and impartial role of the therapist and his informed authority are often the crux of the treatment and the determining factors in overcoming matrimonial sadness and failure.

Unit Family Therapy

Psychotherapeutic methods here bring you together with your spouse and children in simultaneous sessions. At its least it gives each one of you the chance to voice your gripes and encourages respect and tolerance for your and the others' idiosyncrasies and options. Here, too, contracting can synthesize the gains of the psychotherapy and establish a working family relationship. The benefit is derived mostly when primary issues of role delineation are clarified and each one of you knows where you stand and what to expect of each other. Minor and simple behavioral changes may often produce major and enduring accords for happiness between family members.

Conjoint Family Therapy

This is a unique form of group treatment in which two to five families are treated together at the same time. Such methods can aid severely regressed obsessionals a great deal. Close relatives, often confused and dejected by the malignancy of the obsessional's neurosis with which they have been living, rarely comprehend the why of the person's actions. Enlightenment, especially in the company of others with the same troubles, seems to lift the burdens of all concerned.

Marriage Encounters

These are weekend experiences for behavior modification usually conducted under religious auspices. Also called "dialoguing," the accent is placed on the priorities of each spouse and how best to mediate them. Intrafamily communication is improved as a matter of course. You were the wife who said that your O-C husband never answered any of your questions or comments. "He just looks at me with a vacant stare as if I'm ectoplasm. I wonder if he would know I was gone if I just moved out. Well, maybe at suppertime."

After a weekend encounter session you are forced into awareness of each other and you respond. At home you are more alert now to your respective sensitivities. Even small disputes are eased with a mild caress. Instead of memos you both begin to write little love missives. One wife changed from "Out shopping. Back at five," to "I went to buy the things you like. Be back at five. Hugs and kisses."

Other forms of family therapy have arisen, but with or without professional help your personal touch at home can soften the hardships of a maladaptive's hangups. It is called "plain good sense" and even "smothering with love." Nothing lost. Everything gained.

BIOLOGIC THERAPIES

Much research evidence is accumulating which suggests that genetics, hormonal function, nervous system chemistry, body metabolism and numerous other biologic processes participate in personality development and function.

For this reason many physical treatment procedures for bettering, modifying and toning up the biology of nervous system function have been and still are being used in the hope of clearing up severe maladaptive conditions. Within my professional life I have utilized or become acquainted with acupuncture, light and deep anesthesia, narcoanalysis and narcosynthesis (truth serum), carbon dioxide inhalation, insulin coma, hormone substitution by mouth and injection, and neurosurgery.

Whether all are used or not by every psychiatrist, we also have at our disposal electrotherapy, known as electroconvulsive treatment (ECT) or electrostimulation treatment (EST), cerebral electrotherapy (CET or electrosleep), and every kind of psychotropic drug (major and minor tranquilizers, antidepressants and sedatives). Both used and abused are alcohol, cannabis (marijuana), stimulants (uppers, speed), depressants (downers), and hallucinogens (acid or LSD) taken singly or combined with other drugs to relieve uptightness. Then there is the nutritional approach which offers diets, vitamins, minerals and supplements, all meant to stabilize and benefit your metabolic processes and psychic energy flow.

You need hardly be reminded of the "snake oil" promoters and fellow quacks selling every imaginable gadget to relieve tension, spasms and pain. Unfortunately, their very existence indicates the extremes to which many maladaptives will resort in desperation for relief.

When Physical Treatments Help

Undoubtedly, uptight, tense or depressed O-Cs and obsessionals are physically as well as emotionally disturbed. If you are an angry compulsive urbanite, gulping down a quick lunch, you will show a different neurohormonal and metabolic level from that of a relaxed muleteer who dozes through a siesta each day. Stress modifies your hormonal output just as hormonal output creates psychologic and emotional variances. Women brutalized in concentration camps stopped menstruating; even in normal environments hormonal imbalances may cause premenstrual tension. Biologic therapies which set straight the physical and chemical imbalances that relate to maladaptation have helped immeasurably.

The most exquisitely distressing symptoms of neurochemical in-

267

stability appear in the emotions—foremost, depression. Less destructive but painful are panic, anger, fear or agitation. You may experience two or more of these symptoms, for example, when depression includes agitation and fear. Marching right behind and equally intolerable come the psychosomatic symptoms of pain or tightness in the body mass. Relief with physical treatment then becomes obligatory.

Treatment for Depression. Depression hovers over the maladaptive as an omnipresent complication. However, when it does descend it can be treated readily with electrotherapy or with antidepressant drugs.

If the depression is of such severity that it instills you with hopelessness and you dwell on doing away with yourself, then electrotherapy is the treatment of choice. As given today under mild anesthesia and with a muscle relaxant, it is safe, rapid and painless, producing the highest incidence of recovery from depression (80–90 percent) in the shortest possible time.

The misconception about permanent memory loss and the words "shock treatment" have unfortunately frightened away many depressed persons and, in effect, denied them this excellent treatment. Some patients do experience mild, temporary forgetfulness with electrotherapy, but this clears up within two to three weeks after the last treatment. With some techniques there may be little or no transient memory loss. For full details on the use of electrotherapy you are referred to my book *Up from Depression.*

Because the alternative to treatment for depression can be suicide, electrotherapy especially is, in my opinion, a lifesaving procedure.

A large armamentarium of antidepressant drugs is also available for the maladaptive's depression. These psychic energizers can pick you up in about 65 to 70 percent of cases and may have to be taken for two to three weeks before you feel better. The drug should then be continued for several months, usually on a reduced (or maintenance) dose, to prevent any relapse.

The predicament, however, is that as an O-C you may refuse medication, or you grumble about its side effects, such as constipation, weight gain, and a dry mouth. Yet if you do persist with it and your depression is mild to moderate, getting rid of depression is well worth the minimal discomforts of the drug.

When the symptoms of depression dominate your O-C or obsessional maladaptation, the first order of business is to treat the depression and clear it up. While it envelops you it is impossible for your nervous system to respond to behavior therapy or any other kind of psychologic treatment. It would be like working in a fog, and you could not be reached.

Treatment for Panic, Anger and Fear. These emotions are best treated with tranquilizers. Here, too, many such drugs are available on prescription and manage to hold down your threshold of tension to a reasonable enough level, one at which you can at least get along. If you reject pills, you can elect its first-rate substitute, relaxation therapy, with all of its many acceptable advantages.

A recent addition to the biologic armamentarium for phobics and obsessionals is a drug called *clomipramine*. Basically, it is related to the antidepressant *imipramine*. It is hoped that drug therapy in the future will be more directly helpful for the O-C, phobic and obsessional persons than it is now.

Treatment for Agitation. Should you become so chronically uptight that you palpitate with agitation, everyone around you is engulfed in your misery. The major tranquilizers can reduce this state and help you through the worst. Even wine, an ancient and easily obtained tranquilizer, taken at lunch or dinner in moderation, will settle you down. Very often, agitation accompanies depression, and both conditions can be treated by combining a tranquilizer with an antidepressant drug.

Treatment for Insomnia. You may stay partially awake because of persistent drowsy ruminations at bedtime which kill off your sleep.

Quite often insomnia, too, points to depression. When the latter is treated, your sleep pattern improves. In some instances, sedatives are indicated which will give you a fair stretch of sleep.

Electrosleep (CET) is also an excellent assist for insomnia and for tension in selected situations. But for really good slumber, learning *how* to release into sleep becomes the curing agent. For this, the relaxation procedures discussed in Chapter 18 are incomparable when applied to the problem of insomnia.

REACHING FOR OPTIMAL CHANGE

In this book I have tried to present you with authoritative, optimistic insights and guidelines for living without the ambivalence and threats that raise your psychologic defenses and keep you uptight.

All of the treatments that we have discussed, used singly or in various combinations, carefully prescribed and supervised on an individual basis, can ultimately triumph over most of the crises and chronic misery that you, the O-C and obsessional, generate and attract. However, emphasis has been placed on the most recent approaches in behavioral modification to the shaping of new behavior. This therapy holds out the best opportunity for you to regain your mental and physical equilibrium when you believe that you have lost it forever. In restoring your confidence and tapping the secretions of your humanity, you will not be impelled to constant vigilance and control over people or your environment— impossible tasks that are victimizing you. Putting it simply, to survive you must adapt.

True, you may have to learn how to live with a few psychologic handicaps such as some uncertainties, just as another person lives with some physical impairments. To suggest "Aren't we all a bit neurotic?" might be valid to the extent that unequivocal security is given to no one. We all know that we will die. Yet while life is here we want to enjoy its full measure of happiness. The duration and consequences of your maladaptiveness will determine how willing you are to modify. Rigidity need no longer be your identifying hallmark.

It is my hope that the information conveyed here may change the most paradoxic and disturbing person you know—yourself— into someone whom you and everyone else can warm to. I have yet to meet the uptight O-C who could not be liked. As a troubled fellow-being, you deserve an easier, richer, more sensuous and splendid life than the one you have known. In a sense, then, one can say that this is really a book about love, because its underlying thesis claims that love is your due. It can be brought into your embrace by you alone, through the changes that you set out to make.